BEHEMOTH

★

Also by Ronald B. Tobias

Kings and Desperate Men
They Shoot to Kill
Our Man Is Inside (with Diego Asencio)
Insider's Guide to Writing for Screen and Television
Theme and Strategy
Twenty Master Plots
Film and the American Moral Vision of Nature

BEHEMOTH

The History
of the Elephant
in America

RONALD B. TOBIAS

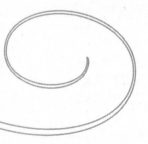

HARPER PERENNIAL

NEW YORK • LONDON • TORONTO • SYDNEY • NEW DELHI • AUCKLAND

HARPER PERENNIAL

HarperCollins books may be purchased for educational, business, or sales promotional use. For information please e-mail the Special Markets Department at SPsales@harpercollins.com.

FIRST EDITION

Designed by William Ruoto

Library of Congress Cataloging-in-Publication Data

Tobias, Ronald B., 1946–

   Behemoth : the history of the elephant in America / Ronald B. Tobias. — First edition.

     pages cm

   ISBN 978-0-06-224485-7

   1. Captive elephants—United States—History. I. Title.

   SF408.6.E44T63 2013

   636.967—dc23

636,967   2013017875

13 14 15 16 17   OV/RRD   10 9 8 7 6 5 4 3 2 1

For Candy
My beloved

Acknowledgments

My gratitude to those who gave me their enthusiasm and advice; to those who contributed their research skills to discover the extent to which elephants have contributed to our society; and to Candy, for her patience and support.

Particular thanks go to the folks in Tennessee: Rob Atkinson, Steve Smith, Angela Spivey, Jill Moore, Christina Cooper, Dr. Susan Mikota, Hank Hammatt, and Professor Doctor Sumolya Kanchanapangka of Bangkok; the folks in Montana: Jared Berent, Catharine White, and Casey Kanode; and the folks in New York: Penn Whaling of Ann Rittenberg, Elizabeth Perrella, and Emily Cunningham at HarperCollins.

Most of all, my gratitude goes to the elephants for their needless sacrifice.

When you have got an elephant by the hind leg, and he is trying to run away, it's best to let him run.

—ABRAHAM LINCOLN

Contents

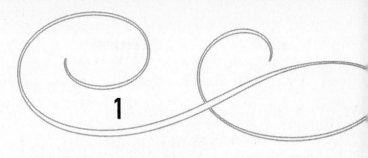

Seeing the Elephant

---◆---

from the Boston *Gazette*, February 23, 1761

THE GORMAGUNT

Whereas a surprising monster was caught in the woods of Canada, near the River St. Lawrence, and has with great difficulty been tamed, and brought to the house of James ELLIOT, at Curler's Hook. This is to inform the publick, that it will be exhibited at said house till the curious are satisfied.

The monster is larger than an elephant, of a very uncommon shape, having three heads, eight legs, three fundaments, two male members, and one female pudendum on the rump. It is of various colours very beautiful, and makes a noise like the conjunction of two or three voices. It is held unlawful to kill it, and it is said to live to a great age.

The Canadians could not give a name until a

very old Indian Sachem said, he remembered to have seen one when he was a boy, and his father called it a gormagunt.*

◆

On February 17, 1796, the sailing ship *America* lay at anchor off St. Helena, an island in the South Atlantic Ocean, twelve hundred miles from the west coast of Africa. A junior officer noted in the ship's log that the crew had spent the day loading supplies, which included among other things "23 sacks of coffee . . . several pumpkins and cabbages, some fresh fish for ship's use, and greens for the elephant." Then he added, in large bold letters that violated the disciplined margins of his log: "ELEPHANT ON BOARD."

By the time Jacob Crowninshield, the master of the *America,* had reached St. Helena, he'd been at sea seventy-six days since leaving India. He was less than halfway across the Atlantic, and it would be mid-April before he'd reach New York. Four months at sea with an elephant in the hold. "We take home a fine young elephant two years old, at $450," he wrote his brothers in America. "It is almost as large as a very large ox, and I dare say we shall get it home safe, if so it will bring at least $5,000."

---

* This joke was well-known and at least as old as Shakespeare, who repeats it. *Gormagunt* is a variant of *gormagon,* defined in *Dictionary of the Vulgar Tongue* (Francis Grose, 1811) as "[a] monster with six eyes, three mouths, four arms, eight legs, five on one side and three on the other, three arses, two tarses [penises], and a [vagina] upon its back; a man on horseback, with a woman behind him. http://www.gutenberg.org/cache/epub/5402/pg5402.html, accessed January 2012.

The fledgling American merchant fleet flourished during the revolution in France in 1789. The Crowninshield family of Salem, Massachusetts, began its career in shipping and trade in the West Indies with a few small ships in the early 1790s, and by 1796 the family business had grown so much that each of the five sons of patriarch George Crowninshield captained his own vessel. With larger ships that could sail to the East Indies—and beyond—they sailed the oceans of the world in search of wealth.

When Jacob Crowninshield found an elephant calf for sale in a Calcutta market, he reasoned that if he could get the calf back from India alive, he might get ten times what he'd paid for her. "I suppose you will laugh at this scheme," he wrote his family, "but I do not mind that, [I] will turn elephant driver . . . so if it succeeds, I ought to have the whole credit and honor too; of course you know it will be a great thing to carry the first elephant to America."

Crowninshield arrived in New York Harbor on April 13, 1796—not quite twenty years after the signing of the Declaration of Independence—and offloaded a dazed two-year-old female elephant that hadn't seen the sun in 120 days.[1] The calf was physically and emotionally traumatized not only from the rigors of the trip but also from being separated violently from her mother. Calves normally stay close to their mothers for two to three years, and although Crowninshield's elephant could feed itself at two years, she still would have been drinking her mother's milk. Given the lack of concern or even basic understanding of care, it was a miracle she survived. Many who came after her didn't. In years following, transoceanic travelers occasionally reported seeing the bloated corpse of an elephant bobbing in the middle of the ocean.

Ten days after he arrived, Jacob Crowninshield took out advertisements in the New York papers announcing he would show an elephant in the Bull's Head Tavern, in the Battery where Beaver Street ran into Broadway. He touted the elephant as the greatest natural curiosity ever presented. Admission was the princely sum of fifty cents; half price for children.[2]

People flocked to see the elephant. Within weeks, a Welshman from Philadelphia named Welshaven Owen offered Crowninshield ten thousand dollars—twenty times his investment—for ownership of the elephant.[3] Crowninshield took the money and retired from seafaring at the age of twenty-six. He entered politics and served two terms as a congressman from Massachusetts. In 1804 Thomas Jefferson nominated him as the secretary of the navy, and the Senate confirmed his appointment a year later, although Jacob declined to serve, citing his wife's poor health. In the years following he advised President James Madison on issues of trade with Great Britain, and he died in 1808 at age thirty-eight.

The junior officer on board the *America* who wrote "ELEPHANT ON BOARD" in the log also died in 1808, of yellow fever in Suriname, but not before he had fathered a girl and a boy. The boy he named after himself:

Nathaniel Hathorne. His son later added a *w* to his last name to become Nathaniel Hawthorne, Jr., author of *The Scarlet Letter* and *The House of the Seven Gables*.[4]

Crowninshield's elephant outlived both men. She spent twenty of her first twenty-two years of life touring between Massachusetts and the Carolinas until she disappeared into the fog of history. Until then, newspapers widely reported her comings and goings. In addition, the Welshman Owen gave out handbills so everyone would know *the elephant was coming*. "It is the most respectable Animal in the world," read his handbill, which paraphrased the French naturalist Georges-Louis Leclerc— the Comte de Buffon—who'd declared the elephant closest to man relative to intelligence and a soul. People slogged by foot, wagon, and horseback through snowstorms, hail storms, lightning and thunder, and rain so heavy the ground turned into sucking mud for a glimpse of Crowninshield's elephant. Then they went home and told their friends and neighbors, *I have seen the elephant!*

For many the elephant was living scripture. As the marvelous beast of Job, Behemoth lived in the space between celestial and bestial. Her eyes, yellow as spice, embodied ancient wisdom, and her skin mapped out countless treks across the Sinai. She even swayed to a gospel only she could hear.

Crowninshield's elephant was as big an attraction in its time as Buffalo Bill's Wild West Show would be a century later. Or Ringling Brothers, Barnum & Bailey Circus for the first half of the twentieth century. She tramped between Charleston, Baltimore, Philadelphia, New York, Boston, and dozens of smaller communities between them, and every day from sunrise to sundown (except the Sabbath), crowds swarmed to see her. In December 1796, she appeared in Philadelphia to support the relief effort for the victims of the fire that had razed much of Savannah, Georgia. Welshaven Owen promised to donate his gate receipts for the day to Savannah. "Generosity is Requested," he begged the public. By the time she appeared on stage at the New Theatre in Philadelphia in the following summer—fifteen months after landing in America—Crowninshield's elephant had grown to three thousand pounds and measured fifteen feet, eight inches from her trunk to the tip of her tail. Her attraction grew with her size. Her character also changed. Rather than a character from the Bible, more people recognized her as a fellow traveler in the American genesis story. She shared their hardships, their frustrations, and their desires. And she drank excessively. "[She] drinks all kinds of spirituous liquors," reads a handbill promoting her appearance in Boston. "Some days [she] has drank 30 bottles of porter, drawing the corks with [her] trunk."[5]

In 1805 Hachaliah Bailey, an enterprising cattleman from

Westchester County, New York, found an elephant for sale among the cattle in the New York City stockyards.[6] Her previous owner, Edward Savage, about whom little is known, had made a living for a year touring his elephant in Hudson Valley, and for some reason had abandoned the idea and put her up for sale for a thousand dollars, the market price for seventy head of cattle.[7]

In addition to his cattle business, Hach (pronounced "Heck") Bailey was part owner of a sloop that ferried cattle, hogs, and sheep down the Hudson River to the slaughterhouses in New York City. He was also the director of the Croton Turnpike Company, a toll road that linked Bailey's hometown of Somers to the Hudson River at Sing Sing (present-day Ossining). Bailey was an innovative man and an aspiring entrepreneur. He decided to prove an elephant was worth more than seventy head of cattle by working her as a draught animal. She could plow deeper, and haul and carry more than any team of horses; she could pump water. With an elephant, he reasoned, he could reduce the number of horses he needed and thus feed fewer mouths.

Hachaliah is an Old Testament name that can be translated either as "enlightened by Jehovah" or "troubled by Jehovah." Whatever the source of his inspiration, Bailey bought the elephant, shipped her upriver on one of his barges, and then walked her seventeen miles to his farm at Somers.[8] By the time he got home, however, he knew his plan wasn't going to work. The animal, which measured seven feet high and thirteen feet around, had an insatiable appetite. The day she arrived she ate Bailey out of all his corn and potatoes and then started on his hay. He also learned that elephants process food less efficiently than horses or cattle, and she'd defecate as often as twenty times a day, leaving behind huge boluses of partially digested grass that weighed anywhere from ten to forty pounds.[9] It didn't take Bailey long to realize his idea was worth less than what he'd paid for her, and that the longer he kept her, the more she'd cost.

He came up with an alternate plan, a plan that would make him, in P. T. Barnum's words, the Father of the American Circus.[10]

A natural-born showman, Hach Bailey followed in the footsteps of Owen and Savage and took his elephant to the road.[11] He named her Bet, perhaps as a tribute to his infant daughter, Elizabeth, and for three years they walked up and down New England looking for barns and taverns to show her to the paying public.[12]

Bailey charged an admission of between fifty and twenty-five cents for adults and half price for children—the same price Crowninshield had set for when she first landed in New York. For those who didn't have cash, he bartered for knives, farm implements, foodstuffs, and even rum. Together with his dog and some trained pigs, he traveled from town to village, mostly in the middle of the night so as to avoid giving a free show. Still, when people heard the elephant was coming, they lined the road at night to see her.

People came from farms and communities as far away as thirty miles (a considerable distance in those days) to see the elephant. So many came that Bailey had to hide Bet behind a canvas to keep nonpaying customers from getting a glimpse of her, thus creating a prototype of the circus tent. He embellished his eighth wonder of the world with stories about India, Africa, and the Holy Land, and how her ancestors had marched with Alexander and Hannibal and with Assyrian, Egyptian, and Babylonian kings. A LIVING ELEPHANT, he wrote as the headline of a newspaper ad in 1808. "Perhaps the present generation may never have the opportunity of seeing an Elephant again," he predicted, "as this is the only one in the United States, and perhaps the last visit to this place." People often paid to see her several times, each time with more family in tow.

Bet paid handsomely, but Bailey itched for greater wealth. In 1807, he franchised Bet to another man so he could raise the capital to buy more wagons, more horses, and more animals so he could sell more franchises. He returned to his farm in Westchester County, bought a tiger named Nero, and gave birth to the germ of an idea that mushroomed in American life for the next century and a half.

Bet toured for another five years before Bailey sold her to an equestrian company named Pepin & Breschard in 1812. Their show, which was typical for the time, provided mainly "Representations of Exercise of HORSEMAN-SHIP, executed in a superior style and by the first talents in that line." Mr. Breschard himself rode two horses simultaneously and performed "a variety of feats of dexterity with apples, forks, cup and ball, bottle, &c."[13] As soon as they premiered Bet, however, Pepin and Breschard realized an elephant outdrew horses, no matter how well they performed. So they trained Bet to stand in the ring while acrobats tumbled on a wooden platform tied to her back, making her America's first performing elephant.[14]

Bet died four years later after a morally outraged Daniel Davis, a farmer in York County, Maine, unloaded both barrels of his shotgun into her ear because he took offense, as the local pastor put it, that Bailey "took money from those who could not afford to spend it."[15] Davis spent two days in jail. There's no record if the court compelled him to pay damages. He became the first but not the last man in America to shoot an elephant.

Meanwhile Bet was stripped of her skin and bones, which were put on display in a curiosity museum in New York City, where she would compete with Ned the Learned Seal and a Genuine FeeJee Mermaid, which was the top half of a monkey sewn to the bottom half of a fish.

After Old Bet died, Hach Bailey bought two more elephants. The first was an eleven-year-old Asian female, which he named Little Bet. She toured until 1826, when six boys with muskets ambushed and killed her near Chepachet, Rhode Island, testing the promoter's boast that a musket ball couldn't penetrate her thick skin.[16] The other elephant was a six-year-old bull he named Columbus, whom he advertised as "the largest and most gracious animal in the world" and the first and only male exhibited in America. He stood seven feet tall and "sixteen feet six

THE LARGE MALE ELEPHANT COLUMBUS,
REPRESENTING A VIEW OF HIS INDIAN SADDLE.

Columbus, 1834.

inches from the end of his trunk to his tail," dwarfing any elephant before him.[17] Columbus was Bailey's star attraction.

In one version of his saga, Columbus dropped dead after giving a performance in Baltimore in 1837. Fearing financial ruin, Columbus's owner substituted a bull named Mogul for Columbus, who spent the rest of his life impersonating the Genoese Explorer.[18] He died four years later after crashing through a wooden bridge over the Hoosick River in North Adams, Massachusetts.[19]

By 1825 Hach Bailey was running his animal menagerie business out of a hotel he'd built in Somers, which
he named the Elephant Hotel. Built on a marble foundation at the intersection of the Croton and Peekskill
turnpikes, the Elephant Hotel was a meeting place for
people in the livestock and menageries trades. Passengers traveling the stagecoach between the state capital
at Albany and New York City usually stopped at the
Elephant. People like Aaron Burr, Horace Greeley, and
Washington Irving shared news with other legislators
and politicians over a meal and cider, and drovers going
to or coming from the New York City stopped at the
Elephant as well, making it a place to find out the latest
market news.[20] The Elephant Hotel still stands at the intersection of U.S. Route 202 and N.Y. Route 100. The
seven bedchambers of the third floor house the Museum
of the Early American Circus. The Somers Town Hall
occupies the first two floors.

Bailey erected a twenty-five-foot memorial to Bet
at the center of the road juncture. A gilded elephant
whose trunk waved up and down crowned the granite
and iron obelisk. As she aged she lost her golden patina
and turned gray. As motor traffic grew heavy, she endured several hits, one that killed a man, so they moved
her out of harm's way. She lost part of her trunk, which
ceased to wave. Bet continues to stand atop her pedestal in Somers, lovingly restored. Once a giant in a
dwarf's land, she is now a dwarf in a giant's land.

Not far from the Elephant Hotel, just over the border in Connecticut, lay the village of Bethel, where a sometime farmer, grocer, livery stable owner, tailor, and barkeep named Philo Barnum scratched through life looking for ways to provide for his wife and twelve children. He had ideas, but they resisted turning a profit.

One of his sons, however, did have a solid head for business. Phineas Taylor Barnum worked as a clerk in his father's country store, where at the age of fifteen he drove "sharp bargains with women who bought butter, eggs, beeswax, and feathers to exchange for dry goods, and with men who wanted to trade oats, corn, buckwheat, axe-helves, hats, and other commodities for ten penny nails, molasses, or New England rum."[21] One lesson he took away from his experience as a clerk in his father's cash, credit, and barter store was that everyone cheated at one time or another. "There is a great deal to be learned in a country store," he observed, "and principally this— that sharp trades, tricks, dishonesty, and deception are by no means confined to the city." People sold rags for linen, literally. Farmers weighed down their grain with rocks, gravel, or wood ash or they'd deliver their contract short. Sharp dealing required a watchful eye and an understanding of human psychology. Barnum had both.

At night and on rainy days when trade slowed, local men would gather at the Barnum store in Bethel to swap stories while they smoked around the cast-iron stove. Barnum loved listening to the town "wits and wags," but he found inspiration in the man from Somers who told captivating stories about his life as a showman.

Finally, in 1835, at the age of twenty-five, P. T. Barnum quit the grocery business and bought a blind, toothless, old black slave so crippled with arthritis she could barely move. He promoted her not only as the world's oldest woman at 161 years, but also as George Washington's mammy.

Heth was so decrepit one might easily suppose she was 161. She looked like a mummy in a sundress. Barnum claimed she weighed forty-nine pounds—and indeed, she was little more than skin draped on bone. Her shriveled hands and arms, locked with arthritis, crossed her chest, and her nails, six inches long, curled around like corkscrew talons. Mostly she talked to herself as she drifted in and out of her reverie, but she'd engage anyone who spoke to her.

Predictably, someone would ask her, *How old are you?*

I was born the year the Dutch took New York back from the English, she'd answer.

Proof of her age came from a printed copy of a bill of sale dated 1727 that conveyed a fifty-four-year old slave named Joice Heth to Augustine Washington in return for "thirty-three pounds lawful money."[22] Born the year the French Jesuit missionary Marquette and fur trapper Joliet first explored the Mississippi River valley, Heth had witnessed the entire panorama of American history. She was twenty when the Salem Witch Trials began and eighty-three when Ben Franklin flew his kite. The Boston Tea Party took place on her hundredth birthday and she turned 110 the year Adams, Franklin, and Jay sailed to France to sign the Treaty of Paris, which ended the War of Independence.

The most important year in her life, however, was 1732, when Augustine Washington's second wife, Mary, gave birth to his fifth child, a son named George. "[Joice Heth] is the first person who put clothes on the unconscious infant [Washington]," Barnum declared, "who, in after days, led our heroic fathers on to glory, to victory, and freedom!"[23] Feeling confident, Barnum booked Heth into Niblo's Garden on Broadway in New York City, which, at 3,600 seats, was the largest indoor theater in the world.

The show sold out. The New York papers lent an air of legitimacy to the affair that made skeptics scratch their heads. "We venture to state," wrote the New York *Commercial Advertiser*, "that since the flood, a like circumstance has not yet been witnessed equal to one which is about to happen this week." The New York *Evening Star* agreed. "From the bill of sale of this old lady from George Washington's father, we can have no doubt that she is 160 years of age."[24]

Those who believed Methuselah lived a thousand

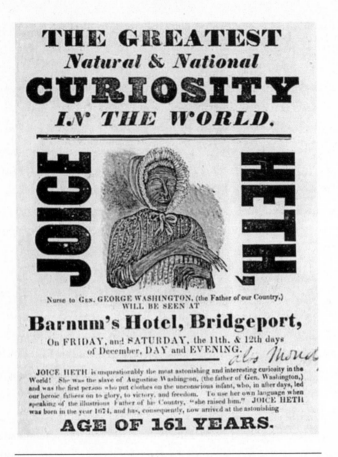

George Washington's Wet Nurse.

years had no trouble believing Joice Heth was 161; after all, Jacob's granddaughter Serach had lived for hundreds of years. But skeptics accused Barnum of fakery. No one lived to 161, no matter whom they were related to.

When attendance started to sag after several weeks, a paper published a letter to the editor mysteriously signed "A VISITOR," which claimed Heth wasn't even human but a "curiously constructed automaton, made up of whalebone, India-rubber, and numberless springs." A hidden ventriloquist gave her a voice.[25]

A fresh surge of people flooded Niblo's to see the mechanical woman. In his autobiography, Barnum admitted writing the letter. "A joke was never given up in Bethel," he wrote, "until the very end of it was unraveled."[26]

In 1841, at which time the population of the United States was 17 million, Barnum opened a curiosity museum that he named the American Museum. By the time the museum burned down twenty-four years later, 38 million people had walked through its doors and marveled at Hachaliah Bailey's elephant named Bet, the Fee-Jee Mermaid, and Ned, the Learned Seal. Twelve times a day Barnum offered a spectacular array of exhibits that included "educated dogs, industrious fleas, automatons, jugglers, ventriloquists, living statuary, tableaux, gipsies, Albinoes, fat boys, giants, dwarfs, rope-dancers, live 'Yankees,' pantomime, instrumental music, singing and dancing in great variety, dioramas, panoramas, models of Niagara, Dublin, and Jerusalem; Hannington's dioramas of the Creation, the Deluge, Fairy Grotto, Storm at Sea; the first English Punch and Judy in this country, Italian Fantoccini, mechanical figures, fancy glass-blowing, knitting machines and other triumphs in the mechanical arts; dissolving views, [and] American Indians, who enacted their warlike and religious ceremonies on the stage."[27]

"I had at last found my true vocation," Barnum confessed in his autobiography.[28]

In December 1848, while the Great Pathfinder, Colonel John Frémont, stumbled through the snowy passes of the Sangre de Cristo Mountains of Colorado in search of a route west, President James Knox Polk confirmed rumors of a gold strike in California. Three hundred thousand people struck out to cross the continent in search of destiny.

About half went by land, the others by sea. At the start everyone shared the same optimism. An outfit calling themselves the New England Pioneers— "twelve stout men armed and equipped and ready for California"—left their homes and families in January 1849 and headed west, determined to hold to their principles "and not to leave one in exchange for every lump of gold taken out." Six months later they were panning for gold on the north fork of the American River in California. George Holbrook Baker recorded the total earnings of the New England Pioneers over three days as $2.40. He described himself as a hapless miner, "one who endures many hardships, suffers many privations, and ventures his health, in a measure, for the golden hope of gain, and often it amounts only to that, as some return with injured health and empty pockets." He quit two weeks later, "satisfied," he said, "with having seen the elephant."[29] Baker shared his disappointment with hundreds of others in mining camps with names such as Poverty Hill and Humbug Flat.

That didn't stop others who painted "Goin' to See the Elephant" on the sides of their wagons and set out to cross the continent.[30] "All hands early up anxious to see the path that leads to the Elephant," wrote John Clark in 1852, at the beginning of his trek west. "Oh the pleasures of going to see the Elephant!" Lucy Rutledge Cooke exclaimed at the start of her journey.[31]

They went via the Oregon, California, and Mormon trails. Not everyone who set out for California made it. Some quit and returned home; others died on the trail. Axles broke, wagons bogged down in mud, river crossings swept away the oxen, wagons, and sometimes, family members. For four to five months they endured Indian attacks, cholera, wild animals, blizzards, and prairie fires. On crossing the desert strait of the western Washoe, Lucius Fairchild wrote in his diary "that desert is truly the great Elephant of the route and God knows I never want to see it again."[32]

The luster of the pilgrimage dulled as they plodded on. George Bonniwell recorded the excruciating details of endless disasters on the trail in 1850. "This is a trying time to the men and horses," he wrote. "I have just been to get grass, and got up to my 'tother end' in mud. I don't know if I shall ever get out. First glimpse of the Elephant."[33] The passage was a heady mix of adventure and ordeal, disaster mixed with awe, and grief leavened with hope. "As we traveled, I saw things that convert the most skeptical to the Presbyterian doctrine of total depravity," wrote Ezra Meeker about life on the trail in 1852, "actions unbelievable brutal and selfish to men and women and dumb brutes alike." Meeker wrote:

> Yet, there were also many instances of self-sacrifice, helpfulness, and unselfishness. It became a common saying that to *know* one's neighbors, they must be seen on the plains. I will vouch for that. The trail brought out the best—and the worst—in mankind. We were beginning, as they say, to *See the Elephant*.[34]

The Elephant appeared as insurmountable hardship. "Lo, the Elephant, the Elephant!" railed Walter Griffith Pigman when his wagon train found itself waist-deep in mire:

> . . . when the mules feet broke through the grass they sank down to the degree that when stripped of harness it was not until assisted that many of them could get ashore. We now had a job to pull our wagons nearly two miles by hand, often to our waist in water. And still there was more trouble ahead. . . .[35]

More profound than hardship, *Seeing the Elephant* meant you'd seen it all, from joy to despair, to success and failure, and birth and death. It implied the loss of innocence and the cost of experience. "We are told that the Elephant is in waiting, ready to receive us," wrote James D. Lyon in his journal in 1849, ten miles east of Fort Laramie; "if he shows fight or attempts to stop us on our progress to the golden land, we shall attack him with sword and spear."[36]

Those who survived the hardships and heartaches of the journey west were disheartened when they reached

Seeing the Elephant, California, 1849.

California and Oregon only to find out that chunks of gold weren't lying on the ground. Mining required unremitting heavy physical labor, which many were willing to give, but luck was capricious and gave of herself indiscriminately.

Have you seen the elephant? a veteran asked the newcomer as he came off the Oregon Trail.

From the tip of his trunk to the end of his tail, the newcomer replied wearily.

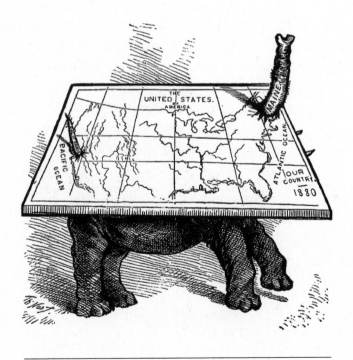

Thomas Nast imagines America, 1880.

One saw the elephant crossing the continent and saw him again in the birth of a new society in the far west, and so the elephant naturally came to symbolize the country physically as well as spiritually. The continent itself took the shape of an elephant. Pioneers, settlers, homesteaders wrote about crossing the great belly of the plains as they marched west to the jagged black spine that divided the continent. The Elephant stood facing east with New England as his head and Florida as his trunk. California was his rump and Baja his tail. The journals and diaries of men and women trekking across the continent described the journey as the crossing of a great body, and no other animal captured the expansiveness of the West more than the elephant. "Thou Elephant of the route," rhapsodized one traveler on the trail, "though wrapped in the storm clouds, thou art now within my grasp."[37]

They found the Elephant in mucking rains, deep snows, and earth baked hard as brick. They found him in cholera, diphtheria, smallpox, and whooping cough. He was the dust devil that danced before the windstorm, the whirling spouts of tornadoes and firestorms, and the titanic scrape of the flood. Both marvel and scourge, the Elephant became the sum of the American experience. He was joy and pain, success and failure, freedom and slavery, and, most of all, he was life and death.

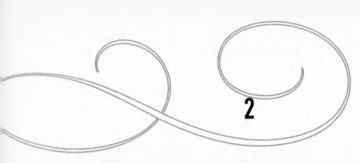

2

The Unfortunate Man Who Won an Elephant in a Raffle

◆

from the New York *Daily Times*, January 16, 1856

A CARGO OF ELEPHANTS

The Charleston *Courier* of the 7th says:

The steamer *Thomas Swan*, which arrived yesterday from Philadelphia, had, as a portion of her live cargo, four elephants, destined for a Southern menagerie.

During the severe weather of Saturday, one of the elephants was lost overboard in the rolling of the vessel; the others are doing as well as could be expected, and will, perhaps, bring their trunks on shore this day—provided the said trunks pass muster at the hands of our officers of customs.

◆

On December 14, 1860, the state of Georgia called for a convention of southern states to ratify an independent nation. A week later, South Carolina approved an ordinance to dissolve the union between South Carolina and other states. Mississippi, Florida, Alabama, Georgia, and Louisiana followed suit in January. By the middle of February 1861, the newly formed Provisional Confederate Congress resolved to capture Fort Sumter in South Carolina and Fort Pickens in Florida.

On March 1, 1861, the editorial writer for the *New York Times* warned of the storm gathering in Florida. "If [Fort] Pickens opens fire upon us, with her tremendous batteries," he warned, "we shall see the largest kind of an elephant." Many didn't take the southern threat seriously, but rather saw it as the dalliance of a "body of impulsive gentlemen who are extremely desirous of seeing an elephant, and who, could they once feel him kick, or get a moderate toss from his trunk, would go home perfectly satisfied."[1] They took the secessionist threat as a bluff concocted by bored Southern drawing room dilettantes who thought it'd be fun to sport with Washington. "It is not positively an eternal Gun-Cotton-dom which they crave," wrote the *Times*, "but simply to see the elephant—to have a great time, and retire." One battle and Jefferson Davis would be done.

Not long after the start of hostilities, a cartoon titled *Jeff. Sees the Elephant* caricatured the Union as an elephant dressed in a blue topcoat and shoes and socks made of Old Glory. With a rolled copy of the Constitution in his pocket, he holds a sword in his right hand, and eight cannons stick out from his chest. Behind him are more arms, stacks of cannonballs, the flag, and in the background the U.S. Capitol.

Jefferson Davis is a donkey, dressed as a dandy, holding up his monocle to peer at his foe. Behind him stand an army of donkeys armed with pitchforks, brooms, and rakes. The lithograph portends the troubles that lie ahead for the South. A gallows waits in the background.

Meanwhile, President Lincoln and Secretary of State William Seward fortified Fort Pickens at Pensacola. Only the South didn't attack the fort in Florida; instead, on April 12, 1861, Confederate cannons under the command of General P. G. T. Beauregard bombarded Fort Sumter,

Jeff. Sees the Elephant, *E. B. & E. C. Kellogg, ca. 1861.*

South Carolina, for thirty-four hours. The hapless fort surrendered the next day.

After the battle of First Manassas in Virginia in July and the battle of Wilson's Creek in Missouri in August, it became obvious Jeff Davis wasn't going to turn tail and run. In fact the Confederacy won half of the thirty-five significant military engagements of 1861.[2]

Bigger, bloodier battles followed: Shiloh, Second Manassas, Antietam, and Chickamauga in 1862. Soldiers suffered through war in the darkest of terms after seeing their comrades shot or their limbs blown off or suffering the horrors of prison camps and field hospitals. Alonzo Bump wrote from the battlefield at Fredericksburg in May 1863, "i have seen the Elephant i am sadisfied and willing to Come home . . . ," and then added plaintively, "i seean Enough at the Last Battle to sadifey me."[3] Hearvey Slutts wrote his father that "we went down to Vixburg they was about 65 thousand in the fleat we seen the elephant there we was down there several days and dun some pretty hard fighting."[4]

Vicksburg, in Jefferson Davis's words, was "the nail head that holds the South's two halves together," and General Ulysses Grant engaged the Army of Tennessee to take the city on the Mississippi. Twenty thousand men were killed or wounded; another thirty-seven thousand were captured. Stragglers wandered the battlefield as Grant laid siege to the city for forty-five days, until the city surrendered on July 3, 1863. The next day, fighting began at Gettysburg. Soldiers wrote home bitterly, *I have seen the elephant.*

Abraham Lincoln had himself seen the elephant. In his re-election campaign in 1864, the Lincoln people used printer's slugs of elephants running at a trot and waving a banner overhead to announce pre-election victories in different states. THE ELEPHANT IS COMING! reads the headline on the back cover of a campaign magazine called *Father Abraham*.

At first the elephant was simply a printer's ornamental device, called a dingbat, that allowed merchants to fill in the banner with a message about their products, which ranged from shoes to pianos. Lincoln changed the elephant town crier into a fully inflected symbol for himself and the Republican Party.

By happenstance, in 1862 Lincoln received an inauguration gift from His Majesty Somdetch Phra Paramendr Mahat Mongkut, Rama IV, the King of Siam, who sent a sword, a picture of His Holiness Rama IV, a picture of his daughter, and a promise to send two sexually mature elephants to start the Royal American Elephant Herd.

The gift was actually addressed to the previous occupant of the White House, James Buchanan, and had taken five years to arrive. By default, the gifts now belonged to Lincoln.

Lincoln accepted the sword and the pictures of His Holiness and his daughter, but refused the offer of elephants. It was the only time in the history of the presidency that the chief executive turned down a gift from the head of a state. "I appreciate most highly Your Majesty's tender of good offices in forwarding to this Government a stock from which a supply of elephants might be raised on our own soil," he wrote gingerly. "This Government would not hesitate to avail itself of so generous an offer if the object were one which could be made practically useful in the present condition of the United States." He explained that the climate in America was generally inhospitable for elephants. He also pointed out the United States was in the process of replacing animal power with steam. The steam engine, Lincoln wrote, would be "our best and most efficient of transportation."[5]

A more troublesome elephant awaited Lincoln. Five days after the Union won at Antietam in September 1862, the Secession Elephant turned into Lincoln's Elephant when he made public his intention to emancipate slaves in any state that did not submit to his jurisdiction by January 1, 1863.

The southern press dismissed Lincoln's proclamation as "a practical humbug of the first [order]." Noting that the governor of the Union state of Massachusetts had refused a federal request to colonize five hundred "contraband" Negroes, the press speculated about where freed slaves were supposed to go since neither the North nor the South wanted them. "They want no more 'colored brethren' in Massachusetts," wrote the *New York Herald*. "They want them neither temporarily nor permanently, and the *Herald* declares the opinion that the idea of colonizing is practically all a sham—and to take the niggers at all, will be to take them for a century." In other words, while the idea of abolition may have had an intellectual appeal to northerners, at a practical level, no state wanted tens of thousands of "pauper negroes" camping in its backyard. Southerners found Lincoln's idea laughable not only for the breadth of its arrogance but also for the depth of its ignorance.[6] Nonetheless, on January 1, 1863, Abraham Lincoln declared in the Emancipation Proclamation that "all persons held as slaves" in any rebel state to be "forever free."

The next issue of *Frank Leslie's Budget of Fun* lampooned Lincoln's elephant with a cartoon of an elephant with the head of a caricatured slave. Dressed in sharecropper's pants, he stares dumbly at things beyond his comprehension. In the lower corner of the picture, the owner of the elephant beseeches the viewer for advice about what he should do with him.

The story of *The Unfortunate Man Who Won an Elephant in a Raffle* had been familiar to people since colonial days. In it, a man wins an elephant in a raffle and is impressed with his good fortune. He takes the elephant home but quickly learns it has no useful purpose, costs a fortune to keep, and is impossible to sell. The Emancipation Proclamation was that elephant. "Washington is full of darkies—men & children & wenches swarm in all directions—," Walt Whitman wrote his mother in 1867; "— I am not sure but that the North is like the man that won an elephant in a raffle."[7]

THE MAN WHO WON THE ELEPHANT AT THE RAFFLE.
Old. Waitel.—"BUT THE QUESTION IS, WHAT AM I TO DO WITH THE CREATURE?"
[See Gen. Weitzel's Report to Gen. Butler, on capturing several hundred wagon-loads of Niggers.]

*"The Man Who Won the Elephant
at the Raffle."
Lincoln's Emancipation Elephant,
January 1863.*

The Republican Party also adopted the elephant as its symbol of choice as Lincoln's elephant morphed into the Republican elephant. In 1874, conservative political car–

toonist Thomas Nast formalized the spiritual connection between the two. His inspiration for that elephant was Jennie, an elephant at the Central Park Zoo, who took part in the *Central Park Zoo Disaster*, that fall.

Jennie was a fully grown Asian of about four tons. She wasn't a spectacular specimen but large enough to impress the people who came to see her. She was well-behaved and a favorite of children who took joy feeding her cakes and oranges; strollers in the park often found her chained to a tree grazing contentedly on the grass or probing the pockets of visitors for treats.[8] During the zoo disaster, however, she was inside her enclosure at the zoo.

The *New York Herald* wrote that the trouble began when Pete, a double-horned rhino weighing two tons, charged his keeper, Anderson, who'd poked him in the eye with a prod by accident.

Anderson watched dumbfounded as Pete smashed through his enclosure and charged him. Another keeper, named Hyland, grabbed a gun and shot Pete broadside as he made for Anderson, but the bullet wasn't powerful enough to penetrate his hide. It did earn Pete's attention, however, and without missing a stride, he changed course for Hyland.

Pete impaled Hyland on his horns and slammed him against an animal cage so hard the panther got out. The zoo went hysterical: monkeys screamed, hogs squealed, and hyenas laughed as Pete took out his anger on the other cages, which "snapped asunder like kindling wood." Then he attacked the cage that held a pair of

African lions, a female and a four-hundred-pound tom named Lincoln.

Lincoln roared and struck out at Pete with his paw but at four hundred pounds he weighed a tenth of Pete and so a charge would've been suicide. Instead, he snagged a hapless man who had the bad sense to run past him, and with a flick of his forepaw, tore the man's "clothes and flesh to pieces." Children cried, women fainted, and men shouted.

And Jennie remained calm.

A tiger and a mountain lion got into a scrap over Hyland's corpse, "rolling over and over, striking at each other with their mighty paws." Then a black wolf jumped onto the back of the tiger. "Between the wolf and tiger the conflict was brief," wrote the *Herald*. "The [tiger], shaking off the feeble hold of the other, turned quick as lightning on his hind legs, and falling, with open, gleaming jaws, upon his less muscular foe, rolled him over in the dust." Meanwhile, the mountain lion gnawed on Hyland's skull.

The cats ran out of the zoo. Pete followed. So did a pair of warthogs, a tapir, a two-toed sloth (it's hard to imagine a sloth making any kind of escape), and two kangaroos. Reports quickly came back that lions were attacking pedestrians on the streets of the Upper East Side of Manhattan.

Men from the zoo and police patrolmen of the Nineteenth Precinct united to hunt down the escapees. They found Pete in the middle of Ninety-third Street and opened fire on him. The rhino shrugged off the bullets, which "confused him momentarily," and then trotted down Ninety-third.

The posse gave chase when the tiger charged them. A zookeeper named Archambeau tried to rope the cat, but it jumped on top of Archambeau instead and would have killed him had not Pete charged them both. The lion got out of the way in time, but Pete stomped Archambeau to death. "A sentiment of horror pervaded the streets," wrote the *Herald*. People on the street were climbing trees and streetlight poles. An Italian man stabbed a man from Flatbush over an argument who would get to climb a certain tree. "From this point it has been extremely difficult to gather anything like a coherent or complete story of the depredations of the uncaged beasts," reported a witness.

And still Jennie remained calm.

The mayor of New York City declared martial law. "All citizens, except members of the National Guard, are enjoined to keep within their houses or residences until the wild animals now at large are captured or killed," read the order. The mayor would fire the cannon at City Hall Park to let everyone know when the streets were safe.

The *Herald*'s story ran upwards of ten thousand words, the equivalent of a forty-page typed manuscript, and detailed the grisly deaths of men, women, and children who fell victim to the marauding animals on Fifth Avenue as they fanned east to the Hudson and south to Castle Pier. Two Swedish men on their way to their farm in Nebraska shot and killed Lincoln, and John Adams Dix, the governor of New York, shot and killed the tiger. When it was over, forty-nine people lay dead. Two hundred more were injured. Fifty-eight animals had died, including Pete, both Lincoln and his "wife," a laughing hyena, a Cape buffalo, a porcupine, a woodchuck, a Derbian wallaby, a guanaco, and two giraffes.

The story so unsettled the city that parents rushed to the schools to retrieve their children, men either deserted work or didn't show up in order to stay home to protect their families, shops closed, and the traffic on the streets thinned to a trickle. The story was so long and the details so graphic most people didn't read the story all the way through. A man in Plainfield, New Jersey, had a fatal heart attack while reading the story about how a lion had seized four children "and mangled the delicate little things past all signs of recognition."[9] But if Henry A. H. Martin had read to the end of the story, he would've realized that "[t]he entire story given above is a pure fabrication. . . . Not one word of it is true. . . . It is simply a fancy picture which crowded upon the mind of the writer a few days ago while he was gazing through the iron bars of the cages of the wild animals in the menagerie at Central Park."[10]

The next day the *Sun* and the *Times* accused James Gordon Bennett, Jr., the idiosyncratic publisher of the *Herald*, of being reckless.[11] Bennett glibly defended himself in the *Herald* the next day.[12] Instead of expressing regret or an apology, he insisted his story was inspired by a genuine concern for the public good. Given the nature of the panic in the city the previous day, he argued, what would it be like if animals from the menagerie *really had escaped*? He cited cases of elephant rampages in Philadelphia and Chicago to prove it could happen in New York if the *Herald*'s warning went unheeded.

Few took Bennett seriously. After all, he was the P. T. Barnum of newspaper publishing, his guiding journalistic principle being "not to instruct but to startle," a lesson he'd learned from his father, who himself once famously advised an aspiring reporter not to ruin a good story by "over-verifying" the facts.[13] A precursor to Joseph Pulitzer's and William Randolph Hearst's gadfly journalism, Bennett knew how to stir the pot to boost sales.[14] Like Barnum, he mixed fact with fiction without regard for category.

Some of his claims were true, such as the *Herald* financing Henry Stanley's expedition to find Livingstone in Africa and underwriting George Washington De-Long's ill-fated naval expedition to the North Pole. Other claims were only partly true and some were completely fabricated, such as the Central Park Zoo Disaster.

One moral lesson of the incident focused on the only animal or human who remained unflapped during the chaos. Thomas Nast saw in Jennie a model of intelligence, patience, and strength of resolve and used her as his model of the Republican elephant. And so she became the star of a political melodrama that would play out in Washington for years.

Bennett launched a second hoax in the same issue as the Central Park Zoo Disaster when he reported that Ulysses Grant had decided to run for a third unprecedented term as president of the United States. George Washington had informally set the precedent when he refused to run for a third term because he said doing so came perilously close to creating reigns. Bennett decried Grant's arrogant ambition to become America's first Caesar.

Grant's wife, Julia, thought her husband should run a third time, but the Hero of Appomattox, whose administration was riddled with scandal and incompetence, had no plans to run again. Speculation was already under way over whose name would be on the Republican ticket. Senators from Indiana and New York had thrown their hats into the ring as did the secretary of the Treasury, a congressman from Maine, and the governor of Ohio. The rumor that Grant would try to run again upset the delicate equations of the party.

Overshadowed by the Zoo Disaster, Bennett's hoax got by nearly everyone except Thomas Nast, who fired back at Bennett on the pages of *Harper's Weekly,* one of the most widely circulated magazines of its time. Nast, the son of a trombonist in a Bavarian military band, who was already famous for creating the modern images of Uncle Sam and Santa Claus, was now inventing icons for the Republican and Democratic parties.

A friend of Grant's, Nast came to his defense when Bennett accused him of designing to become an American Caesar.[15] In the November 7 issue of *Harper's,* Nast drew a cartoon called "The Third-Term Panic," which depicts the *Herald* as a braying jackass dressed in a lion skin.[16]

Nast turned the breakout at the Central Park Zoo of that same week into a political allegory. At the center of the illustration, a jackass brays so loudly it panics timid rabbits, geese, sheep, a giraffe (labeled New York *Tribune*), a unicorn (*New York Times*), and an owl (New York *World*). The temperance ostrich sticks its head in the sand. Only the elephant stands her ground.

But her footing is precarious as the rotten planks of *Reform, Reconstruction*, and *Repudiation* splinter beneath her. She totters above an abyss called *Chaos*.

Her precariousness symbolizes the danger for Republicans of upcoming congressional elections that could—and in fact did—shift the balance of power from the Republicans to the Democrats for the first time since the Civil War. Nast warns his readers not to let braying asses like Bennett distract Republicans, but to hold the course.

Beneath the picture, Nast quotes the first line of Aesop's fable "The Ass in the Lion's Skin": "An Ass, having put on a lion's skin, roamed about the Forest and amused himself by frightening all the foolish Animals he met with during his wanderings." In other words, a braying ass dressed in a lion's skin is still just an ass.

Nast doesn't sign the quote Aesop but rather "Shakespeare or Bacon," a jab at Bennett's crusade to prove that Francis Bacon, not Shakespeare, had written Shakespeare's plays. (Two months earlier, Bennett had published an interview with Shakespeare's ghost, who claimed Francis Bacon was in the room with him but had declined to speak.[17])

The Republican Elephant.
Thomas Nast, "Third Term Panic."
November 7, 1874.

That fall the Democrats crushed the Republicans in the midterm elections of 1874. They lost not only their majority but also almost half their seats in the House of Representatives. Grant's political incompetence and a severe economic crisis soured the American public on Republicans and congressional Reconstruction. On November 21, 1874, *Harper's* published another Nast cartoon that mourned the devastating electoral loss by showing the Republican elephant falling into the abyss of existential helplessness, a hapless victim of the Third Term Hoax.

Between 1874 and 1884, Nast published at least nineteen more cartoons that depict the elephant as Republican. Most of them show the elephant on the verge of one catastrophe or another—often dangling over a cliff—but one cartoon alone shows a positively jubilant elephant.[18]

When Republican James Garfield beat the hero of Gettysburg, General Winfield Scott Hancock ("Hancock the Superb"), by the slimmest of margins for the White House in 1880, Nast drew a cartoon that celebrated the Republican victory on the front page of *Harper's*. Nast's exuberance is palpable. The caption reads, "The Republican Pachyderm Alive and Kicking," as the euphoric elephant kicks up his heels and a new dawn breaks over the nation.

Nast's joy was short-lived. Less than four months after Garfield took office, a delusional assassin shot him. Largely because of the incompetence of his doctor—a man named Bliss, who didn't believe in germs—Garfield took seventy-nine days to die.

The March before the Republican National Convention of 1884, Nast lobbied against the nomination of James Blaine as the Republican candidate for president. Nast's cover drawing for *Harper's*, "The Sacred Elephant," presents the viewer a white elephant upon whom sits a white throne awaiting the party's nomination.

The man entitled to the throne, Nast suggests, must be as pure in his principles as the elephant who bears him. "This Animal is sure to win if it [is] only kept pure and clean and has not too heavy a load to carry," reads the caption.

In June, the Republican National Convention overwhelmingly nominated Blaine as the party candidate.

That November, Democrat Grover Cleveland beat Blaine by three-tenths of a percent of the popular vote.

Nast never drew another elephant.

Thomas Nast, "The Republican
Pachyderm Alive and Kicking."
November 20, 1880.

"The Sacred Elephant."
March 8, 1884.

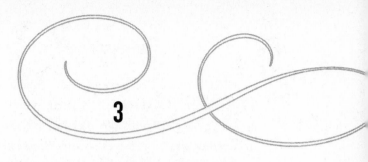

3

Race to the White House

◆

from the Salem (Massachusetts) *Register*, November 13, 1865

"PROCEED WITH THY ELEPHANT"

In Columbiana county resides an old fellow renowned for his belligerent disposition, who is generally known as Friend Shavery. Born and bred a Quaker, he was long since read out of the meeting on account of his quarrelsome propensities, but he still pertinaciously clings to the plain clothes and plain language of his early days, possibly as protection against the wrath he is so continually provoking, by his overbearing and irritable demeanor.

He has always the crossest dog in the neighborhood, the most troublesome, breechy steers &c., and is continually in hot water with some of his neighbors in consequence of the depredations committed by his unruly live stock.

A few weeks since, Van Amburg's Menagerie,

travelling through Columbiana, was obliged to pass his residence. A little before daylight, Nash, the keeper of the elephant Tipoo Saib, as he was passing over the road with his elephant, discovered this *pseudo*-Quaker seated upon a fence by the roadside, watching a bull which he had turned out upon the road, and which was pawing, bellowing and throwing up a tremendous dust generally. In fact, from the fury of the animal's demonstrations, one would take him for one of the identical breed that butted the locomotive off the bridge.

"Take that bull out of the way," shouted Nash, as he approached.

"Proceed with thy elephant," was the reply.

"If you don't take that bull away, he will get hurt," continued Nash, approaching, while the bull redoubled his belligerent demonstrations.

"Don't trouble thyself about the bull, but proceed with thy elephant," retorted Friend Shavery, rubbing his hands with delight at the prospect of an approaching scrimmage, the old fellow having great confidence in the invincibility of his bull, which was really the terror of the whole country around.

Tippoo Saib came along with his uncouth, shambling gait; the bull lowered his head and made a charge directly on the elephant. Old Tippoo, without even pausing in his march, gave his cowcatcher sweep, catching the bull on the side, crushing in his ribs with his enormous tusks, and then

raised him about thirty feet into the air, the bull
striking upon his head as he came down, breaking
his neck, and killing him instantly.

"I'm afraid your bull has bent his neck a little,"
shouted Nash, as he passed on.

"Bent, the deuce!" cried old Shavery, with a
troubled look at his defunct bull; "thy elephant is
too hefty for my beast, but thee will not make so
much out of the operation as thee supposes. I was
going to take my family to thy show, but I'll see
thee and thy show blowed to blazes before I go one
step, and now thee may proceed with thy elephant
and be [damned], please," the "please" being added
as Shavery took a second look at the stalwart elephant keeper.

Over the next forty years the elephant as a symbol of the
Republican Party spread through the ranks of major
political cartoonists such as William Allen Rogers, Grant
Hamilton, Udo Keppler, and Clifford Berryman. The
conspicuous girth of Republican presidents Chester Alan
Arthur, William McKinley, and Theodore Roosevelt
made the association easy, but none so much as William
Howard Taft.

People couldn't help notice how much William Howard "Big Lub" Taft looked like an elephant.[1] He was so
big he couldn't fit into the White House tub, and so tax-

payers built one that could hold his 330-pound frame. He was a larger-than-life man sitting in the backseat of his larger-than-life White Steamer touring car waving to people like a maharajah seated upon the plush howdah of a royal elephant's back.[2] "It is good to see Big Bill Taft enter a room after a number of other men," wrote journalist Frederick Palmer in 1907. "He reminds you of a great battleship following the smaller vessels, coming into port with her brass bright and plowing deep."[3]

As the sitting president, and as the former U.S. solicitor general, governor of Cuba, and secretary of war, and later, judge in the Sixth Circuit Court of Appeals and chief justice of the Supreme Court, Taft had the sort of gravitas that made him a favorite for political cartoonists.

Udo Keppler drew for a mischievous magazine called *Puck*, famous for its no-holds-barred political satire of Republicans. One cover of *Puck* in 1910 shows a frantic GOP mother elephant holding out her child (Taft) to a fireman from the window of her burning house (*Fireman, Save My Child!*), while another shows Taft fumbling with the back of the bride elephant's dress (*Hurry, William, and Hook Me Up!*) as Taft tries in vain to reconcile the party's "Reactionaries" and its "Insurgents."[4]

Keppler's sharpest criticism of Taft, however, came eight months after he took office, when he drew *The Same Rut*, which depicts Taft and the Republican elephant running in circles, Taft holding on to the elephant's tail and the elephant holding on to his.[5]

"Hurry, William, and Hook Me Up!"
Taft Tends to His Party, March 1910.

In 1908, as Roosevelt near the end of his second term, Republican strategists urged him to leave the country so Taft would have at least some chance to emerge from Teddy's shadow. Roosevelt first planned to go hunting in Alaska but changed his mind after he heard stories out

of Africa about white hunters such as Captain Frederick Selous, after whom the novelist H. Rider Haggard
modeled his grand hero, Allan Quartermain, and Colonel
John Henry Patterson, the man who killed the *Ghosts in
the Darkness*, the man-eating Tsavo lions.

Roosevelt went on safari to Africa with his son Quentin between 1909 and 1910 to hunt specimens for the
Smithsonian Institution. Although he forbade the press
to accompany him, it nonetheless followed him, report-
ing Roosevelt's exploits to the American public, which
followed every word. Providentially, he and Quentin
bagged eleven elephants.

Taft trounced the "Boy Orator of the Platte," William Jennings Bryan, in the presidential election of 1908
by promising to continue Roosevelt's vigorous reforms.
The Republican majority held in every state except the
southern swath of states from Maryland to Arizona. A Taft
campaign postcard imagines the country in the shape of an
upside-down elephant. "Invert the map and see how the
G. O. P. blanket is covering the United States!" the headline exhorts.[6] Suddenly an elephant appears, with tusks
protruding from the Great Lakes and a trunk stretching
down New England.

As Taft approached his first midterm, Roosevelt returned from Africa and announced his intention to run
for a third term as president, which dismayed Republican
leaders who were fed up with the Colonel's theatrics.

But Roosevelt's credentials were more impressive
than Taft's. He'd served two terms as president, was the

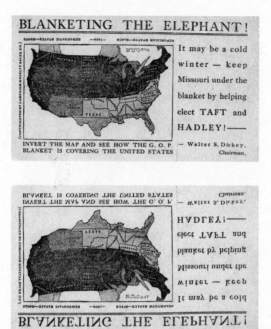

*"Blanketing the Elephant," Taft Presidential Campaign
Postcard, 1908.*

first American to win the Nobel Peace Prize, and had published forty books and dozens of articles about politics, natural history, and exploration. He was an actor in dozens of documentary films about his exploits as a hunter, explorer, and all-around gadabout. And everyone remembered his charge up San Juan Hill.[7]

At age fifty-three, Roosevelt still had great presence. He roared when he talked, relentlessly pounding his fist,

Theodore Roosevelt returns from safari in Africa in 1910 only to find Taft already dancing with the Elephant and Uncle Sam.

demanding action. As he whistle-stopped from town to town during his campaign, he invoked his charge up San Juan Hill with a bugled call to arms. But when Republicans made it clear they intended to stay with Taft, he broke from the party and ran as a Bull Moose Progressive.[8]

In June 1912, all hell broke loose at the Republican National Convention when Roosevelt called Taft "a fat head" who was "dumber than a guinea pig," and Taft then called Roosevelt the most dangerous man in history "because of his hold upon the less intelligent voters and the discontented."

The war escalated from there.

Harper's Weekly published an illustration of the Republican elephant fleeing the big tent of the Republican convention beaten and split hopelessly in two. The heav-

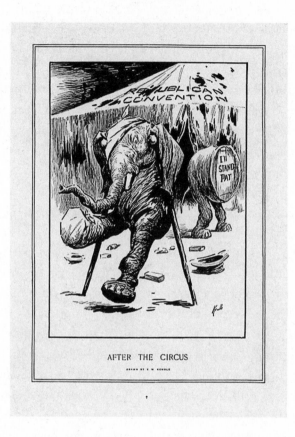

AFTER THE CIRCUS

"After the Circus," by Edward Windsor Kemble.
Taft is the front end, and Roosevelt, the back end.
June 1912.

ily bandaged front half (Taft) walks on crutches while
the rear end (Roosevelt) wanders off aimlessly. Worried
that Roosevelt would split the popular vote and put the
Democrat Woodrow Wilson in White House, loyalist

Republicans cast Roosevelt as a man who endangered the Republican presidential reign, which had started with Lincoln half a century before.

Unlike his flashy Republican opponents, Woodrow Wilson was as plain and skinny as a vanilla bean, but people liked his talk about reforming the banking system, stopping fraud in business, and shortening the leash on monopolies. And he looked like a mule.

Spare and lanky, he had a painfully pinched face he described as "Scotch Presbyterian." He kidded about his looks with the limerick: "For beauty, I am not a star, / There are others more handsome by far; / But my face I don't mind it, / For I am behind it, / It's the people in front that I jar." Publicly, however, his naturally dour manner gave the impression of a sober man as humorless as a mule.

He was a perfect foil to the theatrical Republicans, who preferred the world in black-and-white, with clear heroes and clear villains. They cast themselves as the hero, of course, and Democrats as villains who would put the country out of business and out of work if left to their own devices. During the campaign Republicans mailed thousands of postcards that made their argument visually. In "Lest We Forget," the message is disarmingly simple: *Feast or Famine.*

On the left side of the picture, the Donkey grazes absentmindedly on threadbare ground while organized ranks of jobless and homeless people press forward demanding work. Recalling the great depression of 1893, the steel mills are shut down, their smokestacks still. In

"LEST WE FORGET": Feast or Famine?
The Republican Pledge of Prosperity, 1912.

the foreground, a sign reads WAGES . . . DOING NOTHING, and in the background, darkness shrouds the Capitol.[9]

On the right side of the image, an elephant dances a jig. WAGES are now HIGHEST EVER KNOWN as the mills and factories teem with workers and the smokestacks belch *Prosperity*. A new dawn breaks over the Capitol.

Somewhere along the way, the allegorical race between the Donkey and the Elephant became literal. Perhaps Taft's resemblance to an elephant and Wilson's resemblance to a donkey made the comparisons inevitable; in any case, the idea of racing an elephant and a donkey to the White House came from Fred Thompson, the owner of Luna Park, Coney Island, who'd bet "Uncle Joe" Cannon, the Speaker of the U.S. House and the leader of the Republican Party, that the Democrats would take the election in the fall.

"Not on your life," Cannon replied.

So Thompson bet Cannon a cigar ("the price and quality to be left as a matter of honor on the part of the loser") that a donkey would beat an elephant in a footrace between New York and Washington, D.C.

Thompson supplied the elephant and the mule from his inventory of beasts at Luna Park. He chose the elephant Judy, who was a celebrity even before she joined the race. Hundreds of thousands of people who'd gone to Luna Park over the years had seen her walking up and down the promenade with people seated in the howdah perched on her back.

*Judy giving rides on the Promenade
at Luna Park, ca. 1905.*

Thompson picked Judy because she was physically fit from years on the boardwalk and because she remained unflappable in the constant midst of strange things, strange noises, and strange people. She was deliberate and cautious, which made her seem ponderous. A lot like Big Lub Taft.

The donkey came from a stable of nameless female donkeys—called *jennys*—who worked construction in the park. Lacking creative spirit, Thompson just called her Jennie. She was plain and unadorned, a lot like *the Schoolmaster* Wilson.

At a time when Americans loved a race between anything that could run, hop, or jump, the prospect of a contest between an elephant and a mule sparked the imagination of the public. The race between the Elephant and the Donkey for the White House took on a quality of Aesop fable.

First, Fred Thompson announced the course, which was two hundred miles long. Starting in Brooklyn, they would then go south through Trenton, Philadelphia, Wilmington, and Baltimore, before reaching Washington. Second, he announced the race would start on July 7, 1911, and end about ten days later.

Thompson then hired the United States marshal for Oklahoma, Jack "Catch 'em Alive" Abernathy as the grand marshal for the race. A darling of Roosevelt, who admired him for killing a wolf by ramming his fist down its throat, he had the aura of a dime-novel hero of the Old West.

So were Abernathy's sons, "Bud" and Temple, who had ridden by themselves from Oklahoma to New York

City on horseback. Bud was ten years old and Temple, six. A year later, the boy cowboys found themselves hired to ride the flanks of the race and create a buffer between people, automobiles, and whatever livestock they'd encounter on the road.

The papers devoted dozens of column-inches to Judy's custom-made rubber boots and how she'd be outfitted with a white lantern in front so she could see in the dark and a red lantern in the rear so nothing would run up on her. In an interview with Judy's mahout, he confided his strategy to pack twenty-five pounds of sugar to keep Judy motivated.

Likewise, someone proposed building a contraption that dangled a carrot just out of Jennie's reach to keep her motivated. However, most felt Jennie was plenty tough to see the job done once she set her mind to it.

The lightheartedness of the fable evaporated suddenly five days before the race as the city suffered its first day of a killing heat wave. Between that Sunday and the start of the race on Thursday, 158 men, women, and children died from the heat. "There were cases of quick insanity," reported the *New-York Tribune,* "and the suffering of all manner of mankind and animals was severe." But a rain shower the night before had provided a badly needed relief, and the feeling was growing that the heat wave would break in time for the race.[10]

The day of the race, the temperature again sailed past ninety degrees. When Thompson went to get Jennie from the sweltering barn for the start, he found she'd fainted from heat prostration and strangled in her harness. Quickly,

"TO THE WHITE HOUSE OR BUST," July 7, 1911.
Rising above his son, Bud, Jack "Catch 'em Alive"
Abernathy sits atop Judy.

he found a replacement donkey and named her Jennie II.

Before the start of the race, a photographer shot a portrait of Judy and Jennie. Judy, who weighed ten thousand pounds, stood eight feet tall, compared to Jennie, who weighed two hundred pounds and stood barely three feet at the withers. Unshod, she was barely more than saddle and reins.

The Elephant and the Donkey took their positions on Surf Avenue as a brass band played "Freedom March."

The crowd cheered and whistled, waved American flags, and took snapshots with their Brownie cameras.

Fifty years almost to the day after the armies of the North and the South clashed in the first major land battle of the Civil War at Manassas, Jennie took off at a lively trot down Surf Avenue and was two blocks ahead of Judy before she got much past the starting line.

Their route called for them to cross the Manhattan Bridge and race down Broadway to Battery Park, where they'd take the Staten Island Ferry to St. George. Jennie reached the ferry a half hour ahead of Judy.

But she'd missed the ferry by a few minutes and had to wait for the next one, which gave time for Judy to catch up. Given Jennie's impressive lead over Judy, a reporter asked Frank Walker, Judy's driver, how he hoped to keep up with the spirited donkey.

Walker recalled the race between the rabbit and hare and noted that the race didn't always go to the swiftest. They'd walk all day and all night in order to catch Jennie, and they'd pass her because sooner or later, like all Democrats, she'd lose her focus and wander out into a cornfield.

By the end of the first day, the race was even. The second stage was seventeen miles down Staten Island, starting at the ferry terminal at St. George and ending up in Tottenville, where they'd cross the river to Perth Amboy in New Jersey.

The flat stretch of open road favored Jennie, only somewhere between Clove Lakes and Freshkills, she and Judy both vanished.

The Abernathy boys scoured the route looking for them, followed by flurries of telephone calls, telegrams, and wireless messages. They asked people along the road *have you seen an elephant?* and the answer was always no. Pundits speculated that a socialist lion had ambushed the pair and eaten them. Or maybe a suffragette boa constrictor had swallowed them.

Judy and Jennie showed up late that afternoon, ambling along the route not far from the ferry landing. Their drivers explained that the animals were so physically and emotionally drained from the day before that they needed time to compose their nerves, so they'd gone off into a grass field and let them graze all day. Walker sent a telegram to Thompson asking for another twenty-five pounds of sugar.

On the third day, the pair made it to Perth Amboy. The Abernathy boys refused to ride since it was the Sabbath and "their contract did not call for Sunday riding," so Judy and Jennie marched through Perth Amboy unannounced. Everything went well until Judy spooked a team of horses pulling a milk wagon. The wagon tipped and spilled its milk.

Mayor Albert Bollschweiler of Perth Amboy, a sturdy Democrat, said he was disheartened to learn that the children of Perth Amboy would have to go without their Sunday milk, but he was just as delighted to announce that Jennie was now twenty minutes ahead of Judy. Jennie continued to extend her lead until that afternoon, when she wandered off into a cornfield. By sundown, Judy had again taken the lead.[11]

The race coursed through southern Jersey toward Wilson's Princeton. Democrats, concerned by Judy's lead, worried she might reach Princeton first. Then word came that Judy had picked up a nail in her foot and she had slowed to a crawl. Jennie was quickly gaining ground.

She didn't catch Judy before Princeton, but she did catch up late the fourth day. Again, they were tied, but some speculated Judy was so lame she'd quit the race, making Jennie the winner.

Unfortunately, the fifth day started as just as miserably for Jennie as it had for Judy. After thirty miles, Jennie's unshod hooves had splayed so badly she winced as she walked. The race between the fastest was rapidly turning into a race between the slowest.[12]

Over the next two days they passed Trenton, crossed the Delaware River, and were headed toward Philadelphia when Thompson got a phone call from Jack Evans, the race manager.

"Where are you?" asked Thompson.

"Philadelphia in one of its suburbs. I mean it's—"

"Who's ahead?" demanded Thompson. "How's that donkey? Tell me quickly. How is Jennie?"

"She's all in. I mean out. She's out of the race." And then Evans added, "The elephant has dropped out too." Judy and Jennie were too sore to continue, and not even sugar could induce the elephant to move. Judy was ahead of Jennie when she entered Philadelphia, prompting the *Philadelphia Inquirer* to surmise that Uncle Joe Cannon had won the bet, but Thompson canceled the race and shipped

Jennie and Judy—and the Abernathy boys—back to New York. He declared the race "a simultaneous laydown," in other words, a draw.[13]

Two weeks later Bud and Temple Abernathy left New York on horseback for San Francisco after their father had bet ten thousand dollars his boys could ride 3,600 miles in sixty days without spending a single night under cover. Bud was eleven and Temple was seven.[14] They finished the trip in sixty-two days.

That November, Wilson won forty of the forty-eight states. Roosevelt took six, and Taft took only Utah and Vermont.

The Republicans took the White House back in 1921 and kept it through the reigns of Warren Harding, Calvin Coolidge, and Herbert Hoover. A week before the election of 1932, between Hoover and Franklin Roosevelt, two elephants, named Danny and Eva, visited Hoover at the White House. They wore placards that read *This Is an Elephant's Job—No Time for Donkey Business* and *The Safety of Our Nation Demands Hoover.*[15] The Great Depression was in its thirty-sixth month and popular support for Hoover was flagging. Some accused his policies of making the Depression worse and others were tired of waiting for

"IT'S AN ELEPHANT'S JOB."
The Elephant pushes the economy out
of the Depression while the
Donkey kicks up his heels.
C. L. Robinson, 1932.

progress. Nonetheless, Republicans insisted only a GOP elephant could push "U.S. & Co." out of the muck and toward *Prosperity*, while the Democratic donkey kicked up his heels on a frolic.[16]

Only the public wasn't buying it. It preferred FDR's theme song, "Happy Days Are Here Again." That November, Roosevelt collected 472 electoral votes to Hoover's 59.

Rather than surrender, the Elephant rolled up his sleeve and put his shoulder to the wheel. It would be a long push—twenty years—to pass Roosevelt and Truman to reach Eisenhower.

In 1960, Eisenhower's vice president, Richard Nixon, ran for president against the senator from Massachusetts John F. Kennedy. A day before the election Kennedy told a hometown crowd in Boston Garden:

> I run against a candidate who reminds me of the symbol of his party, the circus elephant, with his head full of ivory, a long memory and no vision. You've seen elephants being led around the circus ring: they grab the tail of the elephant in front of them. That was all right in 1952 and 1956, but there is no tail to grab this year.[17]

It would be another long push—eight years—for Nixon to push past Kennedy and Johnson.

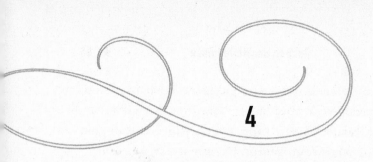

The Voyages of Columbus

from the Cincinnati *Daily Gazette*, December 16, 1878

A CIRCUS THAT HAS TRAVELED

Cooper & Bailey's Circus and Menagerie, which had among its attachés several people well known here, and which more than two years ago started on a tour to the uttermost parts of the earth, has just returned to Philadelphia, where it will winter.

The troupe left California on the *City of Sydney*, October 8, 1876. Since that time they have visited hundreds of cities and towns where the circus ring was a thing unknown. On December 6 the ship arrived at Honolulu, where it stopped for a day. King Kalakaua and his royal suite went on board and witnessed a performance. He seemed highly pleased and made several presents to performers.

The next place visited was the Fiji Islands, and the company then started for Australia, and after a very rough voyage reached Sydney in the latter part of December. In the spring they sailed to New Zealand. As this was the first menagerie ever seen in the south seas, whole tribes of war-like natives flocked from the north to see them. The showmen had a great deal to contend with, as on several occasions the natives refused to leave the tent when the performance was ended and repelled them when force was resorted to. Fever also broke out and a number of attachés and performers were prostrated, among them, the nimble Japanese acrobat, "Little All Right," who died after a few days' illness.

During the return voyage to Australia a number of valuable animals died: among them the performing elephant Babe, a Bengal tiger, two lions, a boa constrictor, and two valuable orang outangs, which had been purchased at Java. The troupe afterward went to Peru, where the *Tycho Brahe* was there engaged for the return to the United States.

A number of the performers have left the show and remained in the South, and out of 150 who went away only fifty returned.

◆

In 1840, circus owners James Raymond and Noel Waring billed Hannibal as the largest elephant who ever lived. He stood at eleven feet, eight inches tall and weighed fifteen thousand pounds, and like many bulls, he went on annual rampages, tearing apart property, chasing people, killing horses, and toppling buildings.[1] When Hannibal's riots became worrisome to the public, the circus explained that his distemper was the result of a broken heart.

Indeed, Hannibal was infatuated with Anne, with whom he'd become "warmly attached" while waiting out the winter in a storehouse outside Pittsburgh in 1843.[2] The two expressed their mutual affection by constantly cuddling and caressing each other. Anne even gently pushed her trunk into Hannibal's mouth, regarded then as "the elephantine style of kissing."[3]

When Raymond & Waring sold Anne to another circus the following spring, Hannibal went into a deep depression.[4] "Hannibal's grief and rage at this sundering of two faithful hearts were terrific," the circus told the public. He went on a hunger strike, refusing to eat for days, bellowing for his lost love, and attacking any man or beast foolish to come near him. His keeper tried to soothe his anguish by giving him whiskey, "and even though he drank eagerly of that consoling beverage . . . his moroseness and fury only increased."

Hannibal went on notable rampages in Pawtucket, Rhode Island, in 1854, in Williamsburg, Virginia, in 1859, and in Philadelphia, in 1861. But the public continued to regard him fondly because of the sympathetic nature of his grief.

When Hannibal killed his keeper in September 1862, however, a formal inquest found he should stand trial for justifiable homicide—"or manslaughter in the fourth degree, at worst," but the judge dismissed the charges against Hannibal after testimony revealed his trainer had been physically abusive.[5]

During his prepubescent years, Hannibal had been an actor in a quartet of bulls owned by Raymond & Waring. Hannibal was the big one. Then there was Pizarro, named after the Spanish conquistador who overthrew the Incan Empire.

Pizarro was Anne's boyfriend before Hannibal.

His name notwithstanding, Pizarro was a paradigm of subservience. He handled easily, didn't make trouble, and reinforced the belief that *the brute shall be subject to the will of man*. According to the circus, Pizarro was so sensitive to human command that all his keeper had to do "to stimulate [him] to the most violent exertions" was give him a certain look.[6]

The third elephant was Virginius. Given a masculine form of the name Virginia, Virginius was also a follower, not a leader. The most junior of the bulls, he was least likely to challenge another bull.

Then there was Columbus.

The first elephant named Columbus who arrived in America was Hachaliah Bailey's big bull (and his putative stand-in, Mogul). The second Columbus arrived in 1831, and unlike Bailey's well-mannered bull, Columbus II was decidedly ill-tempered. He fought everyone and everything, including his own kind. Columbus made the papers for the first time when he picked the lock to his chain so he could go to the other side of the lot and kill a pony with which he was having an issue.[7] The deliberateness of his actions convinced everyone elephants were rational animals, capable of complex thought such as plotting revenge. Those who worked with elephants already knew they were capable of complex reasoning, but as decorated stories that emphasized the intrigues of their lives became increasingly common, the public regarded elephants not only as biological enormities but also as actors in elaborate morality plays. Circusmen told rapt listeners that Columbus's rebelliousness was the result of a conflicted drama, his resistance against the authority of his captors.

Dominion over the animals was nonnegotiable, and absolute dominion required absolute force, a sentiment that was more familiar to the English than to Americans. Americans still remembered what it was like to resist tyranny, and for them Columbus was more of an outlaw hero than a villain that had to be quashed. They admired Columbus's struggle against crushing odds, just as Crocket, Bowie, and Travis had stood up to fifteen hundred Mexicans at the Alamo in 1836. People had grown to admire the outlaw, the underdog, and the brawler, whom they saw as reflections of themselves. Columbus was all of these.

But Columbus wasn't waging an ideological battle against oppression so much as he was just mean. He turned his anger just as easily on his animal brethren as humans, and at one time or another, everyone and everything felt the brunt of his rage. He killed his keepers; he killed other animals in the circus, including a horse, a llama, a monkey, and a rhinoceros; he shredded tents and smashed wagons. Most of all, he intended to topple Hannibal, the lead bull in Raymond & Waring's Menagerie, Museum and Circus United, the same bull who would be charged with manslaughter in the fourth degree.

Columbus couldn't stand Hannibal. Whenever he had a chance, he'd lunge at the larger bull or throw things at him. Hannibal for his part was unimpressed and simply ignored Columbus, which, to hear the story told, infuriated the smaller elephant even more.

The bull men kept Columbus as far away from Hannibal as practically possible and made doubly sure Columbus stayed swaddled in heavy chains. But in 1841, circumstances colluded to create a perfect storm.

By 1841 so many elephants had fallen through bridges that circuses made their heavy stock swim across a river rather than test the strength of bridges that weren't built for their load. Besides, elephants were strong swimmers, and they loved getting wet.

Typically, the keepers would lead the elephants to the shoreline and then push them into the water before Columbus could start posturing with Hannibal. Even in the water, Columbus would catch up to Hannibal midstream and try sparring with him, which mostly resulted in splashing. But on February 23, 1841—five years to the day after the siege of the Alamo—Columbus finally got his chance to pick a fight with Hannibal.

Algiers, Louisiana, is located across the Mississippi River from the French Quarter of New Orleans. Raymond & Waring had split into two traveling shows (which kept Columbus away from Hannibal), but in 1841 the shows unified to play New Orleans. Columbus hadn't seen Hannibal in months.

When he did see Hannibal, Columbus grew restless and agitated, and before the bull men could finish chaining him down, he pulled loose and charged his competitor.

With a fierce swoop from his trunk, Hannibal knocked Columbus "completely off his feet as ever a man was knocked over by a club."[8] Stunned, Columbus staggered to his feet while the keepers hurried Hannibal away. Once Columbus realized Hannibal was gone, he glowered at his trainer, William Crumb, who was saddled on his horse next to him. Columbus whipped his trunk across the head and neck of the horse and sent it sprawling to the ground. Pinned under the horse, Crumb watched in horror as Columbus first gored his horse and then seized him in his trunk and slammed him to the ground with such force "as to break half the bones in his body and cause instant death."[9] Helpless to do anything, the others stood back and watched as Columbus tore apart an animal wagon and killed a llama. Then, suddenly, he took off down the road to Algiers.

Algiers was an industrial entry point for New Orleans. Its citizens built riverboats in shipyards, loaded and unloaded cotton at the docks, and worked the iron forges. Slave traders used Algiers as a holding area to rest and fatten their human stock before putting it for sale on the auction block in New Orleans. The Algiers road was full of landowners, workmen, entrepreneurs, and gangs of men, women, and children in chains, all of whom scattered in panic when they saw Columbus charging toward them.

Columbus caught a black man sitting on a fence and stomped him "piece-meal." He knocked down fences and tents, upset work stalls, scattered the stock, and sent people scrambling for their guns. He killed two mules pulling a dray, killed the driver, and smashed the wagon.

A hastily convened militia opened fire on him in "guerrilla fashion," sallying forth and back as they pursued Columbus or as Columbus pursued them. Wrote the New Orleans *Daily Picayune,* "they felt much more terrified from this invasion than our citizens felt at the approach of the British in 1815." They skirmished nearly an hour until Columbus finally ran out of fight. He'd been shot twenty times with no effect.[10]

That evening Columbus took the ferry to New Orleans and performed the next day as though nothing had happened. Raymond & Waring paid damages to Algiers totaling $21,800. The largest single expense was a slave—the man sitting on the fence that Columbus had trampled—who had been valued at $1,800.

While in Philadelphia in 1847, Columbus killed his keeper, stomped on a monkey, and tore apart so many wagons that he set free a wolf, a hyena, a jackal, and a tiger, all of which "set up the most dreadful and unearthly roars that ever greeted the ears of one who was born out of Africa."[11] When his rampage took him through downtown Philadelphia, the mayor ordered two field artillery pieces and fifty muskets be set up on opposite ends of Walnut Street to contain him. Fortunately the bull men got to him before the militia opened fire.

Later that year Columbus tore the bars off the cage holding the rhinoceros, which he tried to kill, and when the rhino charged him he swatted it to the ground the way Hannibal had swatted him off his feet in 1841. The two beasts parted ways on the outskirts of Philadelphia. The rhinoceros chased horses and cows in a pasture until he found a marsh, where he contented himself by taking a bath while Columbus ransacked the countryside, "dealing destruction wherever he went."[12] Again the citizens rose to arms, and like Algiers, their muskets proved powerless. "They might as well have fired against the side of a stone wall," wrote the *Philadelphia Inquirer*, "as his hide resisted the balls as effectually as he had been encased in iron."

Like Hach Bailey's Columbus, Raymond & Waring's Columbus fell through a bridge and died in 1851. Virginius and Pizarro drowned in 1847 while trying to swim across the Delaware River while chained together, and Anne died after drinking a barrel of icy water in Zanesville, Ohio.[13]

Hannibal went on to glory. In April 1865 he marched bedecked in American flags in a grand procession in Washington after Grant took Richmond, and he marched again in New York after Sherman took Savannah.[14] In Washington, Hannibal knelt in front of the War Department building while a brass band played "The Battle Cry of Freedom" and the audience hooted:

> The Union forever,
> Hurrah! boys, hurrah!
> Down with the traitors,
> Up with the stars;
> While we rally round the flag, boys,
> Rally once again,
> Shouting the battle cry of Freedom.

Hannibal was as close to a war elephant as America ever had.

The great elephant died on May 6, 1865, two days after Abraham Lincoln was laid to rest in Springfield and a month after Lee surrendered at Appomattox. He died in Centerville, Pennsylvania, after being sick for a few days. The *New York Times*' obituary treated him as a war veteran and commended him for his "grave and dignified demeanor" and for refraining from joining "in those playful demonstrations common with the smaller and less distinguished specimens of his species."[15]

As America's growing inventory of heroes gave shape to the dream of a Yankee empire, America insinuated itself into a struggle between Spain and Cuba in 1898 as a pretext to wrest control of territories in the Caribbean and the Pacific from the Spanish.

In many respects the Spanish-American War was the perfect war for America. The Spanish were weary of their imperial ventures on the other side of the world, and the Cuban insurrections had festered for years. America, on the other hand, was itchy to embark on its own imperial venture, and Cuba was only ninety miles from Florida.

Washington insiders like Theodore Roosevelt and Henry Cabot Lodge agitated for war, and publisher William Randolph Hearst printed doped-up stories about Spanish atrocities against hapless Cubans, portraying Spain as a ravening beast prowling America's doorstep. "I think Roosevelt is going mad," wrote a friend in 1898 when Roosevelt quit his job as assistant secretary of the navy to start his own cowboy regiment. "The President has asked him twice as a personal favor to stay in the Navy Department, but Theodore is wild to fight and hack and hew."[16]

America got its excuse to fight on the evening of February 15, 1898, when the battleship *Maine* exploded at anchor in Havana Harbor, killing 266 Americans. The hawks accused Spain of a cowardly act of war that demanded action, not diplomacy. On April 21, America went to war with Spain.

From beginning to end the war took ten weeks. The Spanish wouldn't spend the human and financial capital necessary to protect its colonies on the other side of the world, and so the United States seized control of Cuba, Puerto Rico, Guam, and the Philippines. Fewer than four hundred men died in combat. Another five thousand died of typhoid. And everyone hooted for Roosevelt's Rough Riders as they charged up San Juan Hill.[17]

The third Columbus arrived in America from England at the start of the Spanish-American War. His owner, Lord George Sanger—not a true lord, but the owner of Sanger's Family Circus—had sold Columbus to an American circus run by the Ringling Brothers in order to get him out of the country as quickly as possible after he'd been acquitted by a coroner's jury of murder.

In England, Columbus had been known as Big Charley Lockhart, and the press portrayed him as an angry elephant who'd mercilessly crushed his trainer. The state argued the broadly held view that the elephant was by its nature "the most cunningly malignant animal in existence," and that the only way to control one was to stab it with a pitchfork or beat the soles of its feet.[18] In the state's view, Charley simply had taken "cowardly advantage" of an opportunity to kill a man and did so. There were no mitigating circumstances and therefore he should die for it.

Lord Sanger argued in Charley's defense that the elephant wouldn't hurt anyone who hadn't hurt him. He was an extraordinary animal "of phenomenal sagacity and dexterity," and Sanger had seen himself how Charley picked up a child who was climbing up his leg and set him aside with utmost delicacy. Then there was the time he hugged a worker he hadn't seen in months. He was a sensitive soul who didn't forgive a major grievance against his former trainer, who had abused the bull mercilessly until Sanger had fired him for excessive cruelty.

When the trainer showed up again more than a year later, Charley killed him. "Elephants do not forget injuries," Lord Sanger told the jury. Indeed, he argued, the man's death proved justice had been served.

The jury acquitted Charley of the charges, and Lord Sanger shipped him to America in 1898.

Charley quickly proved himself so ornery that the Ringlings sold him in 1901 to another showman, Colonel George W. "Popcorn" Hall, who changed Charley's name to Columbus and advertised him as the largest elephant "on the globe," purportedly standing a full foot taller and weighing a quarter ton heavier than

Hannibal.[19] Hall estimated his age at 110 years, at least twice his actual age.

Columbus appeared for several years in Hargreaves Big Railroad Circus, performing in the ring as the solo elephant with cake-walking horses, donkey clown carts, a troupe of acrobatic dogs, and an "educated" horse named King Fire, who spoke English.[20] Columbus's trainer was Popcorn Hall's daughter, Mabel Hall, the only woman elephant trainer of her time. The public squealed with delight when she made Columbus stand on his hind legs and wave his forelegs.

Nineteen ten was one in a string of remarkable years in America. In 1908 Henry Ford produced the first Model T; in 1909 four Inuits guiding Robert Peary and Matthew Henson reached the North Pole; in 1910 Barney Oldfield set a land speed record of 131.7 mph at Daytona Beach, Florida; and on April 20, 1910, the comet 1P/Halley streaked across the night sky.

Depending upon one's point of view, Halley's Comet was either a blessing or a curse. In 1066, the comet had been a bad omen for King Harold II of England, who lost at the Battle of Hastings, but it had been a good omen for William the Conqueror, who won it. Comets were known to cause earthquakes and epidemics, make women have twins, and turn good wine into a great wine. They also drove men and elephants mad.

Popcorn Hall blamed Halley's Comet for Columbus's erratic behavior, and as the comet burned its way through the solar system in 1910, he fed Columbus a sweet potato laced with potassium cyanide. The bull died kicking in the hay in a barn at the end of Main Street in Evansville, Wisconsin.

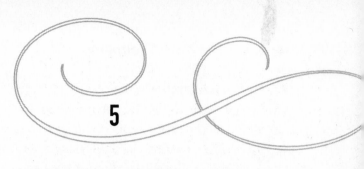

5

Romeo and Juliet, an American Tragedy

from the Washington, D.C., *Critic-Record*, June 28, 1882

AN ELEPHANT-NEGRO BABY

We have been to the home of a colored mother on one of our back streets and found a remarkable monstrosity in a week old babe. It is partly enveloped in an elephant's skin and could not be told from the side of this animal unless seen on a child.

It has a thick, rough, scaly exterior, covered with just enough long hair to easily discern it. The child has a long, pendant ear on that side of the head covered by this skin.

We viewed [it] as a facsimile of the ear of a baby elephant. The skin protrudes a quarter of [an inch] above the natural skin of the child. Its cries are low and plaintive, like an animal, not a human being.

The mother states that she attended a circus last

fall, was frightened by the elephants and regards this as the cause of the child's strange deformity.

The child, or animal, as it may turn out to be, is large and healthy and seems likely to live. What a curiosity it would be if it should live. One of our citizens has offered the mother $1,000 for it.

It is daily visited by hundreds.

In the early 1800s, promoters gave their bulls swashbuckling names such as Mandarin, Hannibal, Emperor, Columbus, Pilate, and Samson. The heroes and villains of Western civilization marched out of story and song, from the first days of the pyramids to the last days of the Civil War. And, in elephant fashion, they marched out of Shakespeare.

The connection between the elephant and Shakespeare was tenuous at best—Shakespeare didn't display any particular knowledge of the species, even claiming in *Troilus and Cressida* that they didn't have knees.[1] But the Victorian injunction that entertainment should be morally edifying created a curious mix of high- and lowbrow as showmen masqueraded elephants as Shakespearean heroes and villains.

In 1889, circus man Adam Forepaugh (whom the public knew simply as 4-Paw) put on a dancing show with "eight mammoth trumpeting pachyderms." Four were female—Desdemona, Ophelia, Cleopatra, and Juliet—

and the other four were male—Othello, Hamlet, Anthony, and Romeo. Together, they danced a quadrille, the formal equivalent of a square dance.

First the elephants in *4-Paw's Famous Troupe of Almost Human Quadrille Pachyderms* bowed to their partners and promenaded forward and back. Then they returned, balanced themselves upright on their rear legs, and ended with an elegant chassé, a gliding triple step of classical ballet. The crowds loved it. "It is as wonderful," wrote one reviewer, "as it is ludicrous."[2] Elephants burlesqued human emotions by playing them out on a large scale. Every movement they made magnified action, and every expression they felt magnified emotion. Audiences expected their tragedies to play out on a grand, rollicking scale. Elephants were naturally romantic. And tragic.

Forepaugh's production of *Romeo and Juliet* was actually a reprise of an earlier performance of the star-crossed lovers that played out in 1852 on the old Mohawk Bridge, near Schenectady, New York.

Located at the crossroads between the Mohawk and Hudson turnpikes, the Mohawk Bridge was designed and built by Theodore Burr, a cousin of Aaron Burr, in 1809. Theodore Burr was arguably one the finest of the colonial bridge makers. His arched bridge was nine hundred feet long and made entirely of wood.[3]

By the 1850s menageries started walking their heavy stock across the river rather than test the rotting bridge, but, in late September 1852, the R. Sands, G. C. Quick & Company's Circus took Romeo and Juliet—along with its camels, horses, zebras, and caged cats—and set out across the Mohawk Bridge.

A man named Dodge had imported the elephant Romeo to the United States in December 1831.[4] Juliet was likely a small female named Caroline, who was shanghaied into the role after Romeo arrived.[5] Billed as "the smallest edition of the species in this country," her owners fashioned her into Romeo's lover. They used adjectives such as *tender, caring, kind, devoted*, and *grateful*. By contrast, Romeo was volatile and brutish. Yet Juliet calmed the masculine storm that raged within his breast.

For twenty years Romeo and Juliet toured, their performance frozen in Act II, Scene II, in Capulet's orchard, when Juliet steps onto the moonlit balcony. But in 1852, the play lurched unexpectedly into the third act when both Romeo and Juliet fell through Theodore Burr's bridge.

Elephants strained colonial infrastructure, bridges in particular. Some, like the Mohawk Bridge, were darlings of architecture; others were either built by local engineers or just improvised. Colonial bridges were made to carry a man with a loaded wagon, not a five-ton elephant, and so when a bridge collapsed under the weight of one, the circus and the community had to suffer through a massive logistical, financial, and emotional shock.

The financial cost was easy to perceive—the death of an elephant often meant the death of the circus—but the emotional cost of a death was even more profound. Horse and oxen teams couldn't jerk the dead weight of the elephant from under the rubble of the bridge, so they had to cut the elephant into pieces and drag it away.

The immensity of butchering so many tons of muscle, bone, and internal organs was traumatic. Men waded ankle-deep in fecal matter as they hacked through sixty feet of intestine, forty pounds of heart, and three-quarters of a ton of bone. More than a hundred gallons of blood covered the men and their knives, axes, and saws; it ran out the bottoms of wagons and turned the road from the bridge into a blood trail.

When Romeo and Juliet fell through the Mohawk Bridge, they fell fifteen feet onto the rocks of the riverbank. Romeo got up quickly, but Juliet broke her shoulder, a death sentence.

Romeo refused to leave Juliet. "[His] attachment toward his unfortunate companion was so great," wrote the *Daily National Intelligencer*, "that no efforts could induce him to leave her in the time of trouble." Romeo ignored his handler's attempts to back him off. "Separating them alive seemed almost impossible," reported the newspaper.

The circus let go the mastiff they used to round up the stock in the hopes it would scare Romeo off, but Juliet was so afraid of the big dog that when she saw it bounding toward them, "the faithful Juliet made a desperate effort to protect her partner."[6]

Once they successfully lured Romeo away, the men built a shed over Juliet, knowing it might take days for her die. "Poor Juliet is past all surgery," lamented a reporter;

" . . . sadly crippled she cannot long survive her injuries, and will *never march again*."

Romeo became increasingly erratic after Juliet's death. He threw a camel over his head; he tried to kill a little boy who threw a stone at him innocently; and he went on public rampages and knocked down everything from orchards to buildings. The circus explained his behavior as a melancholia. But that behavior paled in comparison to what happened in 1853 when Romeo united with a second Juliet at Franconi's Hippodrome in New York City.

Until then Juliet had been called Jenny Lind, named after the Swedish Nightingale, the operatic sensation Barnum was touring with great success. In her new role Juliet learned how to dance for Romeo while he sat on a stool and cranked a hand organ.

They were together only a few months before Juliet left for another circus to become Lallah Rookh, the sultry Middle Eastern heroine of a romance poem written by Tom Moore.[7] There she learned to walk a twenty-foot tightrope suspended four feet from the ground. Halfway across she'd stop, raise a leg, and then wave an American flag.[8] Audiences loved her, and she became a major attraction. She died in 1860 as the result of a publicity stunt when she was forced to swim across the Ohio River at Cincinnati.[9]

Juliet was reborn yet again in the Grand Olympic Arena and United States Circus, which most people knew just as Mabie's. (Over twenty-three years, owner James Mabie had changed the name of the show fifteen times, but the name Mabie was usually in the title, as in Mabie's Grand Menagerie or Mabie's Grand Combined Circus.)

Jerry Mabie was charismatic, a devil of a businessman, and he knew how to put on a good show. He had a seven-and-a-half-foot-tall man with a fifty-seven-inch chest, whom he called the Scotch Giant, "the strongest man in the world." He also had the Holland family of acrobats, a fellow named Neave who was "the bugle champion of Berlin," and the "beautiful" Laura Buckley, who was a bareback rider. In the end, however, Mabie's show depended upon its headline act, *Romeo and Juliet*.

Life in the circus was exceptionally grueling for six months of the year. From May to October of its final season in 1864, the Mabie Menagerie traveled a corridor between seven states from Wisconsin and Minnesota to Iowa and Illinois, then down to Missouri, over to Kansas, and up to Nebraska.[10] Over 161 days, it set up and broke down its circus a total of 278 times. By the time Mabie's reached its wintering grounds in Delavan, Wisconsin, on Halloween day 1864, the animals, the people, and the equipment verged on collapse.

Winter was for recovery. They mended the canvas, replaced worn rigging, refurbished the wagons and harnesses, and rested the stock. Training would resume in the spring. But Juliet, likely weakened by her months on the road, started to suffer from abdominal pain, described as colic. After weeks in acute intestinal pain, she died.

The ground was frozen so hard Mabie dragged Juliet out onto the ice of Lake Delavan and left her there until spring, when she finally sank to the bottom. The only animal strong enough to drag Juliet onto the lake was Romeo. His current handler, an old bull hand named "Canada Bill" Williams, hitched him and pulled Juliet out onto the lake.[11] That winter, Mabie sold his circus to Adam Forepaugh.

The Forepaugh circus would some day challenge Barnum's and Ringling's as *the Largest Show on Earth*. In his words, the Forepaugh circus was *the Most Stupendous Menagerie since the Deluge,* "conceded by Press, Public, and Profession [as] the Wealthiest, Largest, Grandest and most Solid-Tented Exhibition that does now or ever did exist."[12] In 1864, however, Forepaugh was still putting his show together, and one reason he bought Mabie's was for the headline value of *Romeo and Juliet*. With Juliet dead, however, Romeo had little value. So he resurrected her.

Forepaugh claimed he'd found Franconi's Juliet— Lallah Rookh—at a sheriff's sale for a bankrupt circus. The press, distracted by the Civil War, didn't challenge his claim, and so the elephant that had been dead for four years was resurrected.

Forepaugh sensed financial success in reuniting Romeo with Juliet. Only Romeo had since turned into "the most vicious, vindictive and dangerous elephant in the country." He'd already killed three of his keepers (and would kill two more). When he went into a seasonal hormonal balance known as musth, he had to be chained down for weeks at a time, often without food and little water. (During musth, which typically lasts three months of the year, a sexually mature elephant's testosterone levels may soar to sixty times normal.) Romeo was aggressive and easily roused, and Forepaugh couldn't predict how he'd react to a new Juliet.

Forepaugh's older brother George suggested they ease them together by staking Juliet to a hundred-foot chain and then staking Romeo to another hundred-foot chain so the two of them could come together if they wanted or they could stand two hundred feet apart. The idea turned into a catastrophe.

George Forepaugh chained the elephants after dark, when elephants are usually calmest, and waited for Romeo to settle down. Once he was sure Romeo wasn't going to assault Juliet, he left the pair alone for the night.

The next morning he found Juliet had slipped out of her chains and had joined Romeo, who, Forepaugh noted, was "much delighted with his new companion." But when George tried to return Juliet to her chains, Romeo picked him up and flung him into the hay. Then he grabbed the dog that had been his companion for the last two years and bashed it senseless.

George Forepaugh had handled enough elephants to know Romeo had the energy and will of a maniac, and that only a titanic show of force could overcome him. Forepaugh elephants were acrobats, dancers, musicians, and clowns, not thugs. He decided to break Romeo.

Forepaugh called in Stewart Craven, one of the best-known bull trainers, and asked him if he could break Romeo while he was in full musth. Craven said he could, but that would mean "confining him beyond the power of resistance, and then beating him until he trumpets forth his subjection, and yields submission to his tormentors." Forepaugh agreed.

Craven's attitude was typical of the handlers who ruled brutally. For them the relationship between elephant and man was based on a struggle of wills, not trust. Trust got you killed. Craven embodied the ideology of dominion, and in Romeo's case, absolute subjugation required absolute force.

Craven began his intervention by shooting Romeo in the trunk. The big bull recoiled in surprise and pain. Even though most of the birdshot glanced off him, some of the pellets penetrated his thick skin. His anger on boil, the elephant lunged at Craven, and so he shot him again. He took out one of Romeo's eyes.[13]

Romeo was so focused on Craven he barely noticed the men who were tying him with enough block and tackle "to rig a small ship." When they tried to pull Romeo's legs from under him, he resisted, so Craven shot him again. By the time they got the bull on his side and tied down, Craven had shot Romeo more than a dozen times.[14] Only then did the serious work of subjugation begin.

For eight hours, amid the screams of the other animals in the menagerie, Craven "belabored [Romeo] with iron rods, and wounded [him] with the [bullhook] innumerable times, until he was brought under complete subjection and begged long and loud for mercy."

The next morning, Craven announced that Romeo was broken. He was so docile, he claimed, a boy could drive him with a piece of rye straw.[15] "The only evidence of his late bad humor," noted a paper, "being the loss of an eye and scars with which he is marked."[16]

The next season, when Romeo went into musth he knocked down Canada Bill Williams and knelt on his chest until he crushed it.[17] "Williams had not good judgment," Craven reflected, "or he never would have lost his life the way he did."

Wrack and ruin attended Romeo wherever he went over the last years of his life. After Williams, Romeo killed another handler, bringing the total to five, and he tried to kill Adam Forepaugh every chance he got.[18] On February 25, 1872, the *New York Times* noted wearily, "The elephant Romeo has been throwing his keeper into the air again, this time in Philadelphia. Romeo has outlived his usefulness."[19] A hundred days later the great elephant was dead.

During the course of the nineteenth century, handlers started to notice a correlation between an elephant's temper and the health of his teeth and feet. Acute toothaches could drive an elephant to anger and violence, and chronic foot infections were a leading cause of death for elephants who were used to walking thirty or forty miles a day in the wild. Romeo's feet were chronically infected, and when the condition became debilitating, a doctor from the Chicago Medical College examined his feet and found that "numerous small bones of the feet had become broken, detached, and dead." He cut out the dead bones, remarking that the gallons of blood that had bled from Romeo's feet were the human equivalent of "an ordinary attack of nose bleed." Romeo died two weeks later.

In Forepaugh's touching version, he visited his old friend as he lay dying and asked, "How do you get along, old fellow?"

Romeo responded by taking Forepaugh's hand in his trunk and putting it on his forelegs "as much as to say, 'There's where it hurts me; can't you do something to help it?'"

Romeo's infection, certainly antagonized by his foot surgery, spread up his legs and into his body cavity over the next days. Forepaugh stroked him as he endured the misery of septic shock, "his colossal flanks heaving with quick, short gasps, his eyes fixed and filmy, . . . his trunk cold and pulseless."[20] Considering Romeo didn't like Forepaugh and had tried to kill him several times, Forepaugh likely misconstrued the bull's gesture.

"The hero of bloody deeds" died on June 5, 1872. In spite of his sins, which the press enumerated, Romeo struck a chord with people for whom the Civil War was still a fresh wound. They recognized the rebellious spirit that would rather die than surrender to tyranny. They understood how the grand heroic gesture fit hand in glove with tragedy: Gettysburg, Spotsylvania, Chickamauga, Andersonville, and Ford's Theatre. Romeo reminded them of their own willingness to face overwhelming odds. And they admired his fire for independence. In the end, his obituary read, "His pride was unconquerable."[21]

Romeo's ghost returned to Juliet a few months later. Forepaugh reported he was asleep when he was rudely awakened by "an uproar of joy or terror" from the menagerie. When he went outside to see what was causing the trouble, he found the apparition of Romeo standing next to Juliet.

The Rogue Romeo, Delavan, Wisconsin.

"She was in a tremor of ecstasy," he told the paper, "and the two were kindly caressing each other with their trunks."[22]

After his death in 1872, Romeo lingered on in various reincarnations for decades. In 1889 he danced with Juliet in *4-Paw's Famous Troupe of Almost Human Quadrille Pachyderms*. In 1890, Isaac Van Amburgh's Romeo, "the children's pet," performed in Mastodon Shows in Trenton, New Jersey.[23] And in 1900, John Ringling had his intractable version of Romeo shot outside Wichita Falls, Texas. Romeo appeared on the deck of a riverboat with John Robinson's Circus in the 1880s.[24] He played for the Sells Brothers Circus until 1902, and in 1912 he costarred in *An Elephant on Their Hands* with the world-famous silent-film star John Bunny.[25] Today Romeo lives in Polk City, Florida, at the Ringling Brothers Barnum and Bailey Center for Elephant Conservation. He is nineteen years old. Juliet is twenty. She too lives in Florida.

The bones of Franconi's Juliet are still at the bottom of the Lake Delavan. In 1985, the Delavan Historical Preservation Society and Clown Alley #22 erected a life-sized fiberglass replica of Romeo rearing on his hind legs in front of a strip mall on Park Place. A six-foot clown waves from under Romeo's forelegs, the last place anyone who knew Romeo would have stood.

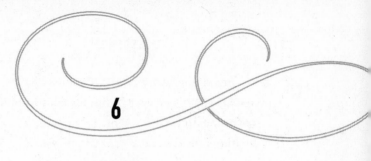

6

Amok

◆

from the *New York Times*, July 21, 1885

THE BIG ELEPHANT ALBERT KILLED

KEENE, N. H. July 20—Barnum's large Asiatic elephant Albert, who killed Keeper James Sweeney at Nashua on Saturday, was taken to a ravine in the suburbs of Keene this afternoon and killed.

He was chained to four large trees and the location of his heart and brain marked with chalk. Thirty-three members of the Keene Light Guard were then marshaled in line at 15 paces, and at the word "Fire" the same number of bullets penetrated the vital spots. The huge beast fell dead without a struggle.

Albert was 30 years old, and had been used as a performing elephant until the last three months, when he had shown such a temper that he was withdrawn from the trained herd.

He was valued at about $10,000. The remains have been presented to the Smithsonian Institution, Washington, D.C.

———————————◆———————————

Being an elephant keeper was an exceptionally dangerous occupation during the nineteenth and most of the twentieth century. For every bull, the saying went, there was a dead keeper. As male elephants matured they became notoriously unpredictable and violent. The press kept an informal head count of how many men an elephant had killed during his career, even though owners often concocted the stories in order to spruce up interest in an elephant with a flagging reputation. But enough of the stories were true, even if the death toll was exaggerated. Maturing elephants seemed to be increasingly incorrigible, and incidences of elephant mayhem always grabbed headlines.

Early handlers had little or no experience with sexually mature elephants because the men who'd first shipped them to America had calculated the risk and costs associated with transporting a juvenile one-ton animal versus a mature six-ton behemoth. As a result the majority of the elephants that came to America were smaller, socially inexperienced, and sexually immature, so it came as a surprise to everyone when males started going into musth.

Early handlers equated musth with the rut, the time when many ungulates mate. Males in rut tend to be combative as they compete for cows in estrus. But elephants come into musth only once a year, usually in winter, rather than timed to cows as they come into heat. Some animal behavioralists regard musth more as a form of dominance behavior than of sexual behavior, although the two are hard to separate. In the wild, young bulls in musth in the absence of older supervisory males attack, rape, and kill rhinoceroses for no apparent reason other than to assert dominance.[1]

The handlers noticed the hormonal discharge that dribbled from the elephant's temporal glands into their mouths while they were in musth, but they attributed their increasingly erratic and violent behavior to psychological rather than physiological causes. Their bursts of rage caught the trainers and keepers off guard as they threw them into the ground, slung them against fences and walls, and gored, trampled, and crushed them. A few men died because they were in the way, but most died because they were abusive, the result of ignorance as much as cruelty.

In 1900, Benjamin Wallace of the Great Wallace Brothers bought Charlie to replace a "deranged" bull named Nero, who'd been killed by an angry mob with pitchforks in Racine, Wisconsin, after he'd killed his trainer.[2] Wallace changed the elephant's name to Big Charlie and billed him as the largest elephant in America, a dubious claim but one showmen liked to make.

When cold weather forced the circus off the circuit and into the barns at the end of the season, the Great

Wallace Brothers settled in for the winter in Peru, Indiana. While most troupers went on furlough until the next season, the trainers and keepers of the big cats and the elephants stayed on to continue caring and working them. Henry Huffman was by all accounts a mild-mannered, patient man who was devoted to his charge, Charlie. The two had been together day and night for eight years, and Huffman knew Charlie's idiosyncrasies. The bond between them was so secure that Huffman was the only human Charlie would let near him during musth.

Huffman liked to fuss over Charlie. He fed him, exercised him, and on sunny days he'd take him down to the Mississinewa River to bathe. Huffman would stand on the shore and watch as Charlie playfully sucked up water in his trunk and showered himself. In April 1901, Huffman led Charlie to the riverbank and took off his lead so he would be free to wade into the river. Locals stopped to watch Charlie as the big bull eased into the water.

Standing in the shallows, Charlie turned around to face Huffman, and without warning, snatched Huffman in his trunk, raised him over his head, and threw him headlong into the river.

Huffman, more startled than hurt, swam back to shore, furious. "Aren't you ashamed of yourself?" he scolded Charlie.

Charlie grabbed Huffman again and this time held him down under water by stepping on him. Horrified, people ran down to the water's edge shouting, waving their arms, and throwing anything they could get their hands on. Charlie shifted his full weight onto Huffman and crushed him as the agitated bull lunged at his tormentors onshore. They ran, and Charlie chased them through the town of Peru and out the other side into a large field, where the furious elephant dug his tusks into the ground and showered the air with dirt.

A crowd quickly ringed the field to watch the drama unfold. While their wives held their children by their shoulders, men from Peru with rifles bickered over the best way to shoot Charlie. The Great Wallace people argued against violent action and asked for them to be patient while they tried to seduce Charlie with cyanide-laced apples, which they threw at Charlie. After a minute, Charlie picked up an apple and inspected it. The wind carried his low, throaty rumble.

While the roadside militia argued heatedly about what to do, one of the men stepped forward and shot at Charlie. All eyes turned anxiously to the great bull to see what he'd do, but Charlie just shrugged off the bullet and continued munching on an apple. Stories had been circulating for years about how elephants were impervious to bullets, and given the relatively weak strength of many calibers, elephants had indeed withstood being shot multiple times without harmful effect. A British elephant known as Chunee had withstood being shot 152 times in 1826 and had to be finished off with a harpoon, and in 1994, police shot Tyke 86 times after he killed his trainer and escaped from the Neal Blaisdell Center in downtown Honolulu and rampaged through the Kaka'ako section of the city. The riflemen of Peru were no better equipped for the job of bringing down Charlie. The most powerful weapon they had was an old Trapdoor Winchester .45-70, the same rifle used by Custer's men and buffalo hunters. They agreed the only possible shot was through the ear into the brain, but the rainbow trajectory of 405 grains of lead made a long shot too risky. The shooter would have to get close to Charlie. Very close.

While the men discussed the best strategy, the cyanide in the apple Charlie had eaten had worked into his system, and he stumbled. He flung his head side to side, whipping his trunk, and slashing his tusks. The earthquake within him sent shock waves through his body. His hindquarters shivered and he urinated and defecated spontaneously. He stumbled again when he couldn't coordinate his legs, and then he fell with a mighty groan. People in the crowd heard the great bellows of his lungs collapse.

His movements no longer voluntary, Charlie's legs began to turn as though he were trying to walk, and then they sped up, churning faster and faster, until they spun. The man with the Trapdoor Winchester stepped forward and shot Charlie through the ear into the brain. Charlie's legs sped up for an instant and then coasted to a crawl. He died mid-stride.

Newspapers ran stories about the elephant that ran amok in Indiana. Charlie had had a troubled past: over the last ten years he'd belonged to four circuses, and by at least one account, he'd killed three men before Huffman. "I knew the big fellow would catch 'Huff' napping some day," said Bill Badger, one of Barnum's bull men when he was told of Huffman's death. "They're the trickiest beasts that live," he said. "They'll fool you for a long time by allowing you to think they love you, when they are just waiting for the chance to put you out of business with a swing of that snaky snout of theirs." Huffman had ignored his advice at his own peril. "I long ago considered the elephant as my enemy, and I will always cling to that belief," Badger told the *New York Times*. "I hate them, though I'm a trainer. I rule them by brutality and fear, not by kindness."[3]

Experts concluded that for reasons either physiological or psychological—or both—maturing males like Charlie suffered from a severe intermittent form of hysteria that made them unstable and dangerous. They described their behavior in pathological terms such as *paranoid*, *schizoid*, and *homicidal*.

When Jennie, the elephant who'd stood rock solid during the Central Park Zoo Disaster of 1874, viciously attacked a camel for no apparent reason, the zoo concluded she was suffering from temporary insanity.

The camel incident occurred on a midsummer's day. Jennie's keeper had chained her to a tree in Central Park so she could browse on fresh grass, as was the custom. The keeper also chained a camel named Cairo to the same tree. The two often shared the tree, and there'd never been trouble between them. The keeper left Jennie as she lazed in the summer sun and Cairo as he chewed his cud "in deep and blinking thought."

Within the hour Jennie turned hysterical and hit Cairo

in the face so hard she fatally crushed his jaw. The keeper found the camel dazed and bloody and Jennie hysterical, lashing her trunk, trumpeting, and pulling furiously at her ankle chain.

Impulsive and inexplicable violence was the hallmark syndrome of elephant insanity. The newspapers ran the story as "Emotional Insanity in an Elephant" and papers all over the country reprinted it for months.[4] Experts speculated Jennie's insanity was the result of a hormonal or nutritional imbalance, and that the problem could be fixed once they fully understood the biophysical mechanism malfunctioning within her. Whatever the cause of her insanity, fortunately, it had passed quickly, like a summer squall.

Curiously, a summer squall did scud through the park the afternoon Jennie went mad. Such squalls were common in Central Park in the middle of summer. The wind turned brisk, the trees swooshed, and their limbs crackled, sometimes accompanied by a clap of thunder and a bolt of lightning. New Yorkers liked them because they took the edge off the sharp afternoon heat of late summer, and the only people who gave them much thought were the people—and perhaps the elephant—caught in their path.

Generally circuses did a good job containing elephant violence when it did occur. They explained the high incidence of trainer and keeper deaths as a risk of the profession—an occupational hazard—much like a trapeze artist who falls off the high wire or a cat man who gets mauled.

But when elephants ran amok in the community, goring and stomping anyone unfortunate or foolish enough to be their way, their violence frightened everyone.

When a bull in musth belonging to Barnum's Great Asiatic Caravan, Museum, and Menagerie got out of line while walking the show from Pawtucket, Rhode Island, to Fall River, Massachusetts, in June 1864, the trainer punished him by making him pick up a four-thousand-pound wagon. Indignant, the bull broke free from his tether and charged down the thoroughfare towards Fall River with intent to do violence. Elephant rampages aren't typically brief affairs; a bull can carry on for hours before he exhausts himself. One witness clocked the speed of the elephant at one mile every three minutes—twenty miles per hour—and so anyone coming from the opposite direction had precious little time to react to the bizarre threat descending upon him.

A man traveling in his wagon to Pawtucket suddenly found himself being charged by an elephant. He put his horse to the whip but was unable to turn his wagon around fast enough, and the bull caught the horse, gored it, and then slung it, the wagon, and the driver into the air. He then picked up the limp body of the horse and threw it fifty feet into a pond. The driver broke his shoulder.

The bull continued down the road to Fall River, found another wagon, and tossed it, the horse, and the passengers into the air. The horse ran away dragging the wagon's forewheels and the elephant gave chase.

He couldn't catch the horse but he happened upon another wagon, which he also crushed. He threw the horse over a fence into a field and stared at it for a minute before knocking down the fence, retrieving the dead horse, and then setting it on the ground next to the splintered wagon.

Continuing his rampage, the runaway bull killed a third horse and chased a fourth until he was so exhausted he collapsed in the bushes alongside the road. He didn't resist as Barnum's men chained him and put him on the ferry to rejoin the show in Massachusetts. Barnum settled with the aggrieved parties for damages and then speculated with a wink how people would pay more to see the Rogue of Rhode Island.

Females sometimes went berserk as well, although their motivations seemed clearer. In 1893, a cow named Dolly rampaged through the World's Columbia Exposition in Chicago after a dog persistently nipped at her heels, and in 1918, Alice broke free from her chains and completely dismantled a railroad car sitting on a siding on Long Island because, according to her handlers, she objected to being sent to Wisconsin.

Alice belonged to the New York Zoological Park. She was famous as a gentle, mellow animal who'd spent years carrying thousands of people on her back up and down the boardwalk at Coney Island. The countless people who slapped, pinched, rubbed, and probed her never seemed to bother her, so when the officials in Madison, Wisconsin, asked the zoo if it would send Alice to visit their schoolchildren, zoo officials saw no reason why Alice shouldn't go. They'd ship her in a specially made railroad car that would keep her comfortable on her trip west.

Alice's trainer loaded her onto the car the morning she was scheduled to leave for Wisconsin. She boarded calmly, and according to a reporter for the *New York Times*, she even winked at him as she walked up the loading ramp into the boxcar. The walls were reinforced with heavy chain plates that held Alice in place tightly enough so she wouldn't stumble into a wall if the train lurched or rounded a sharp curve. Alice grazed on fresh hay while her trainer cuffed her legs with chains. Feeling she was secure and comfortable, the trainer then ran out to grab breakfast before the train left.

He was just starting his breakfast when a roustabout ran in and shouted that Alice had broken her chains and was tearing apart the boxcar. By the time he got to her, Alice had rearranged the boxcar into a flatcar: she'd pulled down the roof and knocked down the walls, and she stood amid the rubble, as nonchalant as ever.

The zoo explained Alice's behavior as her way of making it clear she didn't want to leave her family and go to Wisconsin. Such clear rationales made it easy to forgive females for their misdeeds, but males went off the charts when they went rogue, and no rogue elephant captured the attention of the nation more than Tusko, "the World's Meanest Elephant."

Americans scouting for elephants in Siam first spotted
Tusko stacking logs in a forest work camp in 1902. He
was an astonishingly large bull, at ten feet tall and fourteen thousand pounds. His forehead domes were so big
they looked like battering rams, and his tusks, which
measured seven feet long, were scarred by years of hard
labor. Tusko's body was slung low to the ground—unlike
Jumbo, who was leggier—and his long, arching back
rounded into his massive hindquarters. He was seven tons
of dark, brooding mass.

The Great Syndicate Shows, "a strong rip and tear
grifting outfit" that played out of Kansas City, bought the
elephant and shipped him to Missouri.[5]

They named him Ned, and Ned made it clear from
the start he didn't intend to be complicit with the Great
Syndicate Shows' plan to make him their prized show elephant. He complied grudgingly at best, and during musth,
he had no tolerance for any irritation, real or imagined.
His size so magnified the threat of violence that the owners ordered his tusks be cut off and that he always remain
heavily chained.

Ned was so incorrigible that within a year's time, the
Great Syndicate Shows sold him to W. F. Smith of the
Great Eastern Shows, who turned around and sold him to

the M. L. Clark Wagon Show in the Ouachita Mountains of west Arkansas. For ten years Clark trudged from town to town with Ned in tow—not always willingly—so people could see the elephant. From time to time newspapers carried accounts of his more bizarre behavior, such as in Wilkes-Barre, Pennsylvania, when Ned broke loose one night and did "a moonlight dance on the newly laid asphaltic pavement."

In 1913 a syndicate from Mexico offered Clark $2,500 to pit Ned against a prime Mexican fighting bull in Tijuana. Clark was reticent to make such a long trip south, but he changed his mind when the promoter offered him

Ned in his days with M. L. Clark.

a share of the film rights, which he intended to sell to Edison's company for distribution to theaters nationally. Sensing a big payday, Clark agreed to fight Ned.

Ned's handler was Bill Badger, the same man who'd criticized Henry Huffman for being soft with Charlie. An old black man with a bushy white mustache, "Old Badger" was M. L. Clark's elephant man.

When Badger and Clark got to Tijuana, they learned the Mexicans were promoting a world-class heavyweight fight between the World's Largest Elephant and *five* Mexican bulls. But even at fifteen hundred pounds each, five bulls still only weighed half the total weight of Ned. Badger told Clark not to worry about Ned; he'd take care of himself.

Exactly what happened is a matter of debate. One version has Badger leading Ned into the ring, followed by the *torero*s and five frothy bulls. The bulls took one look at Ned and decided they wanted no part of him. The toreros tried to incite the bulls to attack but they just trotted off, keeping a respectful distance from the elephant. For his part, Ned stood by quietly as the bulls and toreros played keep-away.

The touted clash between titans turned into a Mexican standoff. The crowd got angry, which made the promoters unhappy, and when it became clear nothing was going to happen between Ned and the bulls, the Mexican authorities confiscated the film—which would have been worthless anyway—and fined Clark five hundred dollars, which he and Badger dodged by sneaking Ned across the border in the middle of the night.[6]

Another version of the fight has a "fiery" young bull charging Ned, "but the elephant, exhibiting an equal agility in his actions, did not suffer him to approach" and easily fended him off with a swipe of his long tusks. Foolishly, the bull then tried a frontal charge.

Ned gored him to death in front of a horrified crowd.[7] He then chased the toreros out of the ring, and in an act of supreme defiance, picked up a cape a matador had dropped during his hasty retreat and waved it over his head. It was the perfect ending to a perfect movie.

The Mexicans weren't amused. The authorities seized the motion picture cameras, confiscated the film, and locked Ned in a holding pen pending a criminal review, which would be followed by a judicial assessment, a process, they made it clear, that could last days and perhaps longer. That night Bill Badger went to Ned's holding pen and coaxed him to crash out. They left Tijuana still dragging the gate behind them.

Ned stayed with Clark for the next eight years. During that time his tolerance to humans wore thin. Sensing the growing potential for disaster, Clark sold the unruly bull in 1921 to the Al. G. Barnes Big 4 Ring Wild Animal Circus.

Alpheus George Barnes Stonehouse started Al. G. Barnes in 1895 as a tent show with a pony, a phonograph, and a stereopticon. A ringmaster at heart, his grand manner captivated audiences. By the time he bought Ned, his circus had grown to four rings and included a wide variety of wild animals, including eight elephants. Stonehouse took pride in leading the parade through town seated on the head of his largest elephant, which was Ned.[8]

The Al. G. Barnes Big 4 Ring Wild Animal Circus played small and middle-sized towns from McAllen, Texas, to Devil's Lake, North Dakota.[9] Of all Stonehouse's animals none could match the drawing power of an elephant, and so he reinvented Ned as Tusko, "the Mighty Monarch of the Jungle," the largest elephant in the world.

That spring, Tusko went into full-blown musth in Sedro-Woolley, a town along the Skagit River at the western edge of the Cascade Mountains in Washington State. Tusko "turned a dance into a riot" when he threw his keeper aloft thirty feet.[10] The elephant ran from the circus camp into Sedro-Woolley, flattening fences, knocking over trees in an orchard, and butting down telephone poles. He shredded a chicken coop, knocked down a garage, and toyed with three terrified switchmen huddled in a one-room shanty on a rail siding.

Circus roustabouts mounted two other elephants and ran through Sedro-Woolley after the outlaw elephant. They nearly ran over the town doctor when he stepped out of his house in his nightclothes to get the newspaper. He had to jump into the rosebushes to get out of the way.

The ground trembled. "All of a sudden that whole goddamn building just shook," recalled a man who was playing gin rummy with friends at the pool hall. Even though someone had warned them a mad elephant was headed their way, they assumed the guy was a joker and ignored him, at least until the building started to shake. "We thought he was B.S.-ing," a man in the card game told the local paper. "But, by God, the next time [the building] shook, we realized he *wasn't*."[11]

Sedro-Woolley didn't panic as other towns might have. People knew the circus had arrived and runaway elephants were part of its excitement. "The biggest thrill," the *Courier-Times* wrote the next day, "was not on the [circus] program."

The town watched with amusement as Tusko crushed a Model T like a tin box. Chicken wire still hanging from one tusk, he trotted through the residential neighborhood with a crowd swelling at his heels, waiting to see what he'd do next. When he stopped to look into the front window of a house, boys threw logs from a nearby woodpile at him.[12] He ran through backyards, laundry lines streaming behind him, knocked down fences, and skidded to a stop at the corner of State and Metcalf when he caught a whiff of alcohol.

The crowd could tell something had caught his attention, but not what, and when Tusko turned to face the town's tavern, the crowd roared.

Tusko pushed in the door and perhaps gave birth to the joke, "An elephant goes into a bar . . . " The Great Elephant Drunk of 1922 was under way.

Alcohol was the vice of choice for elephants. Heavy drinkers, they often drank until they passed out, got silly, or went on drunken toots. They drank beer and wine but preferred bourbon and Tennessee whiskey when they could get it. The jackpot, however, was a big pile of sour mash like the one Tusko found in Sedro-Woolley.

As Tusko gorged on the sour mash, the men of Sedro-Woolley took out their own flasks and went on a giant lark as the crowd grew to more than a hundred. "Many [people] acted as if they were chasing a stray horse or cow," reported the paper, "instead of the wildest, largest animal outside of the jungles." The paper also noted that some of the men were so drunk "they could barely discern gray elephants from pink." Said one man, "We had more of a circus following that damned elephant than if we'd gone to the circus."[13]

After gorging on the sour mash, Tusko turned his attention to a small farmhouse sitting at the edge of a field. He trotted over, looked through the windows, and as the people in the house scrambled up the stairs, tried to knock down the building.

The house wouldn't budge. The crowd egged him on, and Tusko tried to move the house again, this time nudging it off the foundation. Tusko then walked to the barn adjacent to the house and helped himself to some celebratory hay.[14]

As it got dark, some of the crowd went home and others stayed to build a bonfire in a field. They sent their boys back to town for warm clothes and more whiskey. Tusko, however, was in no mood to stop and ran off into dark. The next morning they found him strolling along the main road in Garden of Eden, a farming community northwest of town.

Other than Tusko's trainer, who suffered a few bruised ribs, no one was hurt during Tusko's romp. The local paper described the bull as "frisky" and full of "hijinks." The Great Elephant Drunk of 1922 was a smash.

When it was over, Tusko had squashed or overturned twenty automobiles, collapsed the walls to three houses, knocked down a variety of outbuildings, and pushed a farmhouse off its foundation. His swath of destruction ran for thirty miles.[15] Stonehouse paid twenty thousand dollars in damages to the people of Sedro-Woolley and came away with stories in the national press about an elephant so mean it had trampled an unsuspecting town in the woods of Washington. Tusko became the "World's Meanest Elephant," which was good for business for a while, but the elephant's famed incorrigibility rendered him worthless, and the "World's Meanest Elephant" quickly became the "Great Unwanted."

Tusko became so violent that Stonehouse had to keep him off tour. When he went into musth, they shackled, hobbled, and cross-hobbled him. They fitted chain martingales on his tusks so he couldn't lift his head, put him into a heavy chain straitjacket, and forced him into a squeeze chute called a "crush cage," where he stood motionless for three or four months at a time.[16]

Tusko, "the World's Meanest Elephant," in chains, 1930.

In October 1929, another of Barnes's elephants gored a woman to death in Texas and effectively signed the death warrant for every living bull elephant in America. Diamond was every bit as much trouble as Tusko. Like Tusko he was very large, and when in musth, very willful. Unlike Tusko, he killed people.

Diamond was bought and sold eleven times over the last fourteen years of his career.[17] He spent, on average, a few months in one place before he got shipped to another because of bad behavior. During the early twentieth century, circuses went in and out of business almost as routinely, and elephants were big cash investments that failed shows put on the market first when they got into financial trouble. It was in the circus's best interest not to disclose an elephant's behavioral problems, and although elephant men knew them by reputation, the buyers weren't always certain what they were getting. The good elephants went to Barnum, Forepaugh, and Ringling because they could afford top dollar; the bad elephants, however, went to smaller circuses that didn't have the capital to buy better.

In 1924, Diamond joined a small outfit called the Atterbury Wagon Show. Once a herd elephant, Diamond was used to performing with other elephants but had graduated to being a solo performer. Bill Woodcock, one of the great elephant hands of the early twentieth century, and who was with Atterbury at the time, thought Diamond put on "a pretty fair single act." Even though he wouldn't lie down anymore and refused to perform a tub act, he still did a decent three-legged hop and a hind leg stand. He danced his feet, rang bells, and for his finale he gave a bareback ride to several men at a time while doing his three-legged jig around the ring.

Woodcock also noticed that Diamond was becoming less predictable. Woodcock started calling him Black Diamond to reflect his dark mood, and the name stuck.[18]

In 1925, the Atterbury Wagon Show changed its name to the Monroe Brothers. By then Black Diamond's handler was Ben Sweet, or as he called himself, Captain Ben Reed. A veteran bull man, Reed had handled a bull named Tommy for Atterbury for years, until the elephant died unexpectedly in 1919. After Bill Woodcock left the Monroe Brothers, management gave Black Diamond to Reed.

On New Year's Day, 1926, Reed learned too late he was no match for Black Diamond, when the bull crushed him while he was trying to replace a leg chain. Bill Woodcock claimed the bull killed Reed because he lacked respect for him, a more or less formal way of saying Reed hadn't properly asserted physical dominance over the bull.

Two years and two circuses later, Black Diamond joined Tusko at the Al. G. Barnes Circus. It had been six years since Tusko's frolic in Sedro-Woolley. He'd spent three of those years off the tour, in and out of the crush cage. When Al. G. Barnes grounded Tusko in 1929 for bad behavior, Black Diamond stood in for him.[19]

Black Diamond's reputation as a man-killer preceded him.[20] When he went into musth, his new trainer basketed him in chains. He sawed down Black Diamond's tusks and screwed an iron bar between them so he couldn't raise his trunk. In public, he kept the elephant chained to at least two and sometimes three anchor elephants so he couldn't bolt.

A rogue elephant played well to the audience. Chains meant danger and more chains meant more danger. Black Diamond became a celebrity and he developed a following. Then, on October 12, 1929, Al. G. Barnes rolled into

Corsicana, Texas, southeast of Dallas, on the St. Louis Southwestern Railway. The circus was in the twenty-ninth week of a grueling thirty-two-week, 22,000-mile schedule that covered thirteen western states and three Canadian provinces.[21] After a week in Texas, the outfit would head to Arizona and then back to California to close the season. The people, the animals, and the gear were exhausted by the time they reached Corsicana.

But the people in Navarro County, Texas, were feeling good about the cotton crop that year, and they had a few dollars in their pockets to spend on the circus. Excitement ran high as the county crowded the streets to see the procession of wagons and stock rumble from the railroad siding to the show grounds. It'd been two years since the circus had been to Corsicana.

Diamond's handler was H. D. "Curley" Pritchett. Pritchett had been around circuses and elephants a long time, but like anybody who'd been on the road for years at a time, he longed to put down roots. So when, in 1927, Eva Speed Donohoo offered Curley a job as animal man on a cotton plantation she'd just inherited, he shook hands with her on the spot and gave up life on the road with the circus for a more stable life. All Black Diamond knew was that it was the first time he saw Eva Donohoo and the last time he saw Curley.

Pritchett had been Diamond's handler on and off for seven years and knew his habits and moods, his fondness for alcohol and cigars, and his need to bond with a man. Curley bragged to the others how Diamond had wrapped his trunk lovingly around his shoulders and cried when the time came for him to say goodbye.[22] Now, two years later, Diamond was back in Corsicana.

As the locomotive shunted the circus cars to the siding, word spread through the streets the circus was coming and people started to line the streets to see the procession to the fairgrounds.

As the razorbacks unloaded the wagons, the elephant men took out the cows. First they harnessed Ruth, then Lois, Babe, Palm, Jennie, Jenny, Jewel, and lastly Pearl, who had only one eye after a handler had put it out.[23] After they hitched the cows to the railway cars, they started to unload Tusko, Diamond, and the other bulls. That's when Curley Pritchett showed up.

Pritchett asked Jack O'Grady, Diamond's new handler, if he'd let him lead the bull through Corsicana for old times' sake. "I got a lot of friends here who know I took care of Diamond," he explained. "I'd kinda get a kick out of taking him over again."[24]

"Come on in and see if he still knows you," O'Grady replied.

Ruth's bull man, George Washington "Slim" Lewis— who later became Tusko's handler—went along to watch the reunion. When O'Grady opened the door to the iron-bottomed car that housed Tusko at one end and Black Diamond at the other, Curley Pritchett stepped into the car to greet an old friend.

Diamond immediately recognized Pritchett. "If you were one who could interpret the expression on an elephant's face and read [his] thoughts," recalled Slim Lewis, "you would have felt that Diamond recognized him all right, but no longer cared to have him around." But if Diamond felt any ill will toward Curley, neither O'Grady nor Pritchett picked up on it. The bull seemed fine with Curley, and so O'Grady agreed to let Pritchett lead Diamond across town, against his better judgment. For safety, O'Grady anchored Diamond to two other elephants with chains, so that if he did misbehave, he could drag him away.

Everything went well until they reached the fire hydrant opposite the schoolhouse, which they'd opened into a makeshift trough as a quick way to water the stock. The big hurry to get to the show grounds had bunched up everyone at the trough, and so Curley pulled Diamond between two cars parked at the curb on First Avenue to wait his turn.

Then Eva Donohoo stepped out from between the cars and asked Curley if she could touch Diamond. Pritchett knew she was coming because he had arranged for her to see him and Diamond together. "Sure you can pet him," Pritchett replied. "He knows me and he's all right."[25]

Eva reached out to touch Diamond. At that instant he smacked Curley with his trunk so hard he flew over a car. Then he swung back at the startled woman and knocked her to the ground and tried to gore her. Failing that, he pushed a car on top of her.

Three times Diamond's two anchor elephants yanked him away and three times Diamond fought his way back.

When he was satisfied that Eva Donohoo was dead, he turned his attention to Curley Pritchett, who was lying on the ground with a broken arm. Diamond reached over a car with his trunk to grab Curley and when he couldn't reach him, he tried to go beneath the car. It took three elephants to pull Diamond away. Somehow Jack O'Grady managed to get him back into the bull car, where the furious bull flung himself against the iron bars of his boxcar.

Navarro County thought a lot of Eva Donohoo. Once the society editor for the *Houston Post*, the widow worked as a public stenographer in the Rice Hotel in Houston in order to support her little girl.[26] After her father's death, she'd moved back to Corsicana to cope with her inheritance. Now that Diamond had killed her, the town demanded immediate justice. When a vigilante tried to force his way into the bull car with a .45 to settle the score, one of the bull men punched him out.

Meanwhile, Stonehouse wired John Ringling, who'd bought Al. G. Barnes less than a month ago to merge with other circuses to make the Ringling Brothers, Barnum and Bailey Combined Circuses, and asked him what to do about Diamond.[27] While they waited for a reply, the circus put on two performances and sold out both shows, although many who came to see the elephant that had just killed his fourth victim were disappointed when he didn't appear.[28]

Al. G. Barnes was in Bay City on the fourteenth and in Corpus Christi on the sixteenth. By the time Ringling's answer came, it was the seventeenth and they were in

Kenedy, Karnes County, southeast of San Antonio. Ring-ling said only, "Kill Diamond in some humane way." He left it up to Barnes to figure out how.

Newspapers and radio stations called for his execution. Corpus Christi offered to throw Black Diamond into the Gulf of Mexico. The elephant men decided that if the elephant had to be killed, they'd do it, not outsiders who didn't understand how things were. They didn't want Black Diamond to suffer, so they decided to break his neck.

Their plan called to wrap six chains around the elephant's neck and then attach them to four anchor elephants, each of which faced in a different direction. On command, the elephants would snatch up the chains and, best-case scenario, snap Black Diamond's neck. Worse case, they'd strangle him.

They decided to poison him instead. After all, poisoning had worked for the Great Wallace Brothers when they put down Big Charlie in 1901. Stonehouse announced Black Diamond's execution for the following day, to take place about two miles from town in a pasture where they'd dug a hole big enough to bury a seven-ton elephant.

The next day began with the same cry that had rallied the people and the animals to work for the past thirty weeks. O'Grady led Black Diamond, who was anchored by three elephants, to the pasture where he was to be killed. There they could still see the flags waving at the top of center pole for the big tent. Black Diamond walked slowly—perhaps reticently—prompting Slim Lewis to believe he knew he was taking his last walk.[29]

The road was clogged with sightseers. It'd been thirty-six years since Karnes County had a public execution. The crowd had no real emotional investment in the event other than curiosity and a sense that some kind of history was in the making. When Texas Rangers barricaded the pasture, people stopped to listen to the elephants shuffle to the clearing. The Rangers let about twenty others go with O'Grady and Black Diamond. Five of them were armed.

When O'Grady reached the clearing he attached Black Diamond to a chain block that ran between three mesquite trees and a heavy truck axle between them. The plan was to lace bags of peanuts with sodium cyanide and then mix those with bags of untainted ones so the bull couldn't smell the poison. Once he was down, they would shoot him. The honor of killing Back Diamond went to Hans Nagel, the first director of the Houston Zoo.

They put the peanuts into a basket and gave it to Black Diamond as O'Grady patted him. While the elephant ate peanuts, O'Grady whispered something to the bull and then walked away without turning back.

Sodium cyanide works by choking oxygen from the body's cells. A lethal dose of cyanide causes a coma, followed closely by seizures and cardiac arrest. A lesser dose causes confusion, giddiness, labored breathing, and the loss of consciousness. Minutes went by and nothing happened. Black Diamond had eaten only the good peanuts.

Plan B was to give Black Diamond a box of oranges spiked with cyanide, but he rejected them, too. That left only one solution: they had to shoot him.

Hans Nagel and another man, a taxidermist who wanted the elephant's head for a museum in Houston, opened fire on the elephant with submachine guns. "The first burst of lead fired into the body of the nine-ton pachyderm seemed to puzzle the animal," reported the *Corsicana Daily Sun.* "Another burst made him groggy, and he rolled over slowly and took another fusillade in the body."[30] According to reports it took between sixty and 170 bullets to kill Black Diamond.[31] Nagel, visibly shaken, left while the others cut up the bull for souvenirs.[32] Later someone made a commemorative bust of Hans Nagel atop one of Black Diamond's feet.

Curley Pritchett attributed the bull's behavior to jealousy. Eva Donohoo had taken him away, and he never forgave her for that, just as he'd felt Curley had deserted him.

Eight days after Black Diamond's death, Wall Street crashed and America slipped into the mire of the Great Depression, which would last a decade. The death of Eva Donohoo was also the turning point for male elephants in America. From the owners' point of view, these violent outbursts created too much exposure to liability when elephants toppled barns and farmhouses, knocked down outhouses and chicken coops, shredded orchards, flattened every automobile known to man, or worse, killed the rubes. Male elephants were proving themselves to be walking time bombs and no one knew when one would go off.

The solution to the problem was to kill the elephants.

Most people couldn't tell the difference between a male and a female anyway, so the owners decided to replace males with less temperamental females. They tacitly agreed to a major loss of capital in return for the expectation that someday the American elephant herd would be made up of more tractable females. William Hornaday, the director of the New York Zoological Park, noted that circus owners were "afraid to carry on" with males because they were so unpredictable. As a result the American herd was lately made up of "modest and inoffensive spinsters, mostly immature, who . . . make no fuss about 'The Life.'"

Elephants were a constant financial drain. They were prone to foot and tooth infections and respiratory and gastrointestinal ailments; their diets were complicated; they fell through bridges; and outraged citizens shot them as insults to decency. There were susceptible to alcoholism, depression, and fits of violence that sometimes left people mangled or dead.

From the owners' point of view, the male elephant's greatest failure was his inability to reproduce. Owners had hoped they would mate, thus eliminating the cost of commissioning an agent to buy and ship an elephant from Asia or Africa, but the males didn't seem interested in mating. But no one knew anything about the mating preferences of elephants. For that matter, neither did the elephants, who came into maturity unsocialized about sex or rearing young.

As their liability exceeded their value, the owners poisoned, shot, and strangled the males. They recorded their deaths tersely: *euthanized, aggressive*. They usually executed them in private but sometimes performed before a paying audience.

The owners also executed elephants in front of other elephants, and at times the elephants even did the killing themselves. Contrary to the assumption that elephants were indifferent to the deaths of their comrades, contemporary research indicates that elephants do present symptoms of post-traumatic stress disorder (PTSD).[33] According to Gay Bradshaw, author of *Elephants on the Edge*, young elephants who witness the deaths of their own parents or other herd members demonstrate behaviors that reflect severe psychological trauma, including an intensified startle response, dysfunctional social behavior, and hyperaggression.[34] But the worsening economic conditions of the Depression trumped all other considerations. While attendance skyrocketed at zoos, it plummeted for circuses.[35] As profit margins waned, so did owners' tolerance for emotionally and financially exhausting animals. By the end of the Depression, virtually every male elephant in America would be dead.

Fond of Tusko, Barnes decided to sell rather than kill him. He knew the Great Unwanted wouldn't fetch much on the market, but he hoped the bull would at least find a better life.

He didn't. In 1931, at the height of the Depression, Tusko began his new life as property of a carnival huckster named Al Painter, who used him to ballyhoo dance marathons at a "Million-Dollar Pleasure Paradise" called Lotus Isle, near Portland, Oregon.[36] Under Painter's management, Tusko's size increased overnight to twelve feet tall and twenty thousand pounds. Painter hinted he intended to give the elephant to the Portland Zoo, but not before he served as the unofficial mascot of Lotus Isle.[37]

In summer, people from Portland swarmed across the Interstate Bridge and past the hundred-foot tall neon Eiffel Tower that pointed the way east, across the wooden bridge to Tomahawk Island and the pleasure palace that was Lotus Isle.

The park, which covered 128 acres, offered forty amusement park rides, including bumper cars inside a building shaped like a bulldog, a carousel with saddled giraffes and horses, a Ferris wheel, and an endless variety of water slides and chutes. "If I were you for just one day . . . ," a come-on ran in the Portland *Oregonian*, " . . . And that day was tomorrow—Boy! Girl! Believe me! I wouldn't hesitate. I'd know just where to go. Eh?—Where?—Why!—To LOTUS ISLE."[38]

The biggest attraction was "The Buddha-Buddha Temple of Dance," the Peacock Ballroom, "where dancing is deliriously delightful." A cavernous faux-Moorish, faux-Egyptian assembly hall, the Peacock Ballroom held more than six thousand people. Friday and Saturday nights, from 9 p.m. to midnight, thousands of people went to the

Peacock to dance or see the dancers. Al Painter promoted the event as "the greatest athletic contest ever held in the Northwest" as thousands of boyfriends and girlfriends, husbands and wives, and brothers and sisters competed in an endurance contest to claim the thousand-dollar grand prize as the Pacific Northwest Dance Marathon Champion. In 1931 the prize was a new Chevrolet Six Cabriolet that listed for $2,900. The Dance Marathon condensed the years of Depression into days, reinforcing the idea that the strong survived because they were willing to pay the physical or emotional cost, however steep.

Al Painter brought Tusko to Portland because it brought celebrity to his "Walkathons," but the clanking rides, squalling children, and delighted screams of the amusement park did not make a stable environment for an elephant as skittish as Tusko.

The promoter kept the bull chained inside a pavilion near the Peacock Ballroom as a side attraction. Incessantly restless, Tusko tolerated the startling annoyances at the amusement park until a daredevil pilot named Tex Rankin decided to buzz Tusko's pavilion.

Part hurricane and part earthquake, Tusko jerked his chains from the iron deadmen that anchored him to the ground and then proceeded to tear up the pavilion, ripping down walls as though they were made of cardboard. He rampaged through several other buildings, sending crowds of people screaming and scattering everywhere.

Tusko's rampage signaled not only the end of Painter's dance marathons but also the end of Lotus Isle, which was suffering from financial and tragic setbacks that would shut it down after only three seasons. Painter, who wasn't the sort who hung around a place for long, took Tusko to the Oregon State Fair in Salem in the fall of 1931 in order to exploit what value the bull had left. When he couldn't cover his feed bill, the state fair seized Tusko as collateral for Painter's debt of two hundred dollars.

Painter disappeared, and the State Fair Board found itself the owner of an elephant it didn't want. Immediately it put Tusko up for sale to the highest bidder, hoping at least to clear Painter's debt.

The State Fair Board got two bids. The highest bid, $140, came from a rendering company in Albany, Oregon, that had calculated the value of Tusko's fat at a penny a pound for seven tons. Sensitive to public outrage for selling Tusko to a slaughterhouse, the fair instead sold him to the second-highest bid, of one dollar.[39]

One dollar was all that Bayard Gray could afford. A former teamster with Al. G. Barnes, "Sleepy" Gray had no job and no home, but he and his partner, Jack O'Grady—Black Diamond's last handler—saw a chance to start their own show with Tusko in the Pacific Northwest.[40]

Tusko was of a different mind-set: he wanted to kill O'Grady. The web of chains that cinched his body would suddenly go taut, ringing with metallic viciousness, as the great elephant lunged at him. O'Grady knew to keep his distance from Tusko, but one day he got incautiously close and the bull snatched him by the legs and yanked him down.

O'Grady grabbed on to a post and tried to hold on, but he was no match for the giant, who peeled him off and then dragged him within range of his tusks.

"What do you think you're doing?!" shouted a man, who threatened to stab Tusko in the snout with a pitchfork.

The astonished elephant backed a step and dropped O'Grady, who clambered out of reach.[41]

Tusko knew O'Grady from the bad business with Black Diamond in Corsicana three years earlier. He also knew the man with the pitchfork, George Washington Lewis, who'd ridden him to Black Diamond's execution. The bull respected Slim Lewis, who was one of the few men he'd listen to.

O'Grady offered Lewis a job on the spot even though he didn't have money to pay him yet. Together they'd tour Tusko around the Northwest. If they could make some money, too, well then, fine.

The first step of their business plan was to exhibit Tusko at the state fair in Salem. But the people around Salem already knew Tusko from Lotus Isle and weren't keen on paying to see the World's Largest and Meanest Elephant, even if admission was only a dime. What money they did make went to feeding Tusko and when that revenue stream dried up, the men stole what hay they needed to keep him fed.[42]

They decided to move Tusko to Portland, hoping their prospects would improve, but the elephant was entering musth and became increasingly incorrigible. The men couldn't afford a closed truck to transport the tusker, so they moved him on a flatbed trailer. With his legs, body, trunk, and tusks all heavily chained, they slowly guided the animal onto the trailer and watched the leaf springs sag pitifully under the tremendous weight. They took Highway 99 north, Tusko's ears and trunk flapping in the wind. The tongue on the trailer pushed the bumper so close to the road that the chains skittered on the pavement, but the trip to Portland passed without incident, except for when Tusko "lunged insanely" at cars that ventured too close.

They drove Tusko to an old warehouse they'd rented for twenty dollars a month on the east side of Portland, near the foot of the Burnside Bridge. In a city with a population of more than 300,000, the men felt that the prospects for a decent cash income were close at hand. They estimated the interior space of the warehouse could hold fifty people at a time, and if they could keep the line moving, they could move hundreds through per hour. A modest calculation of a hundred people a day would produce $10; five hundred, $50; and on that perfect day, a thousand people would bring in $100. And when that dried up there was always Seattle and Vancouver.

The warehouse filled with people as the World's Meanest Elephant turned into Tusko, the Tramp Elephant. Once the warrior who'd squashed a Mexican fighting bull like a bug, knocked an entire town in the Skagit Valley on its can, and tore down half of Lotus Isle, Tusko now begged dimes on the streets of Portland.

In 1931, Portland felt the sharp pinch of the Depression. Every day, home evictions put more families onto the street. Entire families scrounged and begged to stay fed and clothed. Unemployed men even pried up the planking on the abandoned river docks and condemned railroad bridges to burn in their Hooverville shanties.

On Long Island, Polish-American wrestler Leon "the Ponderous Polack" Pinetzky made headlines when he wrestled a four-ton elephant named Rosie because he couldn't find work. A film documents the mock bout in which Pinetzky tussles with "Roughhouse" Rosie, who indulges his antics patiently. After seventy seconds, Rosie mysteriously goes down for the count and Pinetzky raises his arms in victory.[43] The message is hopeful: one could wrestle the metaphoric beast of the Great Depression and win.

Herbert Hoover had less luck than Pinetzky when it

came to wrestling the beast of the Depression. While he claimed it was "an elephant's job" to push the stalled vehicle of state out of the mud, his promise sounded hollow after three years with no meaningful evidence of economic traction. Democrats said it was time for a New Deal and handed out buttons that read "Get Rid of the White Elephant."[44]

Lewis, O'Grady, and Bayard were having second thoughts about Tusko as well. At first, people had flocked to see the hobo elephant bunked in the warehouse on Water Street. They averaged three hundred people a day, enough to feed Tusko and give everyone a solid day's pay, but as fall segued into winter, people slowed to a trickle, and by Christmas, the men didn't have a dollar between them. With winter coming on, all the men could do was beg, borrow, and steal to keep themselves and their elephant fed and warm. Winter would be hard and lean.

Just as things seemed they couldn't get worse, Tusko went into musth.

As the tusker began acting up, the men shackled his forelegs to the warehouse wall in front of him and then wrapped the chains from his rear shackles around a concrete pillar behind him. His range of motion was so inhibited all Tusko could do was stand in place. Increasingly irritated by his confinement, he started to worry his shackles with his trunk.

Each cast-iron shackle consisted of two hinged halves, locked together by a cotter pin. Most elephants understood not only how their shackles were constructed but also how to unhinge them by pulling out the cotter pins. An elephant's trunk weighs four hundred pounds. A network of forty thousand muscles, it's sensitive enough to smell a grain of rice and dexterous enough to pick it up. Ordinarily the trainer would take the precaution of peening down the pins so the bull couldn't escape during musth, but the men had been so preoccupied with their dire circumstances they'd forgotten to do it. Now it was too dangerous to try.

Unable to stop him, the men watched while Tusko worked the pin out of one of his front shackles.

"What are you going to do about it?" asked two cops who'd come by to tip a cup of Virginia Dare.

"I guess we aren't going to do anything," O'Grady answered as Tusko stepped out of the first shackle and then started on the second.

But letting Tusko escape while in musth wasn't an option. The men knew they had to stop the elephant from removing his remaining shackles. O'Grady came up with a plan.

Since Slim was the smallest of the three men, O'Grady proposed, he should climb into a steel barrel, which O'Grady and Bayard would then roll up to Tusko's leg. Slim could then climb out of the barrel and with a little luck, pound down the pins without setting off the bull.

Lewis agreed to the idea, but only if they tested the idea first. They found a barrel and then rolled it toward Tusko to see how he'd react.

Tusko crumpled the barrel as if it were made from tin foil.

Sleepy Bayard suggested they needed something stronger, and O'Grady remembered seeing cast-iron pipe for a water main on the street. Tusko could stand on that all day and wouldn't dent it. Again, Slim agreed to the plan but only if they tested it first.

O'Grady and Sleepy returned with a length of cast-iron pipe big enough around for Slim to crawl inside. But when they rolled the pipe toward Tusko to see how he'd react, the elephant shoved it out of the way. They tried a second time and Tusko just pushed it back.

The men argued over what to do. O'Grady said the only responsible thing to do was call the police, but Slim objected, saying the police would shoot Tusko. Still, he agreed, even that was better than letting an enraged elephant run loose on the streets of Portland. Out of options, the men gloomily finished the bottle of Virginia Dare while Tusko worked the pin out of his second manacle.

Christmas morning, as Tusko freed his forelegs, O'Grady called the police.

Tusko lost no time attacking the wall to which his rear legs were chained. Old timbers split and reinforced concrete cracked as he tore apart the wall between him and street. But the chains held.

The police wanted to shoot Tusko as soon as they saw what was happening but Slim argued strenuously for a stay of execution as long as the chains held. The sergeant, uncertain how to proceed, called the mayor of Portland and asked for orders.

By then the city newspapers and radio stations had gotten wind of what was happening in the warehouse on Water Street. People showed up by the hundreds to watch Tusko break through the warehouse wall, and when the bull tore open a hole large enough for him to step through, he was met with the approving roar of the crowd.

Portland went Tusko crazy on Christmas Day. The crowd swelled as people jostled to get a peek of the elephant breakout. They sensed a showdown was imminent and that something darkly tragic lay ahead.

In spite of his frantic efforts to get free, the chains around Tusko's hind legs continued to hold. The bull took out his frustration on the concrete pillar that held him, butting it to the cheers of the crowd, but it was no match for him.

Sleepy and Slim worked furiously to come up with a solution that would avert the impending disaster. Hurriedly they fashioned a cable snare that they hitched to the back of the truck, and while Tusko tore sheets of corrugated iron off the face of the building, Slim sneaked the loop end of the cable as close to Tusko as he dared and then covered it with hay. Meanwhile, the mayor went into emergency session with the city council.[45]

The mood of the city—for Tusko and against government—likely contributed to the mayor's decision not to shoot the elephant. In order to protect the public safety, the mayor ordered in the National Guard. Within the hour, a cordon of fresh-faced Guardsmen surrounded the elephant. Tusko turned his attention—and frustration—against the troops and lunged at them. One trooper dropped his rifle and ran away.

Still the chains held. Tusko turned back to the structural pylon he was chained to, put his head down, and rammed it as hard as he could, but still the column resisted him. When he decided to try it from another direction, Tusko stepped into the snare.

Sleepy had been sitting in the idling truck waiting for a signal from Slim, and when he saw him frantically waving him on, he popped the clutch and the truck lurched forward, snapping the cable taut. Caught unawares, the cable nearly yanked Tusko off his feet. Stretched between the column and the truck, Tusko was instantly immobilized. Some didn't find the end satisfying.

The crowd dispersed, the Guard and the police pulled out, and Slim led Tusko back into the warehouse and reattached the shackles, this time with their pins hammered down. Ironically, Tusko's misfortune turned into his fortune as three thousand people lined up on Christmas Day 1931 to see the frothy outlaw. Another fifty thousand came between Christmas and New Year's, more than enough to buy Tusko enough hay to last until spring and to buy the men more Virginia Dare.

In 1932, elephants of every color became the rage. Rampaging elephants appeared in Johnny Weissmuller and Maureen O'Sullivan's first Tarzan film, *Tarzan the Ape Man*, and the George Olsen Orchestra—one of the most popular bands of the day—rose to number eight on the music charts with "Pink Elephants." ("Pink elephants on the table / Pink Elephants on the chair / Pink Elephants on the ceiling / Pink Elephants Everywhere.") When spring finally arrived and Tusko cycled out of musth, a man called the Colonel showed up at the warehouse with a plan to resuscitate Tusko's career as a star.

Slim Lewis called H. C. Barber the Colonel after a breed of self-made men who mined for gold no matter how scarce the dust. They were fast-talking, well-dressed men who peddled hope for a living. The few who were good at it built robber baron empires, but the majority of them just floated from one grift to the next.

The Colonel arrived waving a fistful of cash. In return for part ownership in Tusko, he promised to pay for a truck, a trailer, and a tent so they could travel up and down the Pacific Northwest from venue to venue. He said he'd promote and book Tusko; all the others had to do was care for him and make sure he was where he was supposed to be on time.

The men were adrift and Barber was throwing them a rope. Their choice was simple: take the rope or drown. Less from naïveté than from a lapse of good judgment, they shook hands with Barber. As the legal owner of Tusko, Sleepy Gray signed a contract, which, without knowing it, gave the Colonel full title to the elephant.

Cheery optimism quickly faded to weary pessimism as Lewis, Gray, and O'Grady constantly butted heads with Barber over their expenses. The Colonel wanted to cut back on Tusko's feed, but the bull men refused. Barber's lack of concern for the elephant's welfare troubled them. The Colonel thought of Tusko as freight that needed to be shipped from one place to another according to schedule, and Slim knew he couldn't say for sure Tusko would be at a certain place at a certain hour because that depended upon his disposition, not theirs. He might cooperate and step up onto the trailer happily or he might decide to destroy it. One never knew for sure which elephant would show up. The harder the Colonel pushed, the harder the others pushed back. And then, one day, Barber disappeared.

O'Grady worried something bad had happened to him, but Sleepy and Slim weren't surprised the Colonel had left them high and dry. Fortunately they'd paid rent far enough ahead and saved enough hay to make it through the next several months.

The following winter strained the relationships between the three men. By spring O'Grady had given up his share of the partnership and gone back to his wife, and Sleepy started drinking and ended up in jail on a hit-and-run. That left Slim and Tusko, out of time and out of help.

Desperate, Slim packed up Tusko and on a warm Sunday afternoon went on an unannounced stroll in downtown Portland. The elephant complied gracefully, without any trace of the petulance that had marked him as an outlaw. Unflapped by the flurry of automobiles, buggies, and streetcars that plied the streets, Tusko shambled down the boulevard, his chains sparking on the streetcar rails.[46]

The sudden appearance of a fully grown elephant on the street did not cause alarm; rather, people smiled when they saw Tusko and rushed over to him. Greeters mobbed him and he stood quietly in their midst.

When the police arrived they asked Slim for his permit to parade, which, of course, he didn't have. Slim argued that he wasn't parading Tusko but exercising him after being cooped up in a warehouse for six months. When they threatened to arrest Slim, however, he called their bluff. Go ahead, arrest me, he dared, a*nd good luck taking care of the elephant.* The police backed off their threat and asked Slim nicely to return the elephant to his quarters. He agreed, in return for a full police escort.

A renewed surge of interest in Tusko after his afternoon amble brought in enough money for Slim to rent a truck and trailer so he could get the elephant out of Portland. He lashed Tusko onto a flatbed—as he'd done many times before—and then tramped between tourist camps on Highway 99 between Tacoma and Seattle, Washington.[47] Typically they'd stay in a camp or a day or two before nervous locals or the police would shoo them off. They lived hand to mouth, true citizens of the Depression.

That spring, the Colonel showed up again. He said he'd talked a car dealership and a malted milk company to sponsor them in Seattle, and that they had a schedule of appearances for the season to make. So Slim loaded Tusko onto the trailer and towed him north.

Barber had booked Tusko into a variety of street fairs, parades, advertising promotions, and benefit drives. On July Fourth he'd march in the Independence Day parade, draped with bunting, and in August he was scheduled for a Seattle Indians game at Civic Field. But the city of Seattle did not take kindly to the intrusion of an elephant onto its streets and refused to issue Barber an exhibition license. They couldn't legally show the elephant in public anywhere in Seattle. Barber continued to book Tusko in gigs held in parking lots, car lots, and vacant lots around the city, playing cat-and-mouse with the police, who regarded him more of a nuisance than a criminal. Tusko's hit-and-run appearances made him a lovable scofflaw, an elephant on the lam.

The Colonel turned Tusko's house-smashing talents to good use when a house-wrecking company hired him to knock houses off their foundations as a way to advertise its business. Tusko's name was frequently in the newspaper and on the radio as he traveled through Seattle's neighborhoods standing on his flatbed, his ears and tail waving in the breeze. He and Slim lived in an abandoned miniature-golf course across from the main bus terminal, and some nights they'd walk to the Denny Regrade, a neighborhood that stretches north of Seattle's central business district, taking in the night air. Over the summer, the sight and name of Tusko became familiar enough that Seattle started to think of him as one of its own.

Business dropped in cool weather and stopped in cold weather. By the time the season ended, Slim and the Colonel again found themselves in the same dire financial straits as the year before. Soon they wouldn't have enough money to feed Tusko properly, and then not even at all.

Unknown to Slim, the Colonel arranged to take Tusko to a slaughterhouse in Kirkland to have him killed and stuffed so he could put him on tour without the persistent aggravations of a living animal. "No hay to buy, no elephant man to put up with," Lewis wrote bitterly of Barber in his memoirs, "and best of all a completely docile Tusko he could handle himself."[48] As Tusko's rightful owner, Barber could do what he wanted with the elephant, and Slim Lewis was legally powerless to stop him. But the city of Seattle wasn't. On October 8, 1932, the mayor of Seattle officially declared Tusko a public nuisance.

John Francis Dore had launched his candidacy for district attorney of Seattle in 1930, at a time when the Depression was not something coming but something arrived. Businesses collapsed; thousands of people were out of a job and a home. Relief agencies sagged under the weight of need. Dore declared himself a candidate of the working-man, and to prove his sincerity, he pledged not to take a salary for his job.

Dore's detractors accused him of trying to bribe the electorate and tried to have him disbarred—three times—for what they argued was a flagrant disregard for proper ethical conduct by refusing to accept a paycheck. However clever that bit of legal wrangling might have been, it was the wrong position to take during the worst depression in the country's history. Since 1929, industrial production had fallen by half, and a quarter of the national workforce was out of work. Two million people were homeless. When Dore didn't receive the nomination for district attorney of Seattle after the court cleared him of misconduct in 1932, he ran for mayor instead. "I'm in favor of taking the huge fortunes from those who stole them from the American workers," he declared on the stump.[49]

He won handily.

Dore was in office four months when he impounded Tusko at the Woodland Park Zoo. The director of the zoo, Gus Knudson, denounced Barber as a swindler. "Since [Tusko's] leaving the circus," the city's action to seize Tusko was defensible; "he has been used continually as a racket."[50]

Barber hired a lawyer, who reminded the city that although it had taken custody of Tusko, it still did not own him. He intended to file suit to recover Barber's property, unless the city cared to buy Tusko for three thousand dollars.

Mayor Dore agreed to buy Tusko provided Barber provided a clean title and reimbursed the city for the expenses it had incurred in moving, housing, and feeding him.[51] Barber agreed because his investment had just compounded tenfold.

People who wanted Tusko to stay in Seattle gave their nickels, dimes, and quarters to the public subscription campaign started by Knudson at the Woodland Zoo. Meanwhile, schoolchildren campaigned for pennies to pay for his feed. In his first two weeks, thirty thousand people came to the zoo to visit him. He was a star once again.

That winter Tusko went into musth again. He bashed his drinking tub, threw whatever he could lay his trunk on, and tugged at his chains incessantly. As he came out of musth the following June, he suffered an embolism. As he lay dying, Tusko took hold of Slim's wrist gently with his trunk, and held him there beside him. "I sat talking to him for almost an hour," Lewis wrote. "Suddenly he let go my wrist and began struggling again, finally managing to lie on his side." *May we meet again someday*, Lewis wrote for Tusko's epitaph, *where the grass is tall and green, and there are no chains.*[52]

Someone nailed the two-pound blood clot to the side of the barn, where blood ran like tears to the ground. Four days later, H. C. Barber petitioned for Tusko's remains so he could restore the bull "just as he was in life—even to the heavy chains on his tusks and legs." In this way, Barber promised, "Tusko will live forever."[53] He transported Tusko's body to Kirkland, where he had his skin and bones prepared for mounting.

When Barber couldn't pay his bill, the company boxed Tusko's remains, and to this day they remain locked away.[54]

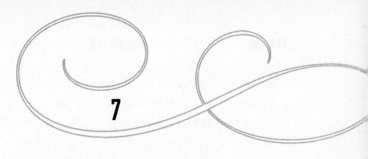

7

Farming with Elephants

◆

from the *Rocky Mountain News,* October 14, 1886

THE WORLD'S LARGEST BAR OF SOAP

Probably no exhibit in the whole exhibition attracts so much attention as the monster elephant shown by John H. and Thomas E. Poole of the Denver Soap Company.

The elephant is an exhibit which attests not only high artistic taste and skill but which shows a wonderful degree of business enterprise. It was built expressly for the exposition. It probably cost a great deal more to put it in place than any other exhibit in the hall.

It is the work of James A. Byrne, who has real and wonderful talent as a sculptor and modeler. There were 7,000 pounds of Denver Best soap used in making the elephant, which is a very perfect model and represents an elephant of unusually large size. The ears, trunk, tusks, sides, legs and feet are all wonderfully like those of the kind of animal kind. The expression of the eye and the general contour of the forehead and head is excellent.

The figure cost $300.

———————————————◆———————————————

The economics of farming and ranching in 1855 invited speculation about the work potential of elephants. Elephants had worked for years in Burma, Ceylon, and Siam, so why not in America? An elephant plowed through hard ground like a hot knife through butter. Some saw it for themselves, while others saw pictures of it.[1]

Plowing Connecticut, 1855.

This scene has the manicured look of a Currier & Ives lithograph. The tusker dominates the foreground as he pulls a plow handled by a mahout dressed "in pink cambric and gold bullion." The train in the background is the New Haven–New York and every day people on the train see the elephant pulling the mammoth plow up and down rows in a field along the tracks. Between the train and the elephant, in the middle ground, the landowner leans on his cane as a gentleman explains to him the progressive economics of farming with elephants.

The man leaning on his cane is P. T. Barnum. It was his farm, his elephant, and his mahout. After he sold his stake in the Great Asiatic, Caravan, Museum and Menagerie, Barnum kept an elephant for "agricultural purposes" on his hobby farm in Bridgeport, Connecticut.

Two months after retiring to his estate, he dressed up one of his hands in Oriental costume, handed him a schedule for the New York–New Haven Railroad, and told him to plow the six-acre plot every time the train came by.

People saw an elephant walk three times faster than a team of horses pulling a subsoil plow that dug down sixteen to twenty inches. Nor did he balk at his work. Remarked one man, "He don't stick up his nose at any reasonable work that his Yankee owner places before him."[2] Newspapers got hold of the story and it spread across the country.

Barnum received a flood of letters "from the secretaries of hundreds of State and county agricultural societies throughout the Union stating that the presidents and directors of such societies had requested them to propound to me a series of questions in regard to the new power I had put in operation on my farm."[3]

Farmers wrote the *New England Farmer*, the first and foremost agricultural journal of its day, and asked, *How many acres could an elephant plow in a day? How much weight could he draw? How much would one cost?* The editor of the *New England Farmer*, Simon Brown, was also the lieutenant governor of Massachusetts. Brown forwarded these inquiries to Barnum and asked for a reply, which put Barnum in a tough spot, because his charade was a hoax to advertise his American Museum in New York City.

In fact, Barnum had been open and honest to those who questioned him about the elephant. When someone asked him how many hours a day the elephant worked, Barnum answered candidly that he worked only in sight of a train.[4] He even joked about how his man had plowed the same field at least sixty times.

Barnum replied to the *New England Farmer* as a husbandman and argued the economics of his experiment. He started out by stating that an elephant ate an average of a bushel of oats and a hundred pounds of hay a day, "Sundays and all." In spite of his large appetite, he had good traits, such as his strong work ethic and his intelligence. "[He] uses ten times better judgment than three-fourths of the 'help' which I am obliged to employ on my farm," he wrote in his reply to Brown, a point of empathy between gentleman farmers that good help was hard to find.

"On the whole he is a very honorable, industrious, intelligent and well-behaved farmer;" Barnum concluded, "nevertheless, I cannot conscientiously recommend elephants as the *cheapest* workers on a farm."

But the class of people who could afford three thousand dollars to buy, feed, and house a fully grown elephant cared about status, not the cost of oats or hay. Barnum had his elephant; now they wanted theirs.

"I began to be alarmed lest some one should buy an elephant, and so share the fate of the man who drew one in a lottery, and did not know what to do with it," wrote Barnum in his memoirs. So he printed a letter marked *Strictly Confidential* and mailed it to those who wanted to know if elephants quarreled with cattle or how old they had to be before they could be bred. "To me the elephant was a valuable agricultural animal, because he was an excellent advertisement to my Museum," he confessed, "but that to other farmers he would prove very unprofitable for many reasons." And then he listed them: they were expensive to buy; they didn't work in cold weather; they were as temperamental as thoroughbreds; and they'd eat everyone out of house and home. "I begged my correspondents not to do so foolish a thing as to undertake elephant farming," Barnum wrote.[5]

Nonetheless, elephants started showing up on farms and ranches anywhere from New Hampshire to the Indian Territory. The American archive of agricultural images includes photographs and newsreels of elephants working on American farms and ranches. They reinforce the notion they were tireless workers as they plowed fields, threw hay, and pumped the well handle for water. "It was found," one critic noted, "that the willing worker [the elephant] performs as well as a good tractor and that the exercise puts him in good humor."

Bad economics turned away those who were in it to save money, but for a few, it actually *made* sense to keep the animals working year-round rather than retire them for the off-season. After all, Barnum's elephant had plowed a field sixty times—a total of 360 acres, *half a section*.

Those who owned elephants looked for productive ways to employ them. The Miller Brothers 101 Ranch in the Indian Territory of Oklahoma combined circus with agriculture. Founded by Confederate colonel George Washington Miller in 1879, the 101 covered 110,000 acres on the Salt Fork and Arkansas rivers south of Ponca, the seat of the famous Cherokee Strip Land Rush of 1893. Miller's neighbor was Major Gordon W. Lillie, better known as Pawnee Bill of Pawnee Bill's famous Wild West Show. Pawnee Bill had encouraged Miller to go into show business.

Although the historian Frederick Jackson Turner had officially declared the frontier effectively closed by 1890, the Wild West shows of Buffalo Bill Cody and Pawnee Bill reaffirmed the prerogatives of Manifest Destiny by reenacting morality plays that showcased the hardships and triumphs of settlers as they overcame tornadoes, prairie fires, droughts, bitter winters, and hostile Indians. They mixed in some trick riding, roping, and shooting

*Circusman Al. G. Barnes and real estate developer Abbott Kinney
hitch a team of elephants to plow a field.*

with Mexican cowboys prettied up in silks (Mexican Joe
Borrero was a favorite), Arab jugglers, Cossacks in red
boots, a human pincushion, some ostriches for roping,
and, of course, an elephant. The 101 toured the United
States, Europe, and South America.

During the off-season the show retired to the 101,
which was the largest diversified farm and ranch in
America in the early 1900s. Besides cattle, bison, hogs,
and horses, they grew wheat, cotton, and corn. Working
hands on the ranch included Bill Pickett (who invented
bulldogging), Bee Ho Gray (given his name by Coman-

che chief Quanah Parker), Will Rogers, Tom Mix, Hoot Gibson, and America's original cowgirl (according to Will Rogers), Lucille Mulhall.

The 101 used its elephant as a draught animal, variously pulling a plow, a hay tedder, a harrow, or a thrasher. Vince Dillon photographed an elephant pulling a harrow in an Oklahoma field in 1910. The elephant in *Elephant Pulling Plow* is a common laborer, and like the workers in the background, she waits for the gentleman in fine clothes to tell her what to do.

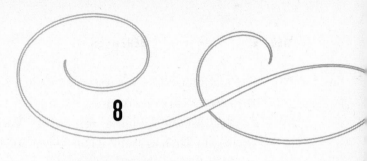

8

Jumbo Nation

◆

from the *New York Herald-Tribune,* January 29, 1886

AN ELEPHANT AS A WITNESS

PICKANINNY TESTIFIES THAT HE IS SORE,
BUT OTHERWISE TREATED WELL

CLEVELAND, Jan. 28 *(Special)* Pickaninny, Forepaugh's trick elephant, was present as witness in a police court this morning in the case against Michael J. Meagher, his trainer, charged with cruelty to animals. Yesterday the beast was taken out to walk three miles in Monumental Park on a wager that he could not do it in thirty minutes. The course was one-fifth of a mile and in the twenty-third minute [of the race], when the elephant was on the last lap, the police arrested Meagher for prodding him behind the ear until the blood flowed. Three thousand persons witnessed the race and consequently there was much interest in the trial this morning and a large crowd was in attendance.

The elephant was unable to ascend the narrow stairway to the court room and the sessions was held in the corridor below. Trainer Meagher was authorized to act as interpreter, and the examination began, the elephant lifting his trunk and taking the oath administered by a notary public.

"Pick, do you feel sore?" was the first question.

In response the animal nodded.

"Are you treated well?"

Pick gave a grunt of assent.

Mr. Wrightman, of the Humane Society, then examined the injured ear and declared that the animal had suffered no harm, whereupon Meagher was dismissed.

While Pick was on the witness stand, he was kept in good humor by the officers of the court, who gave him loaves of bread. After the trial Pick was subjected to the interviewing process and answered inquiries as readily as in the witness box.

◆

The great elephant trainer "Professor" George Arstingstall responded to a question from the *New York Times* about a recent elephant stampede started by a mouse in Madison Square Garden.[1] "The sight of a mouse will make an elephant frantic with fright," he said, further speculating that the reason for such peculiar behavior stemmed from a time in the distant past when wild elephants must have been attacked "by a mole, or some animal resembling the mouse, which fastens itself to their bodies and worries them."[2]

Arstingstall was Barnum's commanding general when it came to his elephants, which at times numbered as many as forty. He'd spent his entire adult life with elephants and through experience had come to know them intimately. He knew the elephant was the root of the circus, and that without one most circuses died. He also knew how to make an elephant obey his commands unquestioningly. He bragged he could teach any trick to any elephant— including standing on his head—within twenty-four hours. His managerial expertise came from his unflinching use of the bullhook.

A bullhook is a goad made of two parts. The head is a sharpened steel or bronze hook attached to a wooden shaft, usually two or three feet long, sometimes called a spear. Indians sometimes carved these shafts out of elephant ivory for their rajahs, but for the most part they were unadorned and utilitarian.

A bullhook inflicts successive levels of "discomfort," to use a common euphemism for pain. The mahout—the driver—uses the bullhook to accelerate, steer, and brake his elephant by sticking the sharp point of the prod in his skin, often drawing blood.

The hook provided more corrective measures. If an

elephant misbehaved willfully, the keeper would dig the hook into the flesh around his shoulder and then push or pull. Elephants shuddered under these attacks, which often drew a great deal of blood.

The bullhook usually ensured compliance. The more pain it inflicted, the more compliant the elephant became. Depending how heavy-handedly a bull man wielded the bullhook, the elephant regarded it with respect at best and dread at worst.

The public assumed such a little stick could hardly be more than an annoyance to such a great animal, but elephant skin is sensitive, and the elephant reacts to being poked, prodded, and, when the handler felt a hard correction was necessary, stabbed. Arstingstall believed in the power of the hook and didn't spare its use. Being in charge of twenty or thirty elephants offered him little choice; the consequences of a stampede were too awful to contemplate.

Although Arstingstall was a keen observer of elephant behavior, he translated what he learned through the ideological lens of the human domination of animals. He perceived the elephants' fear of mice and knew that one scurrying among them could indeed send them into a panic. However, he made an error of perception rather than observation when he attributed an elephant's fear of mice to a behavioral adaption that had evolved over thousands of years. Actually, the adaptation, as Arstingstall called it, had taken less than a dozen years to evolve.

If Arstingstall had had the opportunity to observe elephants in their native environment, he might have noticed they weren't afraid of little animals that scurry. Except for circus elephants, who were famously afraid of mice.

What people politely called a mouse was really a rat. Circus elephants were terrified of the rats that swarmed out at night and gnawed on their sensitive feet and tails. Powerless to defend themselves, the elephants had no choice but to suffer them, and so when they saw anything that looked like a rat, they reacted with horror.

Arstingstall's system of belief, which he shared with most bull men, disconnected him emotionally from the elephants. His guiding principles were corporate, not biological, so he didn't have time or use for the psychology of elephants. An untrained elephant was worth $10,000 and a trained elephant $15,000; therefore, he was responsible for circus capital worth hundreds of thousands of dollars.[3] He had to run a tight ship.

Matthew Scott, on the other hand, took a kindly approach to governance. Originally a parrot-keeper for the Earl of Derby on the gardens of his estate, the Englishman graduated from canaries and kiwis to elands and eventually to the world's most famous elephant, Jumbo, whom he took care of at the Regent's Park Zoological Gardens in London.

Unlike Arstingstall, Scott saw himself as a loving parent. "I have been more than a father to him," Scott wrote of Jumbo in his autobiography, "for I have performed the duties and bestowed the affections of a mother."[4] From the time he first encountered him in 1864 to the last moments of the great elephant's life in 1885, Matthew Scott doted on Jumbo's well-being.

Scott devoted himself to Jumbo and even slept near him so he'd know as soon as something went wrong. "Jumbo heartily hates and abominates rats," he noted. "Very often in the dead of night I have been awakened by poor Jumbo's groans, as if in pain and trouble, and, when I hastened to see what was the matter, I have beheld the rats by hundreds gnawing his hoofs, and snapping viciously at his legs and tail." Scott killed as many rats as he could with a stick, but when that didn't reduce their number sufficiently, he built a network of traps that gradually killed them.

Scott said Jumbo thanked him many times for getting rid of the rats. He also said he and Jumbo talked to each other through words and gestures no one else could hear or see.

Jumbo was captured as a newborn in late 1860 after elephant hunters in the desert highlands of eastern Sudan killed his mother for her ivory. He spent his first years at the Jardins des Plantes in Paris, and in 1864, the French sold Jumbo to the British, who were so desperate for their own African elephant they bought him sight unseen.

If they had seen Jumbo before the sale, the English might have had second thoughts about buying him. "A more deplorable, diseased, and rotten creature never walked God's earth," Matthew Scott wrote about his first encounter with Jumbo. "The poor thing was full of disease, which had worked its way through the animal's hide, and had almost eaten out its eyes. The hoofs of the feet and the tail were literally rotten, and the whole hide was so covered with sores, that the only thing I can compare it to was the condition of [a] man [with] leprosy."[5] Scott nursed Jumbo back to health and to fame, so that by 1866, he was giving rides to thousands of English children, including one lad named Winston Churchill. The English public doted on Jumbo and considered him a national treasure. In the *New York Times'* quirky version of British history, Jumbo gave a command performance to Queen Victoria at Windsor Castle Park, where he gave rides to the royals. Her Majesty would "romp with him by the hour, making him fetch and carry like a dog and rolling with him in innocent delight upon the turf," although it's hard to imagine Queen Victoria rolling on the grass at all, much less with Jumbo. At tea, Jumbo sat at the queen's table, where he begged lumps of sugar "like a trained poodle."[6]

Jumbo was also the people's elephant. He was so popular that a pundit redrew the English coat of arms by swapping the elephant for the imperial lion and changing the country's motto from *Dieu et Mon Droit* (God and My Right) to *Dieu et Mon Jumbo*.

According to Mark Twain, P. T. Barnum decided
to buy Jumbo from the London Zoo the same way he'd
bought the Shakespeare family's twelve-room farmhouse
in Stratford-on-Avon several years before.

When last occupied, the Shakespeare farmhouse was
a butcher shop. The building was in major disrepair, and
rather than spend the money to restore it, the owner decided to sell the property.

Twain said Barnum told him he bought the house so
he could move it "brick by brick" to America, rebuild

Matthew Scott and Jumbo Give a Ride to English Children.
Die-cut Victorian scrap, ca. 1883.

it, and put it on display in his museum. "In America we know how to value anything that Shakespeare's touch has made Holy," he declared. "You'll see."[7]

The thought of Shakespeare sharing the same space as the FeeJee Mermaid and Ned the Learned Seal rankled the British so much, the press decried the King of Humbug for trying to filch their heritage. As Twain related the outrage, "there was an explosion, I can tell you. England rose! What, the birthplace of the master-genius of all the ages and all the climes—that priceless possession of Britain—to be carted out of the country like so much old lumber and set up for a sixpenny desecration in a Yankee show-shop—the idea was not to be tolerated for a moment." Parliament passed emergency legislation that barred Barnum, a foreigner, from moving Shakespeare's house.[8]

In return, Barnum offered to sell the house back to the British. He received several bids, one offering double what he'd paid for the property, rumored to be fifty thousand dollars.

Newspapers on both sides of the Atlantic buzzed with the story. On the foreign shore Barnum was the Yankee Menace; on his own shore, however, he was the Yankee Hero. But Barnum raised eyebrows again when he agreed to sell back the house for what he'd paid for it and not a penny more or less. The offer came with a condition, however. He'd return the house provided the British government promised to restore the building.

The Crown conceded. Barnum gave back ownership of the house and then offered his deepest regrets if he'd offended anyone as he withdrew to America with a better understanding of how to deal with the British.[9]

Thirty-six years later he was back, this time to buy another national treasure—Jumbo, a signature symbol of the British Empire.

In the late 1870s Barnum had dinner in London at the home of Charles Jamrach, the preeminent wild animal trafficker of his time. He'd made his reputation selling exotic animals to zoos and rich people who kept their own personal menageries, such as Lord Rothschild and the English painter-poet Dante Gabriel Rossetti. (Rossetti's quirky menagerie included kangaroos, wallabies, raccoons, armadillos, a woodchuck, and his favorite, an Australian wombat, which he'd bought from Jamrach.) Jamrach's specialty, however, was rhinos and elephants.

After dinner the men drank in Jamrach's "private snuggery" in East London. Jamrach drank port while Barnum, a Universalist teetotaler, drank tea. Barnum offered Jamrach $36,000 for eighteen elephants, an average of $2,000 per elephant. Jamrach had just offered Rossetti an elephant for the market rate of $600, and so he appreciated the potential for a large profit.

Barnum had a condition, however: Jumbo had to be one of the eighteen elephants.

Jamrach laughed. "Jumbo is as popular as the Prince of Wales and the Zoo wouldn't dare sell him," he said. "All of England would be outraged at the idea; he is an English institution and is part of the national glory. You might as well think of buying Nelson's Column."

Barnum sweetened the pot by offering to pay a "round" figure to get the elephant.

"How round?" asked Jamrach.

"Ten thousand," replied Barnum.

The figure gave Jamrach pause. It could happen, Jamrach told Barnum, but it could take time for things to work out.

It took three years. In 1881, Jumbo was changing from a juvenile into a sexually mature male, and his bouts of musth grew increasingly violent and unpredictable. He became so volatile that Abraham Bartlett, the superintendent of the Zoological Gardens at Regent's Park, begged the zoo's council for a high-powered rifle and permission to kill him. The potential for mishap troubled him so much he felt it necessary to have the means and the right to kill him "should such a necessity arise."[10] The council, alarmed by Bartlett's intimations of a rogue elephant plowing through a crowd of men, women, and children, gave him both.

Timed to Jumbo's next round of musth, Barnum sent Bartlett a cable that asked with Yankee bluntness, "What is the lowest price you can take for the large male African elephant?"

"Will sell him for £2,000," Bartlett shot back.[11]

Bartlett had his own intelligence that Barnum had just merged with James Bailey and James Hutchinson to create the Great London Circus, Sanger's Royal British Menagerie and the Grand International Allied Shows United.[12] Barnum's *Greatest Show on Earth* needed an elephant as big as its name, and that meant Bartlett could name his own price, which he calculated at five times its market value.

Bartlett's offer was a fraction of what Barnum would have paid if he'd been pressed harder. He figured Jumbo was worth three times what Bartlett wanted for him, and while Barnum groused about the price publicly, privately he was delighted. No more English buns and oranges for Jumbo; from now on it was peanuts and waffles.

When word of the sale became public, the English swarmed out of their hive and filled the air with buzzing. Newspapers were flooded with letters to the editor demanding Bartlett be charged with treason for selling Jumbo. Others demanded immediate action, and if the government wasn't willing or able, then a citizen committee should take Jumbo back, by force if necessary. A more moderate letter proposed a Children's Defence Fund, which would turn out the nation's schoolchildren to collect pennies to buy back Jumbo.

Meanwhile, barristers flooded the court with petitions to void the sale. One petitioner asked Mr. Justice Chitty in the Court of Chancery to void the sale based upon the assertion it was "morally wrong for the [zoo] to sell a dangerous animal."

While solicitors argued the case in court, the grandes dames of England argued the case in the court of public opinion. A civilized person, they argued, wouldn't tear Jumbo from his wife of twenty years, Alice.[13] They accused Barnum of mental cruelty by forcing Jumbo "to get divorced because of American business enterprises."[14] Then they resorted to heartrending abolitionist metaphors to describe Jumbo's separation from Alice by comparing the pair to the "parting of Uncle Tom from his negro wife down in 'Old Kentucky,' when he was sold in the slave-market."[15]

After one hundred thousand schoolchildren signed a petition to Queen Victoria to keep Jumbo, she felt obliged to step in and ask Mr. Barnum in the politest of terms to return Jumbo to England.

Barnum couldn't have been more thrilled to say no.

Barnum later confessed that "all I want[ed] is a big advertisement." He hoped Jumbo would "furnish me a couple of columns of gratis advertising in every English and American paper for a couple months, and give my show the biggest boom a show ever had in this world."[16]

His strategy worked, although he underestimated how much the affair would dredge up bad feelings between the two nations that had lingered since the American Revolution. On British shores, Barnum was a crass, cold-blooded, and immature Yank, and on American shores he was the mischievous Yankee who'd tweaked the queen's nose. For some Americans, Jumbo immigration symbolized a shift in power between the aged English dowager and the young American pioneer. The hysteria rose to such a pitch that James Russell Lowell, then the American ambassador to the Court of St. James's, later remarked wryly the "only burning question" left between the United States and England was Jumbo.[17]

The emotionally charged atmosphere made moving Jumbo from England to the United States a logistical and public relations nightmare. First Barnum had to build a crate strong enough to withstand a restless or even angry elephant for ten days while at sea, and second he had to convince Jumbo to get into the box, which Barnum knew from experience wasn't likely to go smoothly.

Ordinarily the bull men would have prompted Jumbo to enter the crate by using "appropriate force," defined as the minimum amount of force necessary to change an elephant's behavior. Barnum's men were prepared to do whatever it took to get Jumbo into the box, but to their surprise, Barnum told them *hands off.* The British were looking for an excuse to stop the sale, and he wasn't about to open himself up to charges of physical cruelty. They'd have to coax him with kindness, not cruelty.

The crate was thirteen feet tall and made from sawn oak planks three inches thick and reinforced with heavy iron castings. Closed on three sides, the fourth side left space for Jumbo to stick out his trunk.

Because its designers anticipated Jumbo wouldn't step willingly into such a claustrophobically small space, the crate featured a removable front door and rear wall. By leaving the rear wall open, they hoped to dupe Jumbo into thinking he was walking through a tunnel, not into a box. No matter how much they tried to sweet-talk him into the box, however, he refused, which the English gleefully took as proof of his reluctance to leave the country. Each day Jumbo resisted, the louder the British cheered.

The wind suddenly shifted in the opposite direction when the court upheld the sale. As if understanding its implications, Jumbo resignedly entered the box and let the men close the doors on him for the next ten days.

Jumbo was Barnum's masterwork. A success from the start, Jumbo made more money than any single animal attraction in America. Barnum put him in a class by himself. He was the *Mighty Monarch of his Race*, "The Largest Animal known to Exist, beside whom all Elephants look like Pygmies."[18]

In truth, Jumbo wasn't bigger than several other bulls already in America. He was leggy and tall, which made him seem larger, but he grew in size exponentially because of Barnum's knack for mumbo jumbo.

The etymology of Jumbo's name is a hopeless muddle. It could have come from the Kiswahili greeting *jambo* or from the word *jumbe*, which translates as the big man, the chief. It also could have come from the Zulu word *jumba*, meaning a large package, or from the Mandingo *mumbo jumbo*, a concept British writer Francis Moore explained in 1738 as "a thing invented by the Men to keep their Wives in awe." Over time *mumbo jumbo* broadened its meaning as a form of gibberish whose purpose was to confound.

Whereas the British thought of Jumbo as a willing servant of the empire, Barnum recrafted him so that his size became his preeminent value. Then he connected size to worth. When the *Assyrian Monarch* left the dock in Gravesend, Jumbo was worth what Barnum had paid for him: $3,000. By the time the ship docked in New York Harbor, Barnum had recalculated his worth at $30,000. The bigger the figure got, the bigger Jumbo got.

Jumbo arrived in New York on April 9, 1882. The city showered him with gifts, including chocolate, beer, oysters, and roses. "There was more excitement in this City," quivered the *New York Times*, "than there would be in London if Queen Victoria's imperial knee was swelled to twice its royal size."[19]

Barnum invited the press to the Castle Garden pier at the foot of Manhattan Island to see America's latest—and

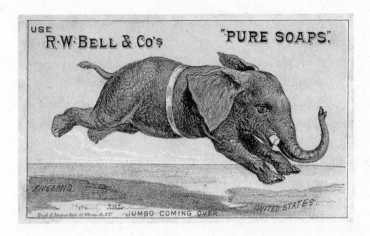

Jumbo Leaps from England to the United States.
Trade Card for Bell & Company's "Pure Soaps," 1882.

largest—immigrant step onshore. The press wasn't shy about accepting his invitation. A steady stream of front-page stories announcing Jumbo's pending arrival had whipped the city into a fever of anticipation.

When the reporters saw Jumbo, however, they were disappointed. He wasn't nearly as large as they'd thought. Barnum had created a Jumbo-of-the-mind that was the size of a giant woolly mammoth, but when fantasy suddenly collided with reality at Castle Garden, the showman explained to his befuddled audience there was "a considerable difference between the actual and the 'museum' height of elephants."

"How high does he reach up with his trunk?" Barnum asked Matthew Scott for the benefit of the press. "Forty-nine feet, isn't it?"

"Twenty-six feet," replied Scott dourly.

"If I were a showman, I would have exaggerated it," Barnum admitted with customary candor, "but there's nothing like the truth!"[20]

Barnum preferred to talk metaphorically about the *Matchless Monarch of Over-Shadowing Majestic Presence.* When a reporter asked how big Jumbo was, Barnum told him the elephant was so big he'd displaced six hundred Irish immigrants from passage on the ship,[21] and when another reporter asked him how long Jumbo's trunk was, he said it was as big as a full-grown crocodile. Then he'd continue with comparisons that had everyone scratching their heads. Jumbo's footprints were so big, exclaimed Barnum, they looked like the "indentation" of a fat man who'd fallen off a high building.

"Then everybody was happy," wrote the *New York Times*, "and looked with increased pride upon the beast."

No one was better at mumbo jumbo than P. T. Barnum.

Thousands of the curious lined up on the street for a glimpse of the team of eight mighty horses that hauled Jumbo in his crate up Broadway. He greeted America waving his trunk aloft as men in the crowd waved their hats and women fell to their knees in astonishment. A full-page picture of Jumbo in *Leslie's Illustrated Family Almanac* shows the horses straining to pull a box that stands two stories tall. The picture's perspective enhances the claim painted on the side of the box: *Monster Elephant JUMBO.*

That night ten thousand people went to see the Greatest Show on Earth at Madison Square Garden, which Barnum had turned into a three-ring *Great Roman Hippo-*

"Jumbo's Arrival in America."
Leslie's Illustrated Almanac, *1882.*

drome with men on horses and camels racing around the oval. The crowds roared and gave Arstingstall a standing ovation when he paraded Jumbo before them while Matthew Scott watched silently from the fringe.[22]

According to Barnum, Jumbo paid for himself in six days.[23] By his third year he would clear a 150 times Bartlett's selling price.

Jumbo was—and remains—the most famous elephant of the Western world. Both real and invented, he was a symbol of American spirit as it equated strength with size. According to Barnum, for something to be jumbo it had to be bigger and stronger than the competitors. It had to possess power "of a Herculean order" that brought "certain destruction to all pretenders and would-be competitors, who foolishly get under his feet or within sound of his trumpet-trunk." Bigger was better, and both America and Jumbo were as big as they got.

Before Jumbo arrived in New York, a *jumbo* was defined as someone who was socially inept, such as a *goof* or a *rube*. A new jumbo came to town in 1882, when the word changed its meaning to anything supersized, with future uses such as a *jumbo jet*, a *jumbo loan*, or *Jumbovision*, which later changed its name to *Jumbotron*.

The word *jumbo* caught fire at every level of American culture. Within weeks of Jumbo's arrival, the Pennsylvania state librarian got into a spat with a state representative and called him a jumbo, an obvious reference to his size. "The epithet is both impolite and inappropriate," one newspaper editor huffed. "The elegant Col. A. K. McClure has nothing in common with Barnum's international elephant."[24] Those who knew McClure understood the comparison at once.

Barnum constantly remade Jumbo into a bigger and bigger giant. Over the first few months he claimed Jumbo had grown several inches, that his tusks had pushed out another foot, and that he'd gained two-thousand pounds. "He is gradually increasing his already monstrous and phenomenal development," touted his promotional literature. "His mastadonic size and really mastadonic shape overwhelm the beholder."[25]

In 1882, the United States became a jumbo nation. Within weeks of his arrival, Easton, Cole & Company built the Jumbo Whistle, the largest steam whistle in America, which could be heard from fifty miles on a clear day.[26] Edison named the big dynamo he built to run the country's first electric generating plant Jumbo, and coal dealers started selling Jumbo peas and Jumbo nuts for an extra penny or two a pound. As the next size after large, Jumbo became an American standard of measure. He was the largest, the longest, the tallest, the heaviest, and the strongest, which made him an analogue for industry, for governance, and a concept for the country itself. The jumbo nation had arrived.

In 1882 Apollo won the eighth running of the Kentucky Derby, Robert Ford shot Jesse James in the back, and Standard Oil of New Jersey incorporated.

Railroads, factories, and foundries were working overtime, and smoke billowing from chimneys was a sign of progress.

Innovations in the printing trade brought down the cost of color reproduction, which made it possible for tradesmen to promote their goods or services on color picture cards they handed out by the hundreds if not thousands. Trade cards and "scraps"—colorful heavy paper stock die-cut into the shapes of things that reflected sentimental Victorianism such as angels, children, flowers, and dogs—became so popular, women collected them in "scrap" albums. An early and effective form of advertising, a trade card consisted of a colored lithograph of something beautiful, interesting, or fun on the front and advertising for a merchant's services or wares on the back.

The Victorian trade card cut a wide swath across popular culture as it embodied the fantasies and realities of daily life in the 1880s. Vendors advertised soap, sewing thread, tobacco, stove polish, hay rakes and plows, horseshoe nails, rat poison, chicken feed, and countless purgatives, emetics, and laxatives.

Circus men used cards to advertise their prize attractions. Isaac Van Amburgh promoted Quedah, "the only living specimen of the supposed extinct mammoth," and Adam Forepaugh promoted his whitewashed elephant, the Light of Asia, "the White Wonder of the Orient." And P. T. Barnum promoted Jumbo.

Tradesmen clamored to use Jumbo to advertise everything from oysters, soap, baking soda, and thread to agricultural equipment. Bell's Soap and Clark's O.N.T. ("Our New Thread") distributed a ten-card series in which Jumbo appears as a gentlemanly citizen of New York, usually dressed with bowler hat and cane, enjoying life as a cosmopolitan. In one card he eats seated at a table in a fancy restaurant with a napkin tied around his neck, and in another, he guzzles beer at a bar. He goes to the opera, plays euchre, gives a violin recital, and, dressed in a stylish bathing costume, frolics in the surf at Coney Island with his little pal, Tom Thumb.

Barnum claimed not only to have the largest elephant in the world but also the smallest. Tom Thumb was a "dwarf" elephant, named after Barnum's star of stars, Charles Stratton, the original Tom Thumb, whom Queen Victoria had dubbed General. Barnum described him as a perfectly proportioned human who was twenty-four inches tall and weighed twenty pounds. He was the first of a Barnum tribe of little people that included Admiral Dot, Commodore Nutt, and Major Atom.

Barnum paired his giants with his dwarfs to empha-

size their size, and he did the same with Jumbo and Tom
Thumb.[27] In Barnum's narrative, Jumbo watched over
the antics of his clownish brother. The two were insep-
arable.

Jumbo and Tom Thumb at Coney Island (1882).

Jumbo and Tom Thumb at Madison Square Garden.
Note Jumbo's legginess.
Trade card, 1882.

Elephants changed from being billboards in a street parade to being corporate advertising campaigns. The Willimantic Thread Company parodied "Jumbo's Arrival in America" in a card that shows two strands of its cotton sewing thread dragging Jumbo up Broadway against his will. "JUMBO MUST GO," reads the caption. A banner waves in the sky, "*AMERICA AHEAD!*"[28]

The Remington Agricultural Company, the mother company of the Remington empire, advertised its new Burdick hay tedder on Jumbo cards, and a soap company in Connecticut called J. B. Williams used him to show that *Ivorine is a Big Thing.* He even symbolized the power of a laxative called Castoria. (*From peasant nurse to highborn lady, All mothers know what's good for baby.*)

The Jumbo family epitomized domestic middle-class progress. On one card for Ivorine (the forerunner of

JUMBO MUST GO, BECAUSE DRAWN BY WILLIMANTIC THREAD!

America Ahead! (1882).

Ivory), Jumbo wears a smoking jacket and his signature red fez and watches contentedly as Mrs. Jumbo washes the dishes with detergent powder rather than a bar of soap. These scenes naturalized Jumbo in the national commercial and domestic landscape.

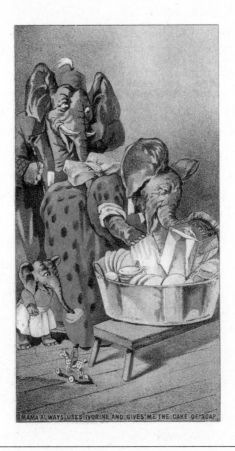

MAMA ALWAYS USES IVORINE AND GIVES ME THE CAKE OF SOAP.

The Jumbo Family uses Ivorine, 1883.

After Jumbo joined the troupe at Madison Square Garden in the spring of 1882, the Greatest Show on Earth went on tour for 186 days. Four steam locomotives pulled a hundred railroad cars packed with the circus from New York to Philadelphia, Washington, Baltimore, Boston, Cleveland, and 123 other, small cities and towns. Jumbo had his own railroad car, painted in red and blue and bordered in gold, called Jumbo's Palace.

Jumbo was Barnum, Bailey, and Hutchinson's star attraction from the day he arrived until the day he died in a tragic train accident in 1885. "He's all we want to see," said one irrepressible visitor, "and we won't look at anything else."

But it was impossible not to look at anything else. In 1883, the circus was a nonstop cascade of irresistible sights, sounds, and smells. One spectator's vivid impression of the show in Madison Square Garden captures the spirit of the circus at the height of its power:

Amid the music of sounding brass and tinkling cymbals, to say nothing of hoarse horns and sonorous drums, a glittering cavalcade wound about the Garden. This was the grand entrée. The animals one by one came out from the caverns in royal purples and gold and sparkling gems. The menials on the dromedaries proudly waved elaborately wrought banners and devices. When the pageant had disappeared Jumbo came forth in all his modern magnificence, with a troop of children on his back.[29]

Then came a band of Sioux Indians, some cowboys, a giant, a bearded lady, the fat boy, a tattooed man, and a Hindu serpent sorceress who wore a necklace of live snakes. There was the clown elephant and an elephantine clown. Professor Arstingstall made the elephants stand on their heads while the Olympians of the sawdust circle—acrobats, strong men, boxers, dancers, and roller skaters—performed nonstop on the stage between the rings. During their finale all the elephants would "tail up" and walk on their hinds legs in a rumba line called the Long Mount. "There was no dissenting voice," wrote the *New-York Tribune*, "that the show was the best Barnum had ever given in New York." His circus had finally earned its acclaim as the *Greatest Show on Earth*.

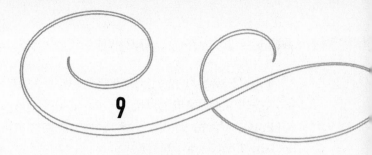

Jumbo Saves the Brooklyn Bridge

from the *New York Times*, August 11, 1890

THE CIRCUS TURNED HIS BRAIN

From the Cleveland (Ohio) Leader, Aug. 9.

Charles Taylor, an eighteen-year-old boy, living on Hicks Street, went to Barnum's circus when it was in this city, and laughed so much that he has been unable to stop laughing since.

He has been behaving himself so foolishly that on Thursday night his friends had him locked up in jail, pending an inquiry into his sanity. He was put in a padded cell, but on Friday morning it was found he had torn all the padding to pieces, so he was placed in another cell. The only thing he could possibly get hold of in this cell was the water pipe, and about noon he wrenched it from its fastenings and a flood of water spread over the jail before his action was discovered.

Taylor's employer says he was perfectly sane until he went to the circus.

◆

Robert Odlum taught young ladies how to jump off
the upper deck of a sinking steamship without getting
hurt. He taught the children of Presidents Garfield and
Hayes how to swim, and he saved Vice President Schuyler
Colfax's son from drowning. At the age of thirty-seven,
Odlum was robust, well built, and had an odd obsession
for jumping off tall objects into the water. He was convinced that a properly prepared person in good physical
condition could jump into the water safely from 140 feet,
the height of the roadway of the newly constructed New
York and Brooklyn Bridge, over the East River. His reason for making the jump was simple: "[I]t will be the
greatest jump on record," he said, "and it will make me
famous."

The Brooklyn Bridge was a technological marvel of
engineering that summed up the progress of the nineteenth century. A hallmark of American ingenuity, the
bridge was dubbed (as were Jumbo and the conjoined
twins Millie and Christine McCoy), the *Eighth Wonder
of the World*.[1] The bridge towers stood head and shoulders above everything in the city except the tip of Trinity
Church's spire. Four massive cables held up sixteen hundred feet of five roadways for people, carriages, wagons,

and trains. The only way to build such a bridge was by taking "one grand flying leap from shore to shore over the masts of ships."[2] No piers, no drawbridges, just one high-flying arch that connected the country's first- and third-largest cities (Brooklyn was an independent city until 1898).

Preceding the Statue of Liberty by three years, the Brooklyn Bridge was the colossus that immigrants saw as they steamed into "the air-bridge harbor that twin cities frame."[3] The bridge was a showpiece of American power, wealth, and innovation.

But suspension bridges had a reputation for falling, either because they couldn't sustain their own weight (its dead load), the weight of traffic across them (its live load), or the force of even moderate winds (its dynamic load), which sometimes twisted the bridges into their cables. The Wheeling and Belmont Wire Suspension Bridge, the first bridge to carry land traffic over a major western waterway, collapsed into the Ohio River after a moderate windstorm in 1854.[4]

Technology had changed in the fifteen years since the Wheeling Bridge disaster. John Roebling, the architect and chief engineer of the Brooklyn Bridge, replaced the iron cables with steel. But New Yorkers were skeptical. They hadn't forgotten that Roebling (with Charles Ellet, Jr.) had designed the disastrous Wheeling Bridge. Building a reliable bridge across the treacherous tidal waters of the East River was a fantasy beyond the skill of any engineer.

Even so, construction started on the Brooklyn Bridge

in 1869 and continued for fourteen years, during which time New Yorkers lost their enthusiasm for it. Rather, people focused on the workers who died in various fires, collapses, falls, explosions, or from the "bends" from diving to the river floor that plagued construction. John Roebling himself died of tetanus weeks after construction began, when a ferry crushed his foot at a pier.[5]

By the time the bridge was completed in 1883, people had grown comfortable with the idea of progress in technology. Since construction had started, American imagination and innovation had produced the incandescent lightbulb, the telephone, the sewing machine, the phonograph record, the lawn mower, and dozens of other marvelous inventions. Skepticism about the bridge faded as the mighty towers rose on either shore.

The Brooklyn Bridge officially opened on May 24, 1883. President Chester Alan Arthur and the governor of New York, Grover Cleveland (who would become the next president), along with distinguished gentlemen of Congress, business and civic leaders, socialites, and thousands of curious onlookers, attended the gala opening on the bridge. The "Dandy" Seventh Regiment of the New York State militia band played "Yankee Doodle" while the luminaries onstage greeted and shook hands with one another. Patriotic banners that hung from the bridge waved in the light breeze. When the military band struck up "Hail to the Chief," cannons from the shore batteries at Fort Harrison and the navy yards fired salutes that boomed across the bay.

Within twenty-four hours of opening, 150,300 people ventured onto the bridge promenade. Hundreds of carriages and trains filled the roadways.[6] Newspapers reported on the first politician to walk across the bridge, the first drunk, the first Negro, the first beggar, and the first musician, a Scotsman playing his pipes.[7] Seventy hours after the opening, more than 400,000 people had been on the bridge.[8]

On the seventh day, disaster struck.

Most businesses had closed their doors on May 30 in remembrance of the patriots who'd fought and died in the wars since the revolution. At a time when the average workweek was ten hours a day, six days a week, Memorial Day was an oasis in a desert of toil.

As the sun burned off the morning dampness, people appeared on the bridge promenade. The distance of the river span between towers was a little more than a quarter mile, so one could stroll the promenade from Brooklyn to Manhattan and back easily in an hour, which included stopping at the top of the bridge to see a spectacular panorama of New York City and Brooklyn from fourteen stories in the air.

To the east they saw the Hudson River and beyond it, the smokestacks of New Jersey lazing smoke into the sky. The river flowed past the bottom tip of Manhattan and into the lower bay, where hundreds of schooners, frigates, tugs, and ferries trafficked the waters. Looking up the East River, paddle wheelers loaded to the rails with passengers churned the water.

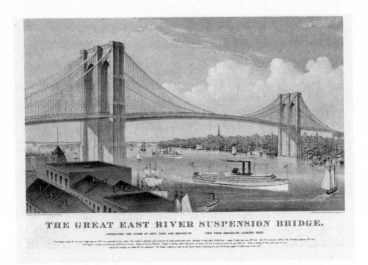

THE GREAT EAST RIVER SUSPENSION BRIDGE.

The Great East River Suspension Bridge, *Currier & Ives, 1883.*
Note the spire of Trinity Church in the background.

From the top of the bridge, people watched stevedores
and longshoremen loading and unloading ships; wagons
arriving empty and leaving full; and streams of people
on foot, horseback, carriage, and bicycle bustling through
the streets. The sight captured a sense of a vigorous nation
going about its business.

On that Memorial Day, a woman lost her balance and
fell down a flight of stairs on the Manhattan approach to the
bridge. The stairwell that led from the promenade down
toward the street was so tightly packed with people she
likely would have been trampled if a security officer hadn't
grabbed her before she disappeared underfoot. (A coroner's
inquest later estimated there were twenty thousand people

on the bridge at the time.) The officer fought vicious currents of men and women who were being funneled into the confining stairwell and managed to get her to the bottom, when another woman saw what she thought was an assault in progress and started to scream, which, in turn, triggered someone to shout, *The bridge is falling!*[9]

The bridge erupted into chaos. People surged toward the exit, compressing those in the stairway so fiercely that some bled from their mouths and ears. Others were pushed forward so hard they tumbled over the bodies of those who had already fallen down. "The bodies were piled four or five deep at the foot of the stairway," wrote the *New York Times*, "and most of those at the bottom were women." And children. The police separated the bodies, some alive, others not. A man who was barely hurt held the body of his smothered son in his arms. They also pulled out a boy whose legs had been crushed but who begged them to save his father when "a man struggled loose from the human pile in the stairway, seized the child, covered his face with kisses, and hurried off with the little fellow in his arms."[10]

Local "roughs"—who likely accelerated the panic by shouting that the bridge was falling so they could snatch anything of value—grabbed what they could as shoes, canes, purses, gloves, and shawls—even clothing—cascaded off the bridge onto the streets and rooftops below. When it was over, twelve men, women, and children lay dead; seven were critically injured, and dozens more wounded.

A disaster of such magnitude demanded declarations of moral and legal liability followed by a swift judgment. Within days, review boards and inquests subpoenaed witnesses and recorded their testimony. The coroner's inquest presented its conclusions six days after the disaster.

To no one's surprise, the president of the New York Bridge Company, the company contracted to build the bridge, insisted the bridge was "perfectly strong and safe." The coroner, however, disagreed. In his view the bridge was a public hazard and should be closed down immediately. "I say there will be another calamity," he warned portentously. "The people of New York and Brooklyn should rise in arms and demand improvements—demand their rights if they are going to be crushed by a certain class of people who are manipulating the political mannerism of both cities."[11] The press repeated his dire prediction.

A prolonged period of finger-pointing, lawsuits, and settlements followed.

In the end, the public was left feeling ambivalent about the bridge. The public translated the panic as an indictment of the safety of the bridge, a charge that had been argued in court but ultimately refuted. Nonetheless, the bridge was too convenient not to use and traffic skyrocketed; bridge trains carried nine million passengers its first year and double that amount the following year.[12] Yet the bridge, a self-proclaimed Eighth Wonder of the World, remained tainted with blood.

The directors of the bridge management company

concluded they had to find a way to mitigate the lingering psychological effects of the disaster. They needed something magnificent, something that would overshadow sadness and gloom with joy and celebration. Barnum gave them the answer.[13]

At the time of the official opening of the bridge, Barnum had offered to pay a five-thousand-dollar "toll" to let Jumbo walk "quietly and secretly" across the Brooklyn Bridge in the middle of the night in order to move him from Madison Square Garden to the fairgrounds in Brooklyn. The toll for a person crossing the bridge was a penny, but no one knew how to calculate the fare for an elephant.

Barnum claimed Jumbo rocked the ferry too much, so crossing the bridge would be safer than capsizing a ferry. Barnum made his offer public, of course, knowing that if the bridge authorities allowed him to cross even at midnight thousands of people would turn out to see his elephant.[14]

The bridge company rebuffed Barnum, but a year later the idea of Jumbo crossing the bridge seemed to offer a solution to the bridge company's dilemma. Indeed, who could resist seeing Jumbo, the Eighth Wonder of the World, walk across the Brooklyn Bridge? The directors of the New York Bridge Company felt they could convince the public the bridge was safe if the largest animal in the world walked across it. The company intended to prove, once and for all, its bridge was safe.[15]

The directors asked Barnum if he still wanted to walk Jumbo across the bridge.

How much is the toll? asked Barnum.

Five thousand dollars, replied the company, *but no charge for you.*

Do I have to cross in the middle of the night?

Cross any time you want.

When it was over, the bridge company agreed to allow Barnum to cross all twenty-one of his elephants and seventeen of his camels. The press speculated the bridge would collapse under the sustained weight of more than a thousand tons.[16] Fear the bridge would collapse and leave the East River fouled with wreckage and the corpses of elephants and camels heightened the inherent drama of the spectacle.

While the bridge company was satisfied the bridge could withstand such a heavy live load, it worried what might happen if the weight weren't distributed evenly across the bridge. What if the elephants bunched up? Worse, what if they stampeded?

Jumbo's keeper, Matthew Scott, had his doubts, too. He worried that if Jumbo decided to act up on the bridge, "he would shake the whole concern down the river."[17] Scott expressed his reservations to Barnum and Arstingstall but they ignored him. "I alone, perhaps, was the only party in the transaction aware of [the danger]," he wrote in his autobiography.

On the evening of May 17, 1884—one week short of the anniversary of the Memorial Day Panic—Barnum's menagerie walked in cadenced single file across the bridge. Thousand of citizens of New York and Brooklyn crowded the roadways on and off the bridge to see "Jumbo, the largest animal in creation, walking on the best and finest promenade in the world." To the people "who looked up from the river at the big arc of electric lights, it seemed as if Noah's Ark were emptying itself," wrote the *New York Times*.

Jumbo came last. Like a king following his retinue, he was the *Matchless Monarch of Over-Shadowing and Majestic Presence*, a monster elephant walking across a monster bridge.[18] The toll collector mugged that he'd let the elephant pass for free since his rate card didn't stipulate a fee for elephants. But when Jumbo put his foot down on the bridge, reported Scott, "the bridge rebounded after the shock given by his foot. The rebound was met by his second footstep, and there was a great vibration caused by it."

As the herd neared the crown of the bridge, a train flew by, spooking the herd, which bunched up suddenly, trumpeting in high dudgeon. "I am said to have a pretty strong nerve," Scott claimed, "but it was something terrible to feel that vibration. . . ." Unnerved by the massive concentration of weight at the center of the bridge, the main engineer ran out to see how the main joint was sustaining the load. Meanwhile, the herd settled down and upon the insistence of their handlers, continued across the bridge. Around them men whistled and women applauded, oblivious to the tremors in the bridge.

A few minutes later, the engineer returned smiling. The main joint hadn't budged.

When Jumbo reached the top, he stopped and walked

to the side of the bridge so he could look at a steamboat pass beneath him. "As we looked down the funnels of the steamboats, and took a glance at the ships from a balloon-point of view," Scott recalled, "it was awfully interesting for me to answer Jumbo's questions, for . . . he had never seen a steamboat on the river."[19]

"His Royal Sacredness," the *New York Times* wrote of Jumbo, " . . . added a new luster to the Bridge last night."[20]

On May 19, 1885, a year after Jumbo's triumphal promenade, Robert Odlum stepped off the center span of the Brooklyn Bridge. Dressed in a red shirt, his body rotated during the fourteen-story fall and he hit the river askew, crushing his chest.[21]

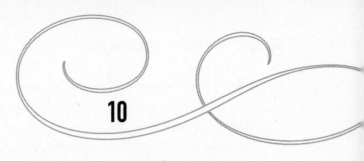

10

The Skeleton and the Manikin

♦

from the *Omaha World Herald*, July 6, 1891

A CIRCUS TRAGEDY

A BABE TRAMPLED TO DEATH BY A FRIGHTENED ELEPHANT.

DENVER. Col., July 5—[Special]—This afternoon an immense crowd gathered at the Manhattan beach, a resort near here, to witness a balloon ascension by a lady. There is a menagerie at the beach and it had been advertised that children would be given a ride on the back of an elephant.

The elephant had made two trips and was just returning to the animal house with eight children on his back when the balloon started up.

The animal became frightened at the balloon and began trumpeting and running about making desperate efforts to unseat the children. They all fell off and all escaped uninjured but one, a little boy named Johnny Eaton, son of a railroad man, who was caught under the elephant's feet and was crushed out of all semblance to humanity.

The keeper of the elephant then stuck a pitchfork into the animal's trunk, and was thrown high in the air by the enraged brute. He, however, was not seriously hurt. By this time other attendants had arrived and managed to secure the elephant with chains.

The parents of the child killed are nearly frantic with grief.

A freight train struck and killed Jumbo near St. Thomas, Ontario, three months after Odlum's death. The saga of the Mighty Monarch prompted two narratives, one of which was a collection of facts and personal impressions of what had happened that night in Canada, and Barnum's version, spun out of cotton candy.

Like any good melodrama, Barnum's story had a villain, which was the mechanical beast hurtling down the tracks in the middle of the night, and it had a hero, the Mighty Jumbo, who in a moment of selflessness sacrificed his life to save a friend.

The circus was in the process of loading the last of its thirty-one elephants onto the train, which was idling on a siding. As usual, the last elephants to board were Jumbo and Tom Thumb, and they were standing on the tracks waiting to be loaded when suddenly an unscheduled freight train came barreling through St. Thomas. Matthew Scott heard the rumble of the train long before it appeared, but no one else heard anything until suddenly there it was, screaming down a grade toward Jumbo and Tom Thumb. They had seconds to react. Barnum later accused the motorman of falling asleep at the throttle, because the train did not slow or even blow its whistle.

The elephants were hemmed in between the circus train on one side and a steep embankment on the other. Scott tried to pull Jumbo *toward* the onrushing train so as to get behind the last car of the circus train, but Jumbo balked. Suddenly it was too late and the train was upon them.

At the last second, Jumbo grabbed Tom Thumb and threw him down the embankment. "In saving his little protégé," the story ran in the papers, "Jumbo had neglected his own chance to escape."[1] Jumbo turned to face the locomotive plunging down the track and then lowered his head to charge. "Not often does an engine confront a living object weighing 15,000 pounds," wrote the *New Haven Register*, "and it paid for the indiscretion by jumping the track." Jumbo derailed the engine and five cars.[2]

The train killed Jumbo by ramming his tusks into his brain. Technically, Barnum argued, the contest between machine and beast was a draw, but it was Jumbo's sacrifice that made him a hero to the men, women, and children of America.[3]

The recollections of those who were there told a different story. The cowcatcher hit Tom Thumb first and sent him flying down the embankment with a broken leg. Then it hit Jumbo, gashing his flank and tearing apart one of his feet. The engine then jumped the track, pinning Jumbo beneath one of the cars. According to Scott, he ran to Jumbo, dropped on his knees, and comforted him as he died. In his last moments, Jumbo reached out with his trunk and touched Scott gently. "The king of Africa's forests met the King of Terrors undaunted," wrote the *New York Herald*.[4]

The story struck all the right emotional chords: love, sacrifice, a heartless machine, and an inconsolable Scott. "Jumbo looked more majestic than ever before," wrote the *Times*. "Then he assumed an attitude of determination, which he maintained until the sands of his life ran out."[5] Even Tom Thumb wept.[6]

One Victorian scrap shows Jumbo lying on the tracks with a grief-stricken Matthew Scott clinging to his side. Jumbo bleeds mostly from his tusks, which the train has just rammed into his brain. To the right, level with Jumbo's eyes, two little girls watch the death scene before them.

In spite of its sentimental embroidery, however, the picture captures the emotional core of the photograph that was taken at the scene around Jumbo's body at the bottom of the embankment. Matthew Scott's grief dominates both versions as he tries to close the emotional gap between man and beast.

Barnum's fictionalized version of Jumbo's death.
Victorian scrap, ca. 1885.

Contrary to Barnum's accusation that the engineer had fallen asleep at the throttle, the man had in fact seen Jumbo on the track and tried to stop the train. Witnesses heard three blasts of the whistle, the squealing of brakes, and the sound of tons of metal scraping the rails, followed by an agonized bellow that made the hair on the back of everyone's neck stand up.

The way the train hit Jumbo also made it clear he wasn't charging the engine but running from it. People also remembered seeing Scott with Jumbo, although no one saw the elephant reach out to touch him. In fairness, everyone was occupied with getting the derailed train off the main track before the next train came through. Dozens of men with ropes and cables struggled to right the train while Scott and Jumbo said their goodbyes.

Once they pulled the train back onto the track, they turned their attention to the dead elephant. A hundred men took half an hour to roll his body off the track and down the twelve-foot embankment. Then they stood around Jumbo's body for a photograph. Matthew Scott leaned against him, his hand placed solicitously on Jumbo's leg.

Souvenir hunters descended on Jumbo's body, scraping his tusks for shavings or cutting swatches of hair, skin, or ear from his body. Someone put up a fence

This picture gives a sense of scale of Jumbo's actual size. Matthew Scott stands in front at the center.
St. Thomas, Ontario, September 1885.

around him to keep people out, which prompted one brazen citizen to charge five-cents admission to see the dead elephant.

The next day Barnum fired Matthew Scott.

Henry Augustus Ward arrived in St. Thomas two days later. He was a former professor at the University of Rochester and had started his own studio, called Ward's Natural Science Establishment, an educational supply house that provided animal and rock specimens to museums. Barnum had arranged for Ward to mount Jumbo. Taxidermy was undergoing a revolution in the late nineteenth century as museums started to shed their stuffy image by displaying their specimens in tableaux called dioramas, which featured an animal set in a dynamic pose in its natural setting. Ward pioneered a new generation of taxidermists, including most famously Carl Akeley, who later built the Akeley Hall of African Mammals at the American Museum of Natural History in New York.

Two years before Jumbo's death, Ward had written Barnum to offer him his services as a taxidermist. Barnum, who often donated his dead animals to museums and universities for study, left orders with his assistants to contact Ward immediately if anything should happen to

Jumbo (*Which Heaven forbid!* he wrote). He also instructed Ward to save Jumbo's skin and skeleton.[7]

Barnum had already promised to donate Jumbo to the Smithsonian. He made the same promise to the American Museum of Natural History, and while the two museums wrangled over rightful ownership of the elephant, Barnum also promised Jumbo to Tufts College in return for a building with his name on it.[8]

Barnum's partner, James Bailey, didn't approve of giving Jumbo away. He felt people would be just as happy to see him stuffed as alive, especially after his heroic last act to save Tom Thumb. In fact, he proposed to make two Jumbos—one from his hide and the other from his bones—that they could exhibit together or separately. And Jumbo didn't require a handler or have to be fed anymore; he was pure profit.[9]

For Barnum profit still trumped ideas he may have had about commemorating his name or contributing to science, so he ordered Ward to build a *double Jumbo* in time for the 1886 season. And when he found out that Jumbo's hide could be stretched to twice its original size, Barnum told Ward, by all means, "let him show like a mountain."[10]

Meanwhile Ward's assistants dismantled Jumbo in Canada. They cut through his belly and removed his heart, liver, and lungs. When they cut open his stomach, they found sets of keys, a police whistle, a handful of English coins, and diverse screws, nails, and rivets. They passed out the coins as souvenirs. Afterward they packed

Jumbo's forty-six-pound heart into one barrel and his brain into another and loaded them onto the railroad car along with his bones, some of which were so big it took two or three men to carry one.[11]

They cremated the remainder of Jumbo in a pyre with four cords of wood. The smell of burning flesh didn't stop enterprising locals from snatching chunks of Jumbo's fat, which they later rendered and bottled as a remedy for ague, malarial fevers, and nervous prostration. When the remains were reduced to ashes, the taxidermy crew sent the rest of Jumbo's bones and hide to Rochester, New York, where Ward and his apprentices began the painstaking process of creating the largest animal mount in the world, a jumbo Jumbo.

Jumbo's collision with an engine on the Grand Trunk Railroad was a moral lesson in the power of human technology over nature. Iron was power, not just in industry but in fleets of battleships that set America on the course of empire when it declared war on Spain in 1898.

The English were furious when they found out the Americans had killed Jumbo after only three years. For them it was the proof Americans cared more about money that the well-being of animals. No one doubted that if Jumbo had stayed in England he'd still be alive, yet that didn't stop the Royal Zoological Society—the same zoo that had sold Jumbo to Barnum in the first place—from selling Jumbo's "widow," Alice, to him three months after Jumbo's death.

Barnum wanted Alice so she could play the bereaved wife to his stuffed Jumbo. He promoted the story that Alice had never recuperated emotionally from her forced separation from Jumbo in 1882, and that she'd remained devoted to him even though she might not ever see him again. One English cartoonist even depicted Alice-in-mourning, wearing the same old-fashioned lace widow's cap that Queen Victoria had worn since the death of her consort, Prince Albert, in 1861.

Meanwhile, Henry Ward and Carl Akeley put the finishing touches on *Double Jumbo*. The manikin was made of straw, leather, glass, beeswax, and paint, draped with three-quarters of a ton of elephant skin tacked to a massive oaken frame. Assembling the skeleton was easier, although Ward had to reglue Jumbo's fractured skull. He mounted the affair on a pedestal fixed with a plaque that read JUMBO AFRICANUS.

Within weeks of the start of the 1886 season, Barnum premiered Double Jumbo to the press in Rochester. Reporters and distinguished guests sat down to a fine meal at the Powers Hotel, toasted to Jumbo with a glass of corn liquor, and then ate a pound and a half of his tusks, which had been ground to powder and served as a jelly.[12]

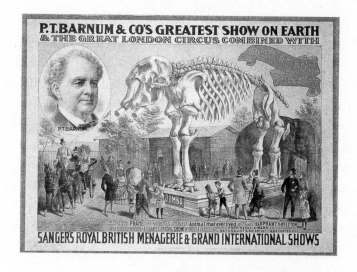

Barnum and Bailey promote Jumbo after his death.
Circus poster, 1888.

In April, Barnum invited another circle of friends and skeptics to Madison Square Garden to participate in the reunion between Alice and Jumbo. Some who came embraced the dramatic conceit of the elephant husband and wife, while others came to see what kind of stunt Barnum had cooked up this time. Either way, it was pure circus.

"Is it real or humbug?" somebody demanded of Barnum.

"Persons who pay their money at the door have a right to form their own opinions," he replied cheerily.[13] Barnum didn't care whether people believed what they saw or not. He cared that people would pay to see his attractions. "Every crowd has a silver lining," he'd say.

The reunion took place on the empty hippodrome track

at Madison Square Garden. During a performance it would be full of men racing each other on horses, giraffes, and ostriches, with elephants jumping hurdles, and Plains Indians in war paint chasing Roman chariots. The track encircled three rings each filled with fat people, skinny people, tall and small people, clowns, acrobats, sword swallowers, trick shooters, and tumblers. In one ring, a young, bare-legged white woman lie on the ground while Indians in buckskins whooped around her; in another, half-naked African tribesmen threw their spears at a lion made of hay. The oval smelled of dirt, sweat, animal flesh, and ten thousand people sitting under the big top.[14] But on this evening, the hippodrome was quiet, and the roar of the crowd was a distant echo.

Barnum's guests watched as men wheeled Jumbo's manikin into the ring. He looked stiff, the result of taxidermy struggling to realize its power, and yet people crowded around him. Some measured him by standing against a leg while others measured him by walking around him. Either way, he was larger than life.

Then Matthew Scott, whom Barnum had hired back to take care of Alice, led Jumbo's estranged wife onto the oval. When she spotted Jumbo standing on the track, she sauntered over to him. At first she "survey[ed] him with wonder," wrote the *Times*. She probed his mouth with her trunk for a few moments and then "gave vent to a groan that made the roof of the Garden tremble."

She took another look at him, groaned again, "and then walked away as though disgusted with the old partner of her joys and sorrows." Scott led her away, he told the crowd, so she could "mourn privately." Later when asked if Alice had really recognized Jumbo, Scott answered, "I can understand elephant talk, and Alice told me that she recognized Jumbo."[15]

For two years Alice marched in the *grand entrée* dressed in black as Jumbo's widow. Maids-in-mourning followed her in faithful procession, dabbing their eyes with over-sized hankies bordered in black. At the end of her second season, she burned to death in a fire at Barnum's winter headquarters in Bridgeport.

In 1889 Barnum put Jumbo's manikin on deposit at Tufts College, near Boston. (He withdrew Jumbo once for a show in London.) The school built the Barnum Museum of Natural History (now known as Barnum Hall) and Jumbo became its mascot. For years athletes put pennies in his trunk or pulled his tail for good luck before a game, and eventually they pulled off his tail, which is preserved in Tuft's Digital Collections and Archives. The rest of Jumbo burned in a fire in 1975. A maintenance man scooped his ashes into a fourteen-ounce Peter Pan Crunchy Peanut Butter jar that still sits in the athletic director's office. Today, Tufts plays Jumbo football, Jumbo baseball, and Jumbo tennis, and his name still appears on the cover of its yearbook.

Jumbo in Barnum Hall, Tufts College, 1942.

Barnum gave Jumbo's skeleton to the American Museum of Natural History, where he remained on exhibition for many years. Gradually his bones began to crumble, so museum staff wrapped Jumbo in plastic and put him in storage, where he stood in darkness until the museum restored him and put him back on display in 1993.[16]

Matthew Scott died in 1915 at the age of eighty in a poorhouse in Barnum's hometown of Bridgeport.[17] Tom Thumb, who survived the train wreck with only a broken leg, recovered fully before disappearing into the fog of history, confounded by his different incarnations.[18]

MUTUAL ADMIRATION.

BARNUM TO JUMBO. "You are a *humbug* after my own heart. You have even beat me in advertising."

BARNUM TO JUMBO: "You are a humbug after my own heart.
You have even beat me in advertising."
Thomas Nast, Harper's Weekly, *April 15, 1882.*

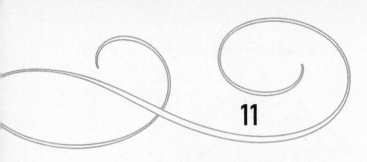

11

White Elephants

◆

from the *New York Times*, June 5, 1904

ELEPHANT LANDS IN JAIL FOR SWIMMING NARROWS

CROSSES FROM CONEY ISLAND TO NEW DORP IN EARLY DAWN

ON THE BLOTTER AS A VAGRANT

Two Fishers Went Sailing Out Over the Deep and Were Jarred by What They Saw

Quaint little old New Dorp had plenty to talk about yesterday. There was a real live elephant in town—an elephant, which, according to police reports, swam all the way across the bay from Coney Island for the simple and, according to the residents, the meritorious purpose of seeing exactly what kind of men and women lived in around the town whence came the Vanderbilts.

At any rate, whether the elephant wanted to see New Dorp or whether he wanted a good swim, or still again, whether he had been coerced into making a four or five mile swim simply to oblige an ambitious press agent, the fact remains that the huge beast did land somewhere on the port side of Staten Island in the early hours yesterday morning.

When he appeared ashore, according to [the] police records at New Dorp, there were at least four fishermen waiting for him, and the monster of the jungle was led a captive in triumph to New Dorp, where he was charged with being a vagrant and locked up.

. . . It was the biggest catch the police of New Dorp have made in years, and one of the them, speaking of it, said that "press agent or no press agent, we got him, and we are going to keep him till a bondsman shows up."

Let thy servant depart in peace," Barnum announced at the ripe age of seventy-three, "but before I go—and I hope to remain for a long time yet—I want a white elephant." Barnum launched a campaign at the height of Jumbo's fame to find his next big attraction, which he decided would be a sacred white elephant from Siam. Whiteness was blessedness, the color of God, a sign of the true race.

Buddhists agreed. When the Bodhisattva saw the time had come for him to be reborn as the Buddha, he entered his mother's womb through her flank while she dreamt of a white elephant bringing her a white lotus. In Siam, a white elephant was a coveted symbol of power, and only royalty were permitted them. Priests carefully tended to their physical and spiritual needs as Buddha awaited incarnation.

The white elephant was a fabulous prize, rarely seen outside the royal palaces of Ceylon or Siam. The British polymath Sir John Bowring declared the white elephant to be so valuable a single hair from its tail was worth "a Jew's ransom."[1] But the American minister to Siam suggested that one could be had if the price was right, but only on the sly since the penalty for buying or selling elephants was death. Barnum sent his man, J. P. Gaylord, to Siam to negotiate the details of the purchase and subsequent export of the elephant.[2] He told Gaylord cost was no object.

When Gaylord got to Siam, the American minister arranged for a meeting with a powerful Siamese lord who offered to sell him a white elephant under the table for one hundred thousand dollars in gold coin. He demanded a quarter of the money in advance and the rest upon delivery.[3] Wary of being deceived or even murdered for such a great deal of money, Gaylord promised to pay but only if the lord agreed to deliver the elephant in Moulmein, a city in neighboring Burma.

In 1883 Burma was split into two. A hereditary despot named Thibaw Min, known as "the gentleman who recently murdered his wives," ruled the upper portion, and the British ruled the lower portion.[4] Gaylord thought it prudent to be surrounded by the British rather than the Siamese.

The Siamese lord agreed to the terms of Gaylord's offer and ordered the elephant prepared for the trip to Burma, which included disguising the holy elephant as an ordinary one by painting it. Before the preparations were completed, Buddhist priests killed the white elephant rather than let him fall into the hands of Christian infidels.[5] Worse, the king of Siam ordered Gaylord arrested for blasphemy.

Gaylord vanished. What had seemed so promising turned into a full-blown disaster: the elephant was dead, Gaylord was missing, and Barnum was out twenty-five thousand dollars in gold coin.

Barnum had a Plan B. Czar Alexander III of Russia had indicated his willingness to sell a white elephant that the king of Siam had sent him as tribute, so Barnum sent three men to Moscow to negotiate with the czar and arrange transport for the elephant to travel fifteen hundred miles overland to the nearest port city.

The men crossed the Atlantic to England, then crossed France, Germany, and Poland until they reached Moscow and the czar's Zoological Park. The men examined the elephant and cabled back that the czar's elephant was an ordinary elephant with scurvy.[6]

Barnum had squandered tens of thousands of dollars and a year of his time with nothing to show for it. But he reckoned a white elephant was easily worth that much money and more as he continued his search for a genuine white elephant.

In June Barnum got a cable from Gaylord, whom he'd given up for dead. Gaylord explained that after the king decided to arrest him, he fled to Upper Burma, where he'd made a deal with Thibaw Min to buy another white elephant. This time he had a bill of sale bearing the royal seal that attested to "the sacred character of the beast." The king was so happy with the deal he'd thrown in at no cost one Burmese native, two Buddhist priests, and three Burmese musicians. Gaylord said the animal was "the equal of any white elephant possessed by the Kings of Siam and Burma," and that he expected him to arrive by ship in San Francisco in four weeks.

Gaylord's next cable was more perplexing. Now he reported having two elephants, a "spotted" one and another with tusks so big they "ran on the ground like the runners of a sleigh and curled up." Barnum wasn't sure exactly what to expect on board the steamship that was making its way from Singapore to San Francisco.

The steamship arrived on time in early July. Neither Gaylord nor the elephant was on board. Nor did the captain know anything about them.

Then Gaylord went missing again.

Months passed again and in the fall, Barnum got a cable from Gaylord saying yes, he had a white elephant and two Buddhist priests named Bo-Chu and Ba-Chu. He'd smuggled the elephant out of Burma by painting it red and blue and then stowed it aboardship in the middle of the night. Since then they'd been making their way around the world via Asia to the Mediterranean. Gaylord and the Sacred White Elephant of Burma expected to reach Liverpool by late January or early February 1884.

In Malta Gaylord cabled more details about the white elephant. His name was Toung Taloung—translated variously as Gem in the Sky, the Sacred Rose of the East, and the Leveller of the Earth—and he had a disposition that was "both kind and gentle," as befitted the dignity of one who was sacred. He was fifteen years old and stood seven and a half feet tall.[7]

The steamer arrived in England two weeks later. By then word had spread that Barnum had a sacred white elephant. The Prince of Wales, the future Edward VII, hosted an exhibition at the Royal Zoological Gardens. Present were the Earl of Derby, the Duke of Sutherland, the American ambassador James Russell Lowell, and "over 1,000 members of the nobility and celebrities in the scientific and literary world."[8] The next day attendance soared as five thousand people elbowed each other for a peek at the white elephant.

In the States, Barnum announced he had plans to build a royal palace car that would transport His Holiness in the United States. "A symphony of gorgeous colors and fantastic carvings," the carriage would be mounted upon elastic springs and contain three sections. The center section would house the sacred white elephant; one end section would contain idols and statues relevant to His Holiness; and the other end section would contain sleeping compartments for Bo-Chu and Ba-Chu and the others who attended the movements of the spirit of Buddha.[9] Anticipation for Toung Taloung (or "Old Tongue," as his name was quickly Anglicized) ran high.

Toung Taloung as imagined before he was seen in the West.
Victorian scrap, ca. 1884.

"The title of a white elephant is one that he merits only by courtesy," sniffed the London *Guardian* after Toung Taloung's premiere at the Royal Zoological Gardens. "He is an ordinary dark-coloured animal, variegated with patches of a tender pink which are ornamented with black spots."

"Spotted," Gaylord had called him.

The scientists who examined Toung Taloung couldn't agree whether the elephant's markings were "a beauty or a blemish." Professor W. H. Flower, the president of the Zoological Society of London, decided he was a partial albino and "therefore piebald from his birth," but a surgeon from the British Hospital for Diseases of the Skin declared he was suffering from a rare skin disease called leukoderma (vitiligo). In any case, he wasn't the creamy white color of one of Huntley & Palmer's sweet English biscuits.

English faunists quibbled over whether a pure white elephant even existed in nature. One expert claimed there was no such animal; another said he'd seen them in China. Gaylord stepped in to settle the dispute. In Asia, he explained, a white elephant wasn't the color of a bar of ivory soap; rather, it possessed a unique set of traits and markings. A white elephant wasn't just an elephant with splotched skin; the splotches had to be in the right places, such as on the front of the trunk, the dewlap, the ears, and the shoulders. He also had to have certain hereditary traits, such as long ears and a long tail that nearly touched the ground, a square chest, hazel eyes, and toenails white as ivory. Since Toung Taloung exhibited all these attributes, he was by definition a sacred white elephant.

The English sourly conceded that Toung Taloung was "the sort of animal that goes by the name of a white elephant in the East,"[10] but even so, *Lloyd's Weekly* in London added, "we do know that the whole affair is a showman's venture."[11]

Stories started circulating that Barnum's elephant was infected with Asiatic leprosy and was contagious.[12] But Barnum thrived on adversity. He had convinced the nation of Jumbo, and he'd do it again with Toung Taloung.

During the Civil War one of Barnum's most popular exhibits at his American Museum in New York had been the "Leopard Girl," a black five-year-old with a severe case of vitiligo. Her head, face, arms, legs, and chest were splotched white and pink, much like Toung Taloung. Barnum turned to scripture, where he found in Jeremiah 13:23: *Can the Ethiopian change his skin, or the leopard its spots? Then may ye also do good, that are accustomed to do evil.* The Leopard Girl was an imperfect human, but wherein did her imperfection lie? Was it her blackness or her whiteness? At Barnum's museum, you could buy a bottle of elixir that restored skin from black to white. Blackness, then, was an imperfection covering an underlying whiteness, and a right tonic or a good scrubbing could return skin to normal.

Soap companies during the 1880s equated blackness with dirtiness and frequently showed images of African Americans being cleansed. Was race simply a function of physical appearance? People wondered. *If you turned a black man's skin white, was he black or white underneath?*

Vying for a share of the burgeoning market in soaps and cleansers, these companies conflated whiteness with

Beat That, If You Can.
Lautz Brothers & Company's soap ad, 1885.

cleanliness, creating a sense of "whiter than white," a standard embodied in the color of ivory. Harley Procter's Ivory soap was "So pure it floats."

The *New York Times* speculated on racial cleansing. "The cleansed Ethiopian will be of a dazzling whiteness, rivaling that of snow," read an editorial. "Probably a method of straightening Ethiopian hair and repressing the exuberance of Ethiopian lips will soon follow the grand discovery of bleaching Ethiopian skin," continued the *Times,* "and in that case all distinctions between the two races will at once disappear and the negro question will vanish from our politics, never to reappear."[13]

Ivorine Pear's, Soapona, and Dreydoppel soap accentuated the theme of underlying whiteness in advertisements that showed a sparkling white Toung Taloung after a brisk scrubbing with their product.

Meanwhile, Barnum steadfastly defended Toung Taloung's *natural* whiteness. He wrote a widely published poem that argued only angels were truly white and that men—and sometimes elephants—were darker shades because they were still imperfect in the eyes of God. "O Barnum has an elephant and advertised it," he wrote in his signature quirky style, "the public then supposed it was a pure snow bright."

> But, says Barnum, I am white and if you'll
> inquire and think,
> "white men" and all sacred elephants are
> "somewhat rather pink."[14]

*The True Story of the White Elephant, Dreydoppel's Soap.
Trade card, 1884.*

At the same time Barnum launched a national contest that offered a cash prize of five hundred dollars to the person who could write the best poem commemorating the arrival of the first white elephant in America. In 1884, five hundred dollars paid a schoolteacher's salary in Winfield, Kansas, for a year and a half. Two years if she was a woman.[15]

Newspapers published the rules for the contest. First, you couldn't poke fun at either the elephant or the owner; second, a poem could not exceed fifty lines; and lastly, there was no room for second-rate poetry, what Barnum called "chaff." He wanted poems that were "masterpieces of descriptive ingenuity, and embroidered with as much ornament as could be bought for the money." To ensure impartiality in the judging, two jurists and a clergyman, three "well-known gentlemen," would decide the winner.[16]

Neither Tennyson nor Longfellow rose to the challenge, although seventy-two thousand people who fancied themselves poets did.[17] The poetry was so bad that neither Barnum nor the judges could make sense of it. "Behind his hallowed stamp of hue revealed," wrote Henry O'Meara from Boston, "Centuple tongues their mysteries have told, / A chiliad of visioned deeds unsealed, / A thousand lustrums' vanished dreams unrolled."

Barnum's favorite poem commemorated (in secondhand doggerel) his contest with John Bull, the English version of Uncle Sam:

> And Columbia smiled On Pee Tee Bee,
> As she had not smiled since she took tea
> In Boston Harbor with one J.B.[18]

Given the lackluster quality of the submissions, Barnum proposed to his partners they increase the amount of the award to attract a better class of poet. *Do what you want*, they replied, *but not a penny more.*

The *New York Times* lampooned Barnum by publishing its own odes to Toung Taloung in the style of poets like Whittier, Swinburne, and Tennyson.[19] "Beginning at a point on the northerly side of / West twenty-first street," read the opening lines of an ode in Walt Whitman's style,

> Distant six hundred and four feet westerly from
> the point formed by the junction
> Of the westerly side of Fourth-avenue and the
> Northerly side of West Twenty-first street . . .[20]

Smarting from these barbs, Barnum pressed the judges to award the prize as quickly as possible. Sixty days after he launched the contest, the judges concluded "so far as they [were] able to judge," that the prize money should be divided equally among the authors of three poems "of equal merit." Joaquin Miller, known variously as the "Poet of the Sierras" and the "Byron of the Rockies," was one of them. "Salaam! And welcome from Siam, / O sun-crowned of the Orient!" he wrote.[21] "Welcome to the Christian West, / From land of dreams to land of deed."

Besides poets, Barnum enlisted scientists and historians who testified under oath to the purity of the white elephant. General Daniel B. Sickles, a former American minister to Siam (and famous for killing the son of Francis Scott Key for sleeping with his wife), declared that Toung Taloung was the finest example of sacred white elephant he'd ever seen. So did Colonel Thomas W. Knox, the only American to have been awarded the Order of the White Elephant from the king of Siam. The Siam correspondent at the *New York Times* agreed. Barnum vaunted these testimonials and published them wherever he could.

He also showed off a document "written upon a palm leaf" and signed by Thibaw Min of Burma, the "King and Lord of All White Elephants" whose ministers certified Toung Taloung was "a specie of White (Sacred) Elephant, and possesses the qualities and attributes of such."[22]

As he had with Jumbo, Barnum appealed to the elephant's authenticity by appealing to cost. People wanted to see the animal Barnum had paid two hundred thousand dollars for, whatever color it was.[23] That amount of money would pay the salary of a female schoolteacher in Kansas for 769 years. Barnum doggedly insisted he was "fully satisfied that, after spending more than $200,000, I have the only 'Sacred White Elephant' ever seen in a civilized country, and a *whiter* one that any in Siam or Burma."[24]

Six days before Toung Taloung arrived in New York with his band of "fifteen Burmese musicians and priests, a sacred white monkey, and a choice assortment of idols," Barnum's chief competitor, Adam Forepaugh, announced he too had an elephant—named Light of Asia (a synonym for the Buddha)—who wasn't splotched or pink, but white as the "ash of a Havana cigar." And his eyes were a "deep, clear blue, this being one of the most unerring signs of pure race."[25]

Barnum roundly denounced Forepaugh's elephant as a fake and dug up witnesses who said they saw Forepaugh's men whitewash it. Outraged, Barnum bleached one of his own elephants "white as snow," derisively renamed it the Light of America, and hung on it a banner that read THE WHITE FRAUD. "Forepaugh has been imitating Barnum for years," he huffed. "For once Barnum will imitate Fore-paugh."

"Liar!" Forepaugh shot back. He insisted his elephant had been carefully inspected and found to be genuine "by the Highest Scientific Authority."

Barnum accused "4-Paws" of being a cheat and prod-ded reporters to investigate. "He [Light of Asia] is a common $1500 small India elephant *painted,* & the paint renewed every week or two," he insisted. He offered Forepaugh ten thousand dollars if he'd swear under oath his elephant was genuine.[26]

Forepaugh responded by calling Barnum a lunatic. "You are an old man," he sneered, "and the vim, vigor and sharp wit and cunning of your youth and manhood have left you."

Forepaugh found experts who testified under oath that the elephant was genuine, including an "international ex-pert on zoology" from Philadelphia. He even convinced the prince of Siam, who was touring America in 1884, to visit Light of Asia while visiting Chicago.

Either no one in the prince's entourage spoke English or the prince declined to engage Forepaugh in conversation, because the visit was conducted in rough Yankee pantomime. Forepaugh walked up to the prince, slapped him on the back, and then pointed at his elephant and said, "There now, Prince, ain't that the kind of elephants you have in your country?"[27]

The prince said a few sharp words in his own language and left. Forepaugh interpreted his comments to be a validation of his white elephant, a point he exploited in his advertising.

Although people noticed that Forepaugh's elephant was whiter on Monday than at the end of the week, they still preferred a fake white elephant to a real spotted one. Disgusted, Barnum started referring to "the masses" as "them asses."[28]

In either case, the public tired of both elephants quickly. By the end of the season, Forepaugh announced that Light of Asia had caught a cold and died. His bones, along with his skin and head, had gone to the Academy of Natural Sciences in Chicago for study and preservation. "I will never buy another white elephant," declared Forepaugh. "The people didn't appreciate the one I had, and they wouldn't appreciate another unless he was white as snow."[29] Roared Barnum in reply, "The owner of this imposition soon announced that it had suddenly died. It was simply *un*-dyed!"[30]

Light of Asia secretly returned to his previous incarnation as an ordinary Indian elephant named Tiny. In fact,

In 1885, the white elephant Light of Asia became John L. Sullivan,
the Boxing Elephant.
Promotional card, 1885.

Tiny was the second incarnation of Othello, who had belonged to the Prince of Wales as recently as the previous
Christmas. Forepaugh had bought Othello in England,
changed his name to Tiny, and gave him a fresh coat of
paint. By the time Tiny got to the United States, he was
Light of Asia. When Forepaugh declared him dead in November 1884, Light of Asia went back to being Tiny, until
he renamed him John L. Sullivan, the boxing elephant.

Ephraim Thompson taught John L. Sullivan how to
punch with a boxing glove tied to the end of his trunk,
and the two would spar together in the ring for a round or

two. Thompson, who was African American, appeared in the ring in whiteface. Once in a while during their scuffles, John L. would scrape the white off Thompson's face, revealing the blackness beneath.

In 1911, Forepaugh sold John L. Sullivan to the Ringling Brothers, Barnum, and Bailey, where he continued to box for ten years. By 1922, John L. made a fifty-three-mile pilgrimage from Madison Square Garden to Hachaliah Bailey's Elephant Hotel in Somers, New York, where he lay a wreath on Old Bet's memorial. "Stiff and rheumatic, like all old stage stars," John L. Sullivan aged gracefully into Old John. Retired from the ring, he did odd jobs around the lot until he died of heart failure in 1932.[31]

Talong Taloung died in a circus fire in 1887.

"I can't say that I grieved much over his loss," Barnum wrote unapologetically.

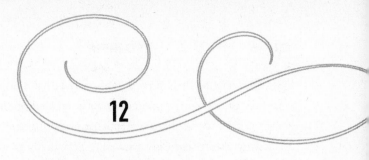

12

Elephant Bizarre

◆

from the *Fort Worth Star Telegram*, March 28, 1906

TRUE ELEPHANT STORY

BIG PACHYDERM COULD UNDERSTAND
ORDERS ONLY IN GERMAN

Several weeks ago, by cable, the Sells-Floto management were offered "the best trained elephant in the world," and it was suggested an immediate reply would be advisable, as others were negotiating for the wonderful pachyderm.

Always on the lookout for any feature that could strengthen the already well behaved performing herd of elephants, William Sells, the director general, at once cabled the shipment of this new marvel, and a week ago "Mogul" trumpeted his respects to the menagerie.

After a few days' rest the wonder was tried out

by one of the trainers, who found that the great beast could or would not understand him, so he reported to the management that Mogul would give no performance, but seemed to be actually growing vicious more and more every day.

Mr. Sells's first inclination was to ship the elephant back to the Fatherland, when the happy thought struck him to send for Herr Zeitz, as the animal had probably been trained in German.

Herr Zeitz reached the quarters and immediately asked for some cinnamon cake, and handing Mogul a chunk, the elephant at once looked pleased and grateful, and making a low bow to the German trainer, threw up his trunk for more. Then the trainer spoke in German, and with words of command the huge beast did everything in the elephant category.

Now the professor is studying up a plan whether to teach him all over in English or make a German elephant school out of the rest of the herd.

◆

On December 5, 1882, James Vincent de Paul Lafferty, Jr., received U.S. Patent No. 268,503, which gave him the sole right for seventeen years to build skyscrapers in the shape of any animal, including fish and birds. Lafferty's patent illustration provided two views of an example of such a building. The first is a broadside view of an elephant with long tusks drinking water through its trunk from a barrel. No larger than mice in comparison, a man and a woman huddle under an umbrella by his front legs, and in the rear, a woman pushes a baby buggy.

The second view looks like an MRI cross section of the main gallery looking down from above. The floor consists of a main hall and several smaller rooms with odd shapes that conform to the contour of an elephant: a Head Room, two Eye Rooms, and a Trunk Room in the front, and two Rump Rooms in the rear. Between the Rump Rooms, in place of an anus, was a window, which became known as "the pane in the butt."

Lafferty began construction of the elephant in southern New Jersey a year before the U.S. Patent Office officially awarded him the invention. The elephant sat on a sand dune two miles south of Atlantic City in undeveloped ocean scrubland.

Lafferty built the elephant because he wanted to lure people who could afford to buy his oceanside lots. Old and new money from New York and Philadelphia had been flowing generously into real estate near Atlantic City for people wanting to build their summer cottages by the ocean. Except Lafferty had a problem. Even though he was only two miles south of Atlantic City, development had stopped abruptly a mile north of his lots because of a tidal estuary that separated his land from the land boom. The city's mule-drawn streetcars stopped at the other side of the wetlands, and people had

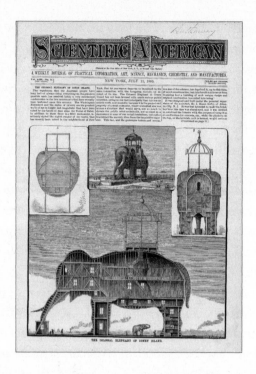

Note the scale, indicated by the life-size elephant standing beneath the structure. Note also the "pane in the butt," in the upper right.

to wait for the tide to go out before they could cross to the other side.

Lafferty needed something that would overcome the natural reticence of crossing the estuary, and so he built the Elephant Bazaar, the country's first shopping mall inside an elephant. In September 1882, Lafferty advertised for sale a hundred choice oceanfront lots in what was now called South Atlantic City. Lafferty claimed the water was cleaner than Atlantic City's, and the swimming was safer, and "last by not least, the Elephant Bazaar, the only building in the world constructed in the novel form of that well-known beast, being 87 feet long, 63 feet high, surmounted by a Howdah or observatory, from which a beautiful view may be had of the surrounding towns, villages, ocean, bay, and thoroughfare."[1] The elephant affectionately known as Lucy weighed ninety tons and was built with a million pieces of wood, including eight thousand ribs shaped by hand, and then covered with twelve thousand square feet of hammered tin. The motto for the Elephant Bazaar was "the only elephant in the world you can go through and come out alive."

A wood and tin elephant six stories tall that towered above all around it, the Elephant Bazaar declared in grand billboard fashion that things were big in America. So gargantuan, in fact, she became an instant navigational reference for coastal freighters, which could spot her eight miles at sea. The Elephant Bazaar was literally and figuratively a guiding light.

People crossed the estuary in droves to go inside her through a door in her rear heel and then climb several flights of stairs to visit the shops that had rented space within her to sell their fancies. Some climbed all 130 steps to the observatory at the top, perhaps pausing to look out "the pane in the butt." The stairs exited onto an observation platform in the shape of a howdah, the royal box in which maharajahs customarily rode. From there people could see a rolling panorama of Absecon Island, a bulwark of land against an expansive sea. For most it was their first aerial view of Atlantic City and the rolling farms, fields, and villages that surrounded it.

But Lafferty got into financial trouble and sold Lucy in 1887. She free-floated through history as a saloon (shut down by the Volstead Act in 1920), the Elephant Café, the Elephant Hotel, a real estate office, a tourist information booth, a children's library, and a summer cottage for an eccentric English couple.

In 1903 a storm buried her knee deep in sand, and in 1904 drunken revelers tipped over an oil lamp that nearly burned her down. She persevered through a hurricane in 1929 that blew off her howdah and another storm in 1944 that wiped out the world-famous Margate boardwalk. She also attracted luminaries such as President and Mrs. Woodrow Wilson, Henry Ford, John Jacob Astor, several du Ponts, and an Indian man who claimed to be the Rajah of Bhong.

After weathering eight decades of gales and hurricanes, relentless salt spray, freezing cold and baking heat, fire, vandalism, and squatters, Lucy gradually slumped into disrepair. She was twice shot with arrows and dented by beer bottles thrown against her. Finally, in 1962, her windows broken, her wooden joints swollen, and her skin peeling away, the city condemned Lucy in order to make way for a high-rise condominium.

A band of Margate citizens known the Margate Civic Association rushed to rescue her, and after a preservation architect pronounced her still structurally sound, the

Lucy, South Atlantic City, New Jersey, ca. 1904.

"Save Lucy" committee raised enough money to move her to a city lot two blocks away, where the long and expensive process of restoration began. In 1971, she became a national landmark in the National Register of Historic Places. It took thirty years to restore her to her original condition.[2] Today visitors can eat burgers at the I Love Lucy Beach Grill, buy a World's Largest Elephant beer mug, and then climb the stairs to the howdah and look out across the implacable Atlantic as the first visitors did more than a century ago.

Two years after starting Lucy, Lafferty built another elephant for the Neptune Land Company, fifty miles to the south in what is today South Cape May, New Jersey. Another publicity stunt to sell real estate on the beach, the history of the Light of Asia is more inglorious than Lucy's.

The name Light of Asia appealed to highbrow types who'd read Edwin Arnold's epic poem about the life of Buddha, *The Light of Asia*. The name also appealed to anyone who knew about Adam Forepaugh's main attraction, Light of Asia, the first truly *all-white* elephant in America.

The officers of the Neptune Land Company chose the name Light of Asia for their elephant in order to exploit the quasi-mystical cachet of elephants, whiteness, and the Buddha, but quickly regretted their decision when Forepaugh's elephant proved a fake.

Forepaugh's Stupendous Humbug, 1884.

That spring, as construction of the Cape May elephant neared completion, a national scandal broke out less than a hundred miles away in Philadelphia. A WHITE WASHED ELEPHANT, ran the headline in the *New York Times*, " . . . A FRAUD ON THE AMERICAN PEOPLE." A man testified under oath that Forepaugh paid him to whitewash an ordinary elephant every week to make her look pure white.

It's hard to say whether this scandal tainted Lafferty's elephant in South Cape May. His marketing plan likely would have failed anyway. Admission and concession fees never covered the cost of construction of the white elephant, much less the cost of maintenance, which was constant. When Barnum busted Forepaugh for faking a white elephant, Forepaugh simply stopped whitewashing Light of Asia and the Buddha disappeared from one day to the next. But the Neptune Land Company was stuck with its white Buddha, and a new word entered the American lexicon: white elephant, n., *a property requiring much care and expense and yielding little profit.*

Like Forepaugh's elephant, Light of Asia dissolved from white to gray as the sea and wind corroded his tin, which caused his joints to slip. At the dawn of the new century, the great white elephant Light of Asia was torn down and burned.

Four years before the Light of Asia went up in smoke, on the evening of September 27, 1896, ships headed up the channel to Manhattan Island would have seen an elephant *fifteen* stories tall burning above the boardwalks of Coney Island. Lafferty's third elephant, the Elephantine Colossus, burst into flame at 10:35 in the evening. At first passersby saw the glass eyes of the elephant, each four feet across, glowing fiercely in the night, and then fire belched from his mouth as though it were a dragon. Finally, his body exploded into flame, a fulmination as bright as any lighthouse.

Promoters called the Elephantine Colossus the Eighth Wonder of the World, and like one of its namesake the Colossus of Rhodes, it stood at the mouth of the harbor to a great port. Unlike the Colossus of Rhodes, which was made out of iron and brass, the Elephantine Colossus was built of 3.5-million board-feet of dry yellow pine, sheathed in 57,000 square feet of tin painted blue. It was five times the size of its sisters in New Jersey. It took a total of 339,270 man-hours to build,[3] and it burned to embers in twenty minutes.[4]

Fire companies came from Bath Beach, Bensonhurst, Gravesend, and Sheepshead Bay to help the West Brighton Beach crew combat the blaze. Two years earlier a fire had devastated West Brighton Breach and the fire captain wasn't going to let history repeat itself. He let the elephant burn and turned his attention to keeping the fire from spreading to the adjoining buildings.

Like Lafferty's other elephants, the Coney Island Elephant struggled financially from the start. The under-capitalized company that financed construction ran out of money before it was done. Suppliers filed liens and the project bogged down as the courts decided who should get paid. Still, the company managed to open the Colossus in August 1884 even though one gigantic ear was still lying on the ground.

According to the promoter, the Coney Island Elephant stood 175 feet tall, was 203 feet long, and was 198 feet around at the middle.[5] The epitome of elephantine, the structure contained thirty-one rooms on seven floors and an observatory at the top. Each room was named after a part of the elephant's anatomy: the Head Room, the Throat Room, the Stomach Room, the Lung Room, to name a few. The Eye Rooms had telescopes so people could look out across Surf Avenue toward the bay and a tobacconist sold cigars from a Hoof Room in the foreleg.

But the Coney Island Elephant was, in the words of one man who watched it burn, "a frost from the start."[6] Originally conceived as a hotel, the Colossus opened as an office building, and when the spaces went unrented, turned into a bazaar with museums, shops, dioramas, and concert halls. The two rear legs contained spiral staircases that went up seven floors to the howdah at the top, which offered a fifty-mile panorama of Manhattan, Brooklyn, and Jersey City. The owner claimed that on a clear day you could see the spray above Niagara Falls, four hundred miles away.[7]

In June 1885 a woman tried to jump off the howdah to her death.[8] A month later a woman got lost inside the elephant and found herself locked inside after closing. Desperate, she slid down the elephant's seventy-two-foot trunk into the Trough Room at the ground level, where she remained trapped until an employee finally heard her cries for help.[9]

That same month, the *Scientific American* chastised the Coney Island Elephant as a crass work of commercial architecture whose only purpose was "to abstract the unwary dime from the inquisitive sightseer."[10] It was, said the magazine, a monstrosity without redeeming value, a particularly odd comment since the Colossus had been built in the middle of Coney Island's tenderloin district, known widely as "Sodom by the Sea" and locally as the "Gut." It was surrounded by shanties that contained saloons, dance halls, gambling dens, drug galleries, and whorehouses, leading even John Y. McKane, the infamous chief of police of West Brighton (whom the press had dubbed "the King of Coney Island"), to admit there was probably no more wicked a place on the planet than the Gut.[11]

The Coney Island Elephant underwent a seemingly endless series of reincarnations as a boardinghouse, dance hall, whorehouse, and flophouse. During its days as a brothel, "Going to see the Elephant" meant to visit the women who practiced their lewd trade from inside a giant wooden elephant.

By the time the elephant caught fire in 1896, the building was abandoned.

Police suspected arson, but since the building wasn't insured, no investigation followed.

"It is not kind to speak ill of the dead," the *Brooklyn Eagle* wrote delicately, "and that indeed is not our intention. We cannot help thinking, however, that if the deceased had not scattered his energies in so many different directions he would have attained a greater degree of success."[12]

In 1892, Lafferty sold the right to build an elephant-shaped building to a group of investors in Chicago called the Colossal Elephant Company. The company then proposed to the organizing committee of the 1893 World's Columbian Exposition to build a monument in the shape of an elephant *twenty* stories tall as its signature landmark.

Celebrating the four-hundredth anniversary of the European discovery of the Western world, Chicago turned six hundred acres of swamp marsh at the edge of Lake Michigan into a glittering exhibition of American progress. The fair captured a national exuberance to show off its agricultural, industrial, and artistic talents.

The fair's organizing committee wanted a landmark structure that would "out-Eiffel" the Eiffel Tower, which had come to symbolize not just the Paris Universal Exhibition of 1889 but France herself. The committee challenged American engineers to come up with a world-class technological marvel that was "original, daring, and unique," something quintessentially American that could serve as a symbol for both the fair and the nation.

The Colossal Elephant Company proposed the great elephant as the fair's landmark. At two hundred feet tall, it would make the Coney Island Elephant look "like a cotton-flannel elephant from some child's Christmas stocking." Elevators in the front legs would carry passengers up and down the floors within the great beast, which would include restaurants, dancing halls, parlors, and luxury apartments. The observatory at the top would give a bird's-eye view of the exposition and beyond to Chicago and Lake Michigan.

The Chicago elephant would not only be bigger than Coney Island's; it would also *move*, making it the largest automaton in the world. The Chicago elephant would swing its hundred-foot trunk, roll forty square feet of eyes, flap six acres of ears, and wag a fifty-foot tail. A steam calliope inside the trunk would simulate his giant roar.[13] The projected cost was $250,000, ten times the projected cost of Lucy.[14]

The idea was met with widespread amusement. How intimate would it be to sit down to dinner with a companion in the elephant restaurant with all that machinery clanking about? And wouldn't the calliope raise the dead? The editor of the *New York Herald* wondered why the creators of such a splendid elephant couldn't also make it walk. "We don't ask that it run, or that it get up on its hind feet and dance, or anything of that kind," he wrote, "but we do insist on a quiet, dignified walk, and we believe that twice the admission fee now contemplated would then be willingly paid."[15]

In the face of such ridicule, the Colossal Elephant Company persisted with its idea to build a two-hundred-foot tall mechanical elephant for the World's Columbian Exposition.

On May 1, 1893, President Grover Cleveland called the exposition "a splendid thing" and pushed an electric button to start the fair. Flags unfurled, fountains gushed, and curtains jerked opened to reveal full-size replicas of the *Pinta*, the *Niña*, and the *Santa Maria*. Over the next six months, 27 million people visited the fair, a quarter of the population of the United States.

One of the goals of the World's Fair was that people learn about food and "how it nourishes their bodies; what kinds and combinations of food are best for health and strength, and how they can obtain the most and best nutriment at the lowest cost."[16] The two buildings dedicated to agriculture and commerce—the Agricultural Building and the Manufacturers and Liberal Arts Building—

contained almost two million square feet (forty-three acres) of exhibits. Canada brought a cheese that weighed eleven tons and Germany brought the world's largest chocolate bar, an eleven-foot statue of a buxom *Germania* sculpted out of three thousand pounds of chocolate and cocoa butter.[17]

The United States brought three Liberty Bells—the original, which was on exhibit in the Pennsylvania State Building, and two life-size replicas—crack and all: one made out of wheat and rye grain and another made out of oranges, lemons, and grapefruits. It also brought Cracker Jack, Shredded Wheat, Cream of Wheat, Juicy Fruit gum, and Aunt Jemima's pancake syrup. It introduced the first commercially viable chocolate bar, the first brownie, the first marijuana brownie, Coca-Cola, and the hamburger.[18] The World's Fair was a sprawling national test lab for ideas about marketing and advertising products for the coming century. Companies vied for gold medals and blue ribbons. After the brewer Frederick Pabst won the title for America's best beer, he renamed his brew Pabst Blue Ribbon.[19]

The culture of the White City was decidedly high: while Winslow Homer won a gold medal for painting in the Fine Arts Building, Antonin Dvorak debuted the *New World Symphony* in the Music Hall. The concert was poorly attended because people really wanted to hear the music coming from the edge of the Midway, where a twenty-four-year-old African American piano player named Scott Joplin introduced the world to ragtime. "Do whatever you have to do, sell the cook stove if necessary and come," author Hamlin Garland prompted his parents in North Dakota. "You must see this fair!"[20]

Over the six months the World's Fair was open, millions of people strolled down the mile-long Midway, where vendors sold them a variety of treats, such as Miss Polly's Entrails Porridge, River Hemp Brownies, Venison Blood Balls, and apples dipped in molasses. The Midway offered men their own treats, such as the International Dress and Costume Exhibit, which hosted the "World's Congress of Beauties," billed as *40 Ladies from 40 Nations*, and on Cairo Street a belly dancer named Little Egypt did the hootchy-kootchy. They came to see the ostrich farm, the camel races, and Carl Hagenbeck's Menagerie, of bears, lions, monkeys, and parrots. They came to see Custer's Last Stand at Buffalo Bill's Wild West Show and an escape artist named Houdini. But "the favorite of the favorites" on the Midway was an elephant named Lily.

Lily wasn't the titan proposed by the Colossal Elephant Company; in fact, she barely reached three feet tall. A "dwarf" elephant from Sumatra, she was billed by Hagenbeck as "the Most Remarkable Zoological Curiosity in the World," at three feet tall, three feet long, and 180 pounds. The public adored her and the press kept close tabs on her, such as the time she got into a vat of beer and drank herself silly. But Lily caught a cold and died by August. "All Midway Mourns," the newspapers lamented, "Sad End of Baby Lil."[21]

Instead of an elephant, World's Fair officials chose as

its landmark structure a 264-foot wheel that stood upright on a forty-four-ton axle that was the largest piece of hollow iron ever forged. The wheel, designed by American engineer George Washington Gale Ferris, Jr., carried thirty-six cars, each the size of a cottage with sixty people in it, which meant the entire wheel could hold more than two thousand people at one time. It would spin around, a revolution in nine minutes.[22] "Ferris is a crackpot," said one of the fair's board members when he first heard the idea. "He has wheels in his head."

Thirteen years later, two hundred pounds of dynamite reduced the Ferris wheel to 2 million pounds of iron scrap. Although the Eiffel Tower of the 1889 Paris Universal Exposition still stands, the world is filled with Ferris wheels.

Lafferty's Patent 268,503 expired at midnight on December 4, 1899. As of that date anyone had the right to build a structure in the shape of an animal. Over the past century a few buildings have appeared, such as the giant muskie that houses the National Freshwater Fishing Hall of Fame in Hayward, Wisconsin, or the Big Duck in Flanders, New York, but no one has tried to build another elephant on the scale of Lafferty's.

Yet hundreds of other elephants stand in front of car washes, Laundromats, pawnshops, antiques malls, gas stations, firework stands, supper clubs, and package stores from New York to California and Michigan to Texas. They average between ten and twenty feet tall and are made of wood, metal, fiberglass, and cement. They strike the same pose: four legs on the ground, head up, and trunk raised. They come in a variety of colors, including white, red, blue, glitter, and psychedelic, but mostly they come in pink.

A pink elephant holds up a martini in his trunk and wears sunglasses to hide his hangover. He stands on the street and in parking lots next to the Pink Elephant Cocktail Lounge and the Pink Elephant Tavern. He is the hallucination of choice for drunks. Over the years, however, he migrated to car dealerships, bowling alleys, and flea markets as they gradually became part of the social landscape.

Pink elephants also lent themselves to the hallucinogenic counterculture of the 1960s and 1970s. For years, a pink elephant stood on water skis wearing a blue bikini with yellow polka dots in front of a sporting goods store in Cookeville, Tennessee. At Mister Ed's Elephant Museum and Candy Emporium in Orrtanna, Pennsylvania, Miss Ellie Phant flaps her ears while she talks from a speaker in her trunk.[23] ("Everyone always asks me the same two questions," she says, rolling her eyes. "How old am I and how much do I weigh?") A pink stucco elephant stands forlornly behind a chain link fence next to a Dunkin' Donuts in Brandon, Florida, and Pinkie, who bears a frightening resemblance to Groucho Marx, stands at a Citgo gas station in DeForest, Wisconsin.

In 1782, the United States officially adopted the bald eagle as the chief visual element in the Great Seal of the United States. An emblem of imperial power and authority, the eagle bears an escutcheon with stars and bars. He holds an olive branch in one talon, and thirteen arrows in the other. The seal appears only by authorization of the president or as prescribed by law, such as on foreign treaties, trade agreements, stamps, and money.

No elephants adorn official United States documents or currency. As an alien the elephant couldn't contend with native species for these honorifics, but Thomas Nast unofficially christened the elephant as the national emblem in 1871 in an illustration for *Harper's Magazine* called *Our Rising Generation*, in which he bemoans a loss of vigor in the national trade ethic of "An Honest Day's Work for an Honesty Day's Pay." Behind the figures that caricature the alienated generation of youth who now feel entitled to the hard-fought gains of their parents and grandparents is a portrait of an elephant on a broadside affixed to the storefront of American business. The Elephant is the *Young America Brand*.

The eagle never competed with the elephant when it came to embodying American sentiments and values. No eagle worked on the railway or in the mines or out in the fields, nor understood the meaning of compassion, sacrifice, betrayal, or a broken heart. Unlike the bestial strength of lions and bears, the elephant tempered brute strength with reason and compassion. The elephant spoke in national dialogues about capitalism, governance, and morality. A moral lesson about size and strength, the elephant was part of the DNA of the nation's steel that built the rails, bridges, and building in the new century of American progress.

The elephant fanned out across the American social stream. Today we know him as Jumbo, Dumbo, Elmer, Horton, Lumpy, and Kabumpo, the Elegant Elephant of Oz. He is Bart Simpson's pet elephant Stampy, and Snorky from *The Banana Splits*. He is Abraham Lincoln, Ronald Reagan, and George W. Bush on Pennsylvania Avenue, and Horatio and Aloysius Snuffleupagus on *Sesame Street*. And since 1902, he lives in every box of Barnum's Animal Crackers.

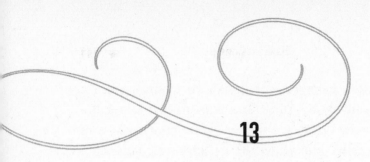

13

Born in the USA

◆

from the *New Haven Register*, October 17, 1883

ELEPHANTINE RECEPTION

BIRTHDAY PARTIES

Society circles will watch for their invitation to [Bridgeport's] second birthday party. Last year Mrs. Queen issued invitations to her lady and gentlemen friends; also to the boys and girls attending Professor George Arstingstall's school for elephants. Jumbo was present, but took up so much space in the winter quarters' drawing room that it's just possible he may not get another invitation.

The baby last year was dressed in a short pink silk, with facings of petit polonaise, backstitched to a *jun d'espirit*. She wore roses and smilax on her head, and as she entered the ring and invaded the ranks of her guests, murmurs of admiration from the elephant beaux present were quite audible.

This year Mrs. Queen's daughter will appear in something new—the very latest. Miss Columbia is also having a new dress made at David M. Read's. The overskirt of *sacre bleu entre saint gris*, cut bias on the off side, is expected to create considerable attention.

◆

In 1882 Barnum dodged a hefty import tax on Jumbo by signing an affidavit with the U.S. Department of Agriculture declaring he was importing the elephant for breeding purposes, even though he knew the giant had never exhibited any sexual proclivity. From time to time Barnum did actually try to interest Jumbo in a female, but he knew from experience that captive bulls generally enjoyed females as companions, not as lovers.

Although not always.

On May 30, 1875, Seth Howes's Great London Circus was making its way to Kansas City by rail when Babe (known formally as Hebe, after the Greek goddess of youth) went into labor. The train stopped outside St. Joseph, Missouri, unloaded Babe with her trainer, and then continued to its scheduled date in Kansas City.

The next day Babe gave birth to America's first native-born elephant. His name was St. Joe, or more simply, Joe, in honor of the city in which he was born. By the time the circus returned two days later, Joe was dead.

Some people in St. Joseph were curious enough to walk out to the fairgrounds and see the baby elephant, and the local paper reported the story. "St. Joe is happy," the story read joylessly. "It is needless to add that the mother and baby do not belong to the city. Its name is St. Joseph."[1]

The writer limited his remarks to fifty words. No headline, just two column inches snugged into the thicket of news on page four. St. Joseph dismissed its namesake because no one from the circus was there to tout the significance of the *First Elephant Born in America*. The absence of an authorial voice made the story hardly worth remembering, and so St. Joseph the city shrugged off St. Joseph the elephant. The circus further erased Joe when it returned the day after his death and put on a performance without saying a word about the passing of the first elephant born in America. Joe was a trivial piece of news, barely recorded.

Which is how the second elephant born in America got to be the *First Elephant Born in America*. Three years after Babe gave birth to her ill-fated calf in Missouri, she got pregnant again by the same bull. By then Seth Howes had sold Babe to James A. Bailey of Cooper & Bailey Company, and so it came as a surprise to the owners when, on March 10, 1880, Babe gave birth to a female at the circus's winter headquarters in the City of Brotherly Love.

Bailey, the brains behind Cooper & Bailey, argued that Philadelphia wasn't just a one-night stand on a long list of stops—it was *home*. That made Babe's infant a native daughter, and Bailey appealed to his fellow Philadelphians to choose a name for her, a strategy that invested them in her well-being.

Before long, dozens of ideas poured into the editorial offices of the newspapers. One man, not appreciating the fact the baby was female, offered a "magnificently broidered robe" if they'd name the elephant after him. Others suggested names of heroines of popular literature such as Thomas Moore's "Lallah Rookh," and Longfellow's "Evangeline," with still others riffed on the words *Philadelphia* and *elephant*. In the end, however, the name that won the contest was the one that held the most meaning for the Cradle of Liberty: *Columbia, Young America*.[2]

A young woman bursting of pubescence, Columbia had been a metaphor for the European colonies in the New World since 1738, and as a symbol she deftly combined notions about sex, land, and nation. Draped in flowing neoclassical robes, often with the American flag pressed tightly against her body, she would beseech the help and comfort of her protector with outstretched arms. As Columbia's incarnation, Babe's little girl became a symbol of America not just as her namesake but also as a first daughter born on American soil.

From that day, P. T. Barnum coveted her.

Barnum was impressed with James Bailey, the serious young man who'd shouldered his way through the circus ranks by the time he was twenty-five with the arrival in 1876 of Cooper, Bailey & Company's Grand International 10 Allied Shows.

Bailey's real name was James Anthony McGuiness. He had changed his name to Bailey after a tobacconist in Cardiff, New York, named George Bailey took in the runaway and taught him the family business. Bailey was the nephew of circus pioneer Hachaliah Bailey and later became the mastermind of the best-known if not the best hoax of the nineteenth century, the Cardiff Giant, after he dug up a ten-foot stone giant behind his barn in 1869. (Bailey had a disagreement with his pastor about whether giants really walked the earth in ancient times. Bailey insisted they did and dug one up behind his barn to prove it.)

George Bailey's young protégé, James, was an aggressive thinker. In 1877, while his colleagues were plodding through their routes in New England, the South, and the West, Cooper & Bailey were playing in Fiji, Tasmania, and Australia. In 1879 his show played in South America.

The big change came in 1879 when—only months after Edison announced the electric light—Bailey became the first to light up the big top so he could give evening performances. Most distressing to Barnum, however, was that Bailey had bought Seth Howes's circus, the Sanger's Royal British Menagerie and Grand International Allied Show, making Bailey the first man to rival him for the title of Biggest and Best.

Bailey not only employed Barnum's methods; he refined them. His slogan was "Better than the Best, It's Equal Not on Earth." Cooper & Bailey's ran acts like Martinho Lowando, the Brazilian Hurricane Rider; Mademoiselle de Granville, the Lady with the Iron Jaw; and "The Wonderful Egyptian CALLIOPE."[3] When it came to elephants, however, Barnum always had been the biggest and the best. His bulls were the best trained, the best adorned, and had characters worthy of Dickens. No one had ever rivaled him.

Until Columbia.

Bailey grasped immediately that Columbia was his ticket to beat Barnum. Taking his lead from Barnum's book on how to make money (*The Art of Money Getting*, 1880), Bailey embroidered a story that glorified motherhood and childhood in ways the circus rarely employed. The circus men catered to more of a male demographic with animal beasts and human freaks, but Bailey designed a campaign that appealed to women based upon sentimental virtues of maternity.[4]

Babe was a model of maternity unhampered by human confusion; a natural Madonna. Men and beasts alike celebrated the birth of her baby on the straw. The elephants were so emotionally involved, wrote *Harper's Weekly*, they "sent up a tremendous bellowing, threw their trunks about, wheeled around, stood on their hind-legs, and cavorted and danced in the highest glee, as though they had gone mad."[5] As the elephant chorus rejoiced, Babe caressed her baby to her feet and then tucked her into the protective crook of her trunk.

Madonna and Child, 1880.

Only Babe wasn't the mother America imagined her to be. In fact, she challenged the idea that motherhood was instinctual. At birth, she picked up Columbia, raised the squealing infant above her, and then threw her twenty yards. Not lobbed, *threw*. She then yanked herself free from her chains and went on a rampage, smashing railings and demolishing the stable's stove while men struggled to pin her down with ropes and chains.[6] "The big elephants set up a tremendous roar," reported the *New Haven Register*, "threw their trunks aloft, reared up, and swayed about in great excitement."[7] But her behavior was not as anomalous as the men believed; after all, she'd grown up socially stunted and didn't know what a mother was, much less how to act like one. When Columbia nudged her breasts for milk, she just pushed her away.

In 1882, Barnum produced a thirty-four-page booklet called *History of Animals; Leading Curiosities & Features*, which the circus sold for a few cents as a souvenir. The magazine contained stories and hand-colored pictures of exotics like tigers, lions, and rhinoceros.

The cover of *History of Animals* depicts a grotesquely distorted Babe, her breasts swollen with milk, about to toss her squealing infant, Columbia. On first look, the image seems out of synch with the story that made Babe and Columbia the first superstars of Cooper & Bailey. But the public didn't know about Babe's bad behavior and saw the picture as a mother celebrating her child by holding it up for all to see. *Behold!* she seemed to say flush with milk. *Rejoice!*

Barnum conceded Bailey's show was hurting business. "It draws all creation," the old showman groused, "and the ladies especially seem half crazy over it."[8] Rather than imitate Bailey's success, however, he decided to buy it, so he offered Bailey one hundred thousand dollars for the act. Feeling cocky, he printed up broadsides that he sent to the forward men on tour who plastered them on the sides of barns, liveries, and stores along the route. "Wait for Barnum!" they exhorted. "Don't spend your money on inferior shows!"

Barnum loved to scramble fact and fiction. Chang and Eng were really Siamese twins and Madame Clofullia's beard was real, but Jo-Jo, the Dog Faced Boy who growled

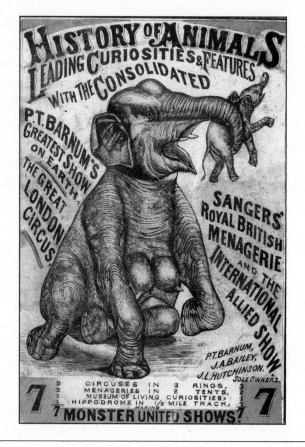

Babe (Hebe) and Columbia, Little America.
Cover of Barnum, Bailey, and Hutchinson's History of Animals,
1882.

and hissed at the rubes as they filed by, also spoke three languages fluently. Waino and Plutano, whom he promoted as
the original Wild Men of Borneo, were really Hiram and
Barney Davis, the sons of a Connecticut farmer.

Then there were the beasts from fairy tales and fables like the FeeJee Mermaid, the Woolly Horse, and the only ELEPHANTUS-HIPPO-PARADOXUS known to exist in the world, a "remarkable pachyderm from the interior of Africa, which even the savants of Europe have not been able to classify." (The animal weighed two tons, had the head of a hippopotamus, the tusks of an elephant, the hide of a rhinoceros, the body of a lion, and the feet of a camel.[9]) In 1880 Barnum's big act was Madame Zazel, "the Human Projectile," who shot out of a cannon and swooped a hundred feet through the air to the other side of the tent and into a net. Her Eagle Swoop was sensational, but no match for baby Columbia. So Barnum made Bailey an offer he couldn't refuse.

"Will not sell for any price," Bailey replied tartly, and then printed Barnum's hundred-thousand-dollar offer for Columbia in his advertising with the headline WHAT BARNUM THINKS OF OUR BABY ELEPHANT. Bailey had out-Barnumed Barnum. "I found that I had at last met a foeman 'worthy of my steel,'" Barnum later wrote in his autobiography.[10] He would never underestimate Bailey again.

The situation grew worse for Barnum as publicity for Columbia continued to grow. Perhaps prompted by Bailey, scientists and naturalists rushed to Philadelphia for an opportunity to make the first studies ever of an infant elephant.

These men of science established three primary research questions: First, the fact no elephant had bred successfully in captivity in over eighty years had generated the hypothesis that elephants either couldn't or wouldn't breed in captivity. With the birth of Little America, that hypothesis now begged clarification: *Was her birth an exception to the rule?* or *Was breeding elephants in captivity really possible?*

The second question was simpler: *How long was the gestation of an elephant?* Estimates ranged from eighteen to thirty-six months, and since no one had seen the physical union between Babe and Mandarin, the exact date of conception would be hard to pin down, but they hoped at least to refine the estimate.

The last question reflected the depth of American ignorance about elephants: *Did infants drink milk through their mouths or their trunks?*

Oddly, the answer to the third question proved the most difficult. That the mother had rejected the infant meant the infant could not suckle her mother naturally. To keep the calf alive, keepers had to milk the female into a funnel and tube that ran into the infant's mouth. Although it was obvious to those feeding Columbia that she drank through her mouth, some argued the evidence unreliable.

Not three weeks after Columbia's birth, Dr. Henry C. Chapman, professor emeritus of physiology and biology at Jefferson Medical College, the curator of the Philadelphia Academy of Natural Sciences, and prosector of the Zoological Society of Philadelphia, presented a disquisition to the Academy of Sciences regarding the order *Pachydermata.* (A prosector dissects cadavers in order to

illustrate anatomy or to determine the cause of death.)
Drs. Boyd from Chicago and Muzzy from Cincinnati attended as well as prominent scientists and physicians from
other major cities and universities to hear and discuss Dr.
Chapman's conclusions.

Dr. Chapman first concluded that elephants did in fact
breed in captivity. He gave several reasons to support his
contention. First, elephants were better husbanded since
the day when circuses walked their stock from stop to
stop. No more pushing, pulling, and straining, no more
standing in bad weather or spending winters in poorly
heated barns. Second, circuses that used to have only one
or two elephants now had as many as five or ten, enough
to allow a partial resuscitation of the social structure of
their herd. As a result, elephants were better adjusted
emotionally. Lastly, nutrition and medical care had improved significantly, which made for healthier animals.
For these reasons, Dr. Chapman concluded, elephants
could indeed mate.[11]

Chapman also calculated the gestation of a female elephant at twenty months. He was short by two months,
but he did accomplish the goal of refining the previous
estimate. He also concluded that an elephant's height
equaled twice the circumference of its leg, and that calves
suckled through their mouths, not their trunks.[12]

All the attention made Columbia a celebrity as people
followed her progress through teething. Late in 1880, Barnum, exasperated and concerned by the quality of competition against him, offered Bailey a truce and a com-

promise: rather than fight a costly battle of attrition, he suggested they merge into a single circus: Barnum, Bailey, and Hutchinson's Consolidated Great London Circus & Sanger's Royal British Menageries and the International Allied Show, or more simply, the *Greatest Show on Earth*.[13]

Merging was a smart move. Barnum's show alone filled fifty-one railway cars, and employed 316 people including five clowns, two dancing midgets, and a Chinese giant. He owned 149 horses and ponies, twenty racing camels, ten elephants, ten giraffes, three Nubian cattle, and the only "huge black hairy Rhinoceros ever captured alive." But Barnum, who'd just turned seventy, was suffering from a debilitating gastrointestinal condition that had reduced his weight from 215 to 144 pounds. His health had made him appear weak and distressed.

From a distance, Barnum may have looked like an old herd bull ready to topple. Bailey agreed to a trial merger, in part, he said, because he needed Barnum's money. "My name as a circus man stands above yours," he told Barnum, "but I need more money, and you've got it."[14]

And so Bailey underestimated Barnum.

Eighteen eighty-one was a year of wonders and horrors. A mentally unstable lawyer named Charles Guiteau shot

President Garfield in the back, Clara Barton started the Red Cross, and the Earp Brothers and Doc Holliday shot it out with the Clantons and the McLaurys for thirty seconds near the OK Corral in Tombstone, Arizona. It was also the year Barnum united for the first time with Bailey and his new partner, James Hutchinson, to create the Greatest Show on Earth.[15]

Their "7 Monster United Shows" included a museum, a racing track, two menageries, and three circuses presented for the first time in three rings, all packed into a tent that could seat ten thousand people.[16] Launching its first season in 1881, Barnum, Bailey, and Hutchinson shows included fifty-seven performances—many of them presented simultaneously. The hippodrome—the oval track inside the tent—was a half-mile long and filled with elephants, horses, and jockeys on ostriches and giraffes spurring them to run. There were Egyptians, Romans, Zulus, a Scotsman in a kilt doing high jumps, clowns, dancers, and aerial acrobats. "The number of daring bareback riders, the vast army of gymnasts, the scores of clowns, the multitudes of jugglers, aerial performers, tumblers, wrestlers and 'specialty artists' that appeared in the course of an evening were positively bewildering," glowed the New York *World*.[17]

The sideshows included Myrtle Corbin, the Four Legged Girl from Texas (who actually had four legs); Che-Mah, the Chinese Rebel Dwarf (who was the son of a Jewish merchant in London); and Major Atom, a man "so small that all little men are giants by his side."

They had giants from Arabia, China, France, Ireland, and Texas, and an animal-man who Barnum claimed had been trapped "during a gorilla hunting expedition near the Gambia River in western Africa," and whom Barnum variously advertised as *The Monkey Man, The Missing Link,* and *Zip the Pinhead*.[18] (Zip was actually William Henry Johnson from New Jersey and was born with microencephalitis, a sloping, underdeveloped head.)

The show confounded the senses. William Batcheller, the Champion Leaper of the World, did a double somersault over fifteen elephants, and Madame Zazel shot out of a cannon and did her famous Eagle Swoop.[19] Still, no act was as precious as Columbia, America's firstborn. "She wandered restlessly around an enclosure," wrote the *New York Sun*, "switching her diminutive tail, waving her little trunk, and winking her small eyes in a curiously ludicrous imitation of Hebe, her mother, who stood chained, and constantly weaved from side to side. . . ."[20]

On February 3, 1882, a fifteen-year-old female elephant named Queen gave birth to an infant while chained to a heavy post in the middle of a sawdust ring at Barnum's winter headquarters in Bridgeport, Connecticut. The blessed event was witnessed by the circus, the press, and nineteen other elephants who, according to the *New York Herald*, resented the intrusion of the crowd of humans who came to watch. "[They] seemed to take a gloomy view of the situation," read the newspaper, "and while continuously swaying to and fro, winked in an ominous manner or flapped their blanket-like ears as though preparing to strike terror to the hearts of those of the human race who stood close to the outer circle of the ring."[21]

The elephants had reason to be distressed. George Arstingstall, originally Bailey's chief bull man, described Queen as "exceptionally vicious and treacherous" compared to Babe. Fearing a repeat of Babe's violent reaction to her newborn, Professor Arstingstall had ordered Queen tied down. Roustabouts pinned her in a web of ropes, each end held by a man, while Chieftain, the father, "shrieked like a calliope" and repeatedly kicked the wall.

Flattened to the ground, in a position that went against the instincts of a mother, Queen gave birth to an unimaginably small infant. When she started kicking, Arstingstall tightened the ropes on her hind legs. The elephant chorus wailed louder and then the big cats and a peacock joined in.

George Arstingstall was a practical man. While he ruled the elephant roost with an iron fist, he was also a watchful man who learned snippets of elephant biology and psychology over the years. To everyone's astonishment, he suddenly told the men to let go of the ropes.

The crowd instinctively backed away.

The men holding down Queen thought the order was either a mistake or a bad joke, because it made no sense, and when they realized Arstingstall was serious, they refused to comply.

Arstingstall repeated the order.

One man, anxious to be the first to leave, let go of his rope and scampered away. The rest pulled harder. As Queen's fury intensified, other men had second thoughts, and one by one they dropped their rope until holding on became impossible.

Queen was a big elephant with a big temper, angry for being held down, and she quickly rose to her feet, ropes draped across her back. She lashed out with her trunk but didn't charge. Rather, she tended her calf.

The calf weighed forty-five pounds, less than 1 percent of the mass of her mother, the equivalent of a woman giving birth to a twenty-three-ounce child. Queen steadied her tottering daughter as her child reached out and touched her with her seven-inch trunk.[22] Arstingstall gave Queen loaves of bread, pans of oatmeal, and crackers soaked in rum, and then cabled Barnum the good news.

"What is it," Barnum asked, "a boy or a girl?"

"A girl," said Arstingstall.

"That's good," answered Barnum, "but be careful of her; there's $100,000 on that straw that can be trampled out in a second."[23]

That night, long after Queen and her calf were asleep, Chieftain continued to sway at his stake.

Barnum named his newest elephant America. Columbia, who would turn two years old in a month, was losing her cachet as a baby. Every day she grew a little larger and looked more like the other elephants in her herd. Barnum even sounded apologetic in his advertisements:

> Some may come to see
> COLUMBIA,
> The Baby Elephant, born here two years ago. No longer an infant in arms, but one of the best performers in the lot.[24]

Barnum saw the chance to replace Columbia with America so he could continue to exploit the public's fondness for baby elephants. After all, Hachaliah Bailey had supposedly swapped Mogul for Columbus and people barely noticed.

By the following morning, however, Barnum changed her name to Bridgeport, in honor of his hometown in Connecticut. By his reckoning, if Columbia had been worth $100,000, then Bridgeport was worth three times that much, so he insured her for $300,000 for an annual premium of $52,000—a thousand dollars a week at a time when the average wage earner made twenty cents an

Bridgeport's First Christmas, 1882.

hour. "All my thoughts and cares at present are locked up in two *trunks*," Barnum wrote, "one of which belongs to *Jumbo* and the other to little Bridgeport."

Demoted to the second rank, Columbia faded into oblivion. She gained notoriety briefly in August 1902 when she gored her keeper and again a few weeks after that when she got into a free-for-all with three African lions at Thompson and Dundy's Luna Park on Coney Island. (Columbia threw a big tom into a crowd of people who'd gathered to watch the scrap.[25]) She survived her battle with the lions, but five years later, in 1907, when she was twenty-seven, her keeper declared her "neither safe nor sane" and ordered her execution. Five men threw a rope around her and with a block and tackle choked her to death while twenty-one elephants, including Columbia's mother, Babe, watched.

Her teeth were made into paperweights and her legs into umbrella stands. Her skin made fine leather for gloves and shoes.

William Randolph Hearst's paper, the *New York Sun*, called Barnum, Bailey & Hutchinson's opening performance in Madison Square Garden in March 1882 "the Greatest Show in the World." "[S]o much was going on incessantly from the moment when the show opened to the concluding moment, in which a handsome performer was hurled through space from a tremendous Roman catapult. No one pair of eyes could take it all in," continued the *Sun*. "The roof was a mass of trapezes, and men and women in fresh and costly tights flashed through the breadth of the Hippodrome as though they had wings."[26]

Like Columbia before her, Bridgeport performed for the kings and kingmakers of the day. At six months, she capered before the VIP boxes "with strange glee and a measure of grace about the feet of its slow and decorous mother." She enchanted former president Ulysses S. Grant, U.S. senator Roscoe Conkling, who'd been falsely accused of being behind the assassination of President Garfield in 1880, and General Daniel B. Sickles.[27]

Bridgeport wore a pink silk dress to her first birthday party, "with facings of *petit polonaise*, backstitched to a *jun d'espirit*." Her headstall was woven with roses.[28]

Barnum took Bridgeport out of the show when her health started to fail in late 1885. She died the following April. "Bridgeport will not be buried like a common baby," wrote the *New York Herald-Tribune*, "but will be turned over to the tender mercies of Professor Ward of Rochester," who was instructed as he had been with Jumbo to make two Bridgeports—one of hide and one of bone.[29]

That fall, Bridgeport went on display next to Jumbo at the Barnum Museum of Natural History at Tufts College, where she could be viewed at no charge on weekdays from three to five o'clock. Her tusks were two inches long.[30]

On Easter Sunday 1908, Abraham Lincoln appeared at Madison Square Garden wearing a spring frock made of crimson plush trimmed with rhinestones. The *New York Times* gloated that such a fine personage would grace New York, and audiences applauded thunderously.

Lincoln was a four-week-old elephant, born at Barnum's in Bridgeport, who weighed less than two hundred pounds and stood about three feet tall. The sober image that normally accompanied the sixteenth president of the United States clashed with the tiny elephant who drank milk from a jumbo baby bottle. Before she turned six weeks old, Barnum recast Abraham Lincoln as Baby Bunting.

Baby Bunting was a bigger hit than Lincoln. She rocketed to headline status in newspaper advertising, bumping an act called *Autos That Pass in the Air* into second place.[31] She was, in Barnum & Bailey's words, "the Crowning Attraction of the Largest Menagerie in the World and the Prize Exhibit in the Biggest Herd of Elephants in America."[32] She was the "Bottle Baby" and women and children flocked to see her. "No child of blood royal or infant born to the people receives more careful attention and sentimental care than Baby Bunting," ran one national story that obsessed over details about the baby's diet ("rice, milk and baby food") and her feeding schedule. The moment Baby Bunting picked up her bottle and pulled milk from its oversized nipple, she transcended beast and became a child star.

Barnum brought Baby Bunting to the children's ward in St. Mary's Hospital, on Thirty-Fourth Street in Manhattan. She arrived with her keeper, a monkey, a cat, and Princess Weenie Wee, "the littlest midget in the world."

"Oh-o-o-o-o-o!" she shrieked upon entering the ward.

The children bolted upright in their beds. The *New York Times* described the sound as "a mixture of thunder and fire engine whistle, so astonishing big in quantity and quality that it did not seem possible that such a very small elephant could have kept such a large noise bottled up inside and not burst in the effort."[33] Baby Bunting's keeper, a clown, explained that Baby Bunting was telling them how very sad she was to see so many children in their beds.[34] She went around the room and shook hands with those brave enough to take hold of her trunk.

Newspapers urged their readers not to miss "the bottle fed baby" as she toured the country. In her first two hundred days of life, Baby Bunting had made 148 stands in thirty states, one Canadian province, and the District of Columbia. In early November she retired with the troupe of Bridgeport for the winter. She was 247 days old.

Then mysteriously she disappeared. She survived the winter because she was on the road for the beginning of the next season, but after Kalamazoo, Michigan, she suddenly vanishes from the record. Publicly at least, Barnum & Bailey never mention her again. She was a meteor that streaked across the sky, stunned the eye for second, and then was gone.

A few circus historians believe Baby Bunting died in late 1909, two months before her first birthday. Others think she lived a lot longer even though no infant elephant born in America had ever survived past a year. Their argument had a fairy-tale quality about it as a story about graduating from puberty to maturity. The death of

Baby Bunting's narrative in 1909 was the death of Baby Bunting but not the elephant, who slipped into a new identity. In August 1909 a newspaper noted Baby Bunting was learning how to perform like the other elephants in the Barnum & Bailey herd. Without her bottle, she was just one more elephant in the long gray line.

If Baby Bunting did survive, she would have been the only elephant born in America to survive infancy. Of the eight calves known born in the United States between 1900 and 1918, none survived longer than a year. Most died of maternal neglect within days or weeks. Their mothers rolled over them, stepped on them, and shunned them. Princess Alice at the Hogle Zoo in Salt Lake City gave

Prince Utah.
Like all elephants born in America before 1962, he died before his
first birthday.

birth to four calves after Abraham Lincoln/Baby Bunting. Baby Hutch was the first in 1912, then Baby Tambon in 1914, Little Miracle in 1916, and Prince Utah in 1918.

Like Babe, Princess Alice was a dysfunctional mother. Baby Hutch died at the age of forty-two days, after Alice knelt on him, "leaving him flat as a pancake."[35] Baby Tambon survived only one day, and Little Miracle survived a miraculous five months. The greatest hope had been for Prince Utah, who was fifty days shy of his first birthday when Princess Alice rolled over him.[36]

No elephant would be born in America for another forty years.

After graduating from the Juilliard School of Music in New York, H. Morgan Berry joined a band that played cruise ships in the 1930s. His true passion, however, was wild animals. Over the next thirty years, Berry and his wife, Fern, went "sleuthing" for animals in Africa and the Far East. "We like traveling and we like the animals," Berry said. Fern cared for the babies. "She's a real help—I couldn't get along with her," he boasted. Besides trading in exotic animals, Berry was also the elephant handler at the Woodland Park Zoo in Seattle. He was, by default, the resident elephant expert in the Pacific Northwest.

Berry loved elephants. People got a kick out of seeing him drive around town in his convertible with an elephant in the backseat. He'd show up for community social events with anything from a python to a monkey that he and Fern had brought back from overseas, and he'd regale everyone with their wild adventures in India, Siam, and Africa.

When the Berrys left for their ninth trip overseas in search of elephants, cobras, and gibbons for zoos in 1958, the story made the second page of the daily edition. ANI-MAL TRAINING SEATTLEITES EN-ROUTE TO ELEPHANT AUC-TION, the headline read in the *Seattle Daily Times*. In the picture Mr. and Mrs. Berry hold up a motion picture camera. Berry said he hoped to film an elephant roundup in the wild.[37] Morgan and Fern Berry reminded people of Martin and Osa Johnson, the couple from Kansas who went to Africa to make adventure movies about elephants, lions, and rhinos in the 1920s and '30s.

Six months earlier, Morgan Berry made the front page of the *Daily Times* when he lost control of his truck at the intersection of Phinney Avenue and North Sixty-Seventh Street and turned over a trailer with four elephants in it. Berry, who owned the elephant ride concession at the zoo, was ferrying his animals to an event in Everett when the trailer spilled four elephants onto Mrs. F. E. Ungar's front yard. "I've never seen anything like it," the elderly Mrs. Ungar told the paper. "Imagine elephants all over my front lawn."

The children eating lunch outside at the John B. Allen

School near Mrs. Ungar's house watched in amazement as one by one the elephants rolled over, stood up, and lumbered off on their separate ways. While the teachers tried to round up the children, Morgan and his son Kenneth tried to round up the elephants.

Once the Berrys managed to gather them, they herded the great beasts through the city rather than wait for a replacement truck and trailer. Berry knew that four spooked elephants could do a lot of damage in a short time, and so he kept them distracted by herding them through the streets of Seattle. People poured out of their homes and businesses to watch. Like Mrs. Ungar, they'd never seen anything like it.

In 1958, Berry returned from Asia with a sexually mature and vigorous bull named Thonglaw. During the past forty years, owners and trainers had continued to shy from owning males, given their violent and unpredictable history, but as people like Berry learned more about the biology and psychology of elephants, the less uncertain they were of them. Owning a bull, they realized, was a management—not a behavioral—problem.

Berry had two female elephants. At eight Belle was old enough to mate with Thonglaw, but not Pet, who, with her "girlish figure," was only five.[38] Thonglaw showed no interest in either of them.

Berry alternated taking Thonglaw, Belle, and Pet for extended visits to the zoos in Seattle and Portland. Seattle had no resident elephants, but Portland had two maidens, Rosy and Tuy Hoa (pronounced Tee-Wah), neither of whom had experienced the company of a sexually mature male. "There might be a romance in the air," the *Oregonian* speculated. "[Thonglaw] tickled [Rosy] under the chin and started pitching elephant woo before he had even been formally introduced."[39] Thonglaw had a girlfriend.

Berry made the newspaper again in 1959 after a monkey on the set of a children's television show called *Buttons and His Buddies* badly frightened Pet. Berry barely got her out the studio when she set off on a tear across the campus of the University of Washington.[40]

Three days later, at the annual coronation of the Seafair Queen, Berry redeemed himself. The front page of the newspaper had a picture of Queen Judy Peterson waving to the audience at the Girls' Fun Frolic from atop Thonglaw.

In her interview, Queen Judy said she enjoyed riding the elephant, but that getting on him in her royal gown was a pain.[41]

Berry left Thonglaw, Belle, and Pet in the care of the Portland zoo in October 1960 while he and Fern went back to Asia. The zoo was happy to have houseguests for the winter because it had just proposed a tax levy for zoo expansion and hoped the publicity from Portland's new "pachydormitory" would stimulate interest.

No one knew Belle was three months pregnant. Her pregnancy went undetected by everyone until the summer of 1961. The zoo decided to keep the news private given the precarious nature of elephant pregnancies in the past. In October, however, a rumor surfaced that Belle was "elephanticipating," but the story really didn't break until January 1962, when she went into labor.[42] For the first time, biologists could fix the actual number of days it took for an elephant to gestate.

Based upon the calculations of the zoo's director, Jack Marks, and its veterinarian, Matthew Maberry, Belle wasn't due to deliver until March. It was eighteen weeks early but within the predicted time frame of eighteen to twenty-four months. The phone at the zoo rang off the hook with women calling to ask how long it took for an elephant to carry a baby to term. "I told one the period of gestation was anywhere from 17 to 24 months," Jack Marks said. "She just said 'My Gawd,' and hung up."[43]

Maberry stressed that no one really knew how long gestation took in an elephant, but when Belle's baby dropped twelve inches in three days, the consensus was that "the ship is ready to launch." She was eating more rocks and dirt than usual, too—half a wheelbarrow load a week.[44]

A woman's group called to say they wanted to give a baby shower for Belle; others sent flowers, candy, and bags of fruit and peanuts. People surged into the zoo and stood four deep to watch Belle as she swayed back and forth. The Greater Portland Elephant Watch had begun.

On the fifth day, at 4:10 p.m., Belle started having labor pains a half-hour apart. Her temperature fell one degree in six hours. The muscles along her back relaxed and her pelvis spread, and the baby picked up kicking the mother. When a reporter asked Marks if the baby would be a boy or a girl, he said he thought it would be a girl because he'd read that elephant babies at eighteen months were always female. A reporter then asked Maberry if he foresaw any problems with the delivery. He replied only, "Nature will take its course."

Belle's labor continued for hours while the reporters drank coffee and played poker, using Belle's brown and yellow pills as chips. Against doctor's orders, they fed Belle peanuts and black coffee while they waited for her to deliver. Meanwhile Maberry checked Belle's uterus for obstruction. "No luck," he reported. "I tried to reach the posterior border of the pelvis, but it was too far back."[45]

Inexplicably, the spasms stopped the next day. Maberry called Dr. Errmano Bronzini of Rome for a consult. Bronzini had presided over the successful birth of an elephant in the Rome Zoo in 1948, but when he couldn't reach Bronzini, Maberry called Dr. Emanuel Amoroso, a reproductive veterinarian at the Royal Veterinary College in London, instead. Amoroso had worked with elephants and had attended births in the wild.

A local radio station broadcast their conversation live. The doctor in London confirmed the diagnosis of the doctor in Portland; Belle was in labor, which normally lasted from six to twelve hours, but it wasn't unusual to take longer the first time.[46] Amoroso counseled patience.

Maberry ordered an electrocardiograph so he could check the strain on Belle's heart. Her heart—all thirty pounds of it—pumped strongly and regularly. With the baby in position for birth, Maberry predicted Belle would give birth within forty-eight hours.

A week later, he was still waiting. And three months after that.

Meanwhile, Thonglaw went into musth. "The expectant father had suddenly turned into a homicidal maniac," wrote Shana Alexander in *Life* magazine. He disappeared from public view. "[He] isn't himself right now," explained the *Oregonian*. "He's been in 'must [*sic*],' a form of elephant insanity accompanied by amnesia."[47]

On April 14, 1962, after five hours of labor, Belle gave birth to a male infant, 166 years almost to the day that Jacob Crowninshield landed his elephant in New York. Concerns about Belle's competence as a mother quickly vanished as soon as she "gave her newborn son a couple of swift kicks in his fuzzy flanks" to get him on his feet. Then, "gently shoving with her trunk and forelegs, Belle nudged his head around to her breast."[48]

"Despite what you may have read," wrote Alexander in *Life*, "the Elephant's Child is born with his trunk fully developed and firmly attached. It is pink-tipped and hairy and, when the Child is hungry, it makes a noise like a leaky balloon."[49]

The elephant house turned into a maternity ward and a local radio station issued hourly "Belle Bulletins" that updated the progress of the newborn. Stuffed elephants flew off the shelves of the stores and schoolchildren drew baby elephants named Ding Dong, Nogero (Oregon spelled backward), and Belle Boy. People flooded the zoo with gifts. One person sent a set of gold-plated diaper pins. Another sent Belle three hundred roses, and when the keeper gave them to her, she picked off the blooms and ate the stems.

The zoo pampered her with a diet fit for elephant royalty: a bale and a half of timothy, three gallons of oats, six pounds of bread, fifty pounds of carrots, half a box of apples, twenty-five pounds of bananas, a quarter box of oranges, and ten pounds of freshly dug dirt.[50] Zoo attendance skyrocketed. Everyone wanted to see Belle and her baby.[51]

Then came a bombshell: the Chicago zoo offered Morgan Berry fifty thousand dollars to buy Belle and her calf. Berry expressed his condolences to the people in Oregon and Washington, but Chicago's offer was too good to ignore. He was willing to offer a compromise, however. He'd discount Belle and her baby to thirty thousand dollars for Portland if the city could come up with the cash before the Chicago deadline.

The sum was woefully beyond the financial wherewithal of the zoo. But a grassroots campaign to raise money crossed all political, business, and social boundaries. Radio station KPOJ launched a prime-time drive to name Belle's baby. Anyone could vote in return for a dollar to help buy Belle and her calf. Television station KPTV launched a "Ring the Bell for Belle" telethon to raise money and set up a remote camera in the elephant house so people could see live shots of the baby and his mom. (The station promised not to quit until the city had reached its goal of thirty thousand dollars.) A local bowling alley announced a "Bowl for Belle Tournament" and firemen placed "Belle-tins" around the city to collect donations in public places. Children rolled "Peanuts for Belle" in the city parks.

Portland sold shares in Belle. A pound of her sold for $6. Five thousand pounds would bring $30,000. The employees in X-ray and medical records at the hospital donated $12.05. Pacific Power & Light bought fifty shares for $300, and the East Side Rotary donated $120 and a poem that urged others to contribute:

> We need a pot that's filled with dough
> for Fuzzy and Mama Belle;
> 'Cause if we want to keep them,
> boys, we'll have to dig like . . . Well?[52]

Businesses pledged their profits; churches and social groups took up collections; and citizens made pledges. Then the result of the radio station's contest came in: it had collected three thousand dollars and popular consensus had named the baby Packy, short for Pachyderm. When the Chicago deadline came, however, Portland had collected only $18,087.68.

Berry knew Portland wouldn't forgive him for selling Belle and Packy to Chicago, so he took the zoo's IOU for the balance remainder and then added Thonglaw and Pet for the same price so the family could stay together.[53] Little did Portland know that Thonglaw had impregnated not only Belle, but Rosy, Tuy Hoa, and the young Pet as well.

The following October, Rosy gave birth to Me-Tu. The next year Tuy Hoa gave birth to Hanako and Pet gave birth to Dino. In one year Portland's elephant population went from two to eight, making the city, in Berry's words, "the undisputed pachyderm capital of the world."[54]

Morgan Berry's wife, Fern, died the year after Packy was born. Thonglaw died under anesthesia in 1974. By then he'd sired fifteen calves, making him the most prolific bull in captivity.[55] Belle died in 1994 of a foot infection. She was forty-five, and Packy was her only child.

By the time Morgan Berry died in 1979 on his ranch in Cowlitz County, Washington, he'd trained more than a hundred elephants. "He was one of the people who could read an elephant's mind," said a trainer who'd worked with Berry over the years. "He could sense what it would do before it happened."

At the time of his death Berry had nine elephants in his

barn. He was training a bull named Buddha when, speculation arose, the six-ton bull had either gone berserk and trampled Berry or Berry had died of a heart attack and Buddha had trampled him afterward.[56] An autopsy was inconclusive.[57]

Berry's son Kenneth, who'd grown concerned when his father didn't answer the phone that day, drove to the ranch to make sure everything was okay. Berry had a bad heart and was living alone since his companion, Eloise Berchtold, had died the year before after being trampled by an elephant during a circus performance in Quebec.

Kenneth found his father at the feet of Buddha, who repeatedly picked up his limp body and flung it. A spokesman for the zoo explained Buddha's behavior was a gesture of respect, a tribute to a great man.[58]

Buddha remained chained to a tree for five months while Kenneth Berry sold the ranch and the elephants. Finally he shot Buddha where he stood.[59] "He wasn't safe to handle," he explained. "I had to turn down the money and dispose of him."[60] He buried Buddha at the base of the tree.

In 1962 inflation stood at 1.2 percent, a gallon of gas cost twenty-eight cents, and Ford built a space-age concept car called the Mustang. The first black student enrolled at the University of Mississippi, escorted by federal marshals; the Soviets put missiles in Cuba; Senate Majority Leader Mike Mansfield returned from Viet Nam unconvinced by the argument for war, and Richard Nixon lost his race for governor of California and famously stated, "you won't have Dick Nixon to kick around anymore."

Nineteen sixty-two was LSD, "The Peppermint Twist," *The Beverly Hillbillies*, and Andy Warhol. On New Year's Day, Decca Records auditioned the Beatles and turned them down. Bob Dylan was writing his third album, *The Times They Are A-Changin'*. It was the dawning of the Age of Aquarius.

A quartet of live births at the Portland Zoo signaled a new age in the relationship between elephants and people. Whereas circuses were transient and the elephants traveled with histories manufactured by showmen, zoos anchored themselves in a community, allowing the citizens of Portland to invest emotionally and financially in the lives of Thonglaw, Belle, Pet, Rosy, Tuy Hoa, their children, and their children's children.

Although zoos learned a lot from Packy's birth, they still didn't know enough about their needs to keep them alive long. Eleven of the fifteen calves Thonglaw sired died, eight before their fifteenth birthday. Still, the survival rate was better than before 1962.

Packy is one of four siblings who survived. In 2005, the zoo gave him a "Father of the Year" award for being the first first-generation elephant captive to mate successfully. In all, he's sired seven offspring, although only three survive. Rama and his sister, Shine, live with their father in Portland. Rama likes to throw egg-based paints across a canvas, which he sells at "trunk shows." Rama's brother, KC, lives with three females at the Dickerson Park Zoo in Springfield, Missouri.

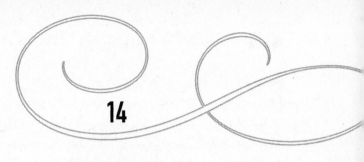

14

Matriarch

◆

from the *Jackson Citizen Patriot*, June 25, 1890

AN ELEPHANT HUNT IN SEATTLE

Pittsburgh Dispatch.

Two elephants of a circus were being driven on board a steamer at Seattle, Wash., for a trip to Ferndale, when they refused to step on a gangplank and both made a break up the street.

The largest, named Queen, was pursued by a crowd of men and boys into a lumber yard, where she made a stand and trumpeted several times. The crowd pressed her with clubs, and in a moment she charged them.

In the scramble a big pile of lumber was upset and four men were buried.

After an hour's chase Queen was captured.

◆

Babe has had at least twenty-six known incarnations as an elephant in America and likely there were double or even triple that many, most of whom left little or no trace of their lives. She was known variously as Babe, Baby, Little Babe, Big Babe, and Babe Ruth; in her present incarnation she's Babe Sh-bang at the Niabi Zoo in Coal Valley, Illinois. She was the Babe who gave birth to America's firstborn Joe and Columbia (*The Latest Arrival: A Baby Elephant Is Born with its Mother in Captivity*, 1880) and became a reason why Barnum joined forces with Bailey. She was also the Babe who panicked after finding a dead mouse in her trough (*Stampeded by a Dead Mouse*, 1893); the Babe who had a toothache (*Pulling an Elephant's Tooth: It Took Ten Men with a Pair of Mechanic's Forceps*, 1900); the Babe who went for a jaunt (*Four-Ton Elephant Cuts Loose Awhile*, 1902); and the Babe who went on a killing spree (*Elephant Gores Keeper to Death at Zoo in Toledo*, 1914).

Once during her twenty-six lives she was male (*An Elephant on a Tear: He Drank a Gallon of Whisky and Had a High Old Time*, 1892). A rich man bought another Babe and her private railroad car for fifteen thousand dollars, and once the Woman's Humane Society rescued an elephant named Babe after a circus abandoned her in St. Louis.[1] She was a star attraction in zoos in San Francisco, New York, Chicago, New York, Milwaukee, Fort Worth, and Washington, D.C. She worked at least twenty different circuses, including Al. G. Barnes, Forepaugh-Sells, Gentry Brothers, Cole Brothers, Clyde Beatty, Sam

B. Dill, the Ringling Brothers, and Barnum and Bailey's Greatest Show on Earth.[2] She loved pedicures, got drunk now and then, and liked to pick the pockets of those who visited her. She went to states before they were states; she went to the Indian Territories and the western provinces, where she dragged logs for cabins and yanked stumps out of the ground. In Bellingham, Washington, she won a pulling and pushing contest against teams of men, horses, oxen, camels, and a hippopotamus named Euphrates. (A team of a hundred men dragged 6,700 pounds; Babe pulled 12,000. The oxen refused to budge.[3])

After Jumbo, she was the most well-known elephant in America. "Nearly every little man and woman in the country who is old enough to go to the circus has seen Babe," wrote a paper in 1904, "who has been traveling about the country in the Barnum & Bailey circus ever since there was such a thing. . . ."[4] She marched in parades, weddings, and funerals. She celebrated old war victories, jubilees, and barn raisings. In 1935 the 101 Ranch offered baseball great Babe Ruth seventy-five thousand dollars to ride Big Babe "preceded by a calliope playing 'Take Me Out to the Ball Game.'"[5] Ruth, who was busy looking for a job as the manager of a ball club at the time, declined the offer, but late that summer, when his prospects weren't looking so good, a reporter asked him what he'd do if things didn't work out for him. Ruth told him he'd join Billy Rose's musical, *Jumbo.*

"What will you do in that?" the reporter asked.

"Ride an elephant, I guess," Ruth answered. "That is

if they can find one big enough—and dumb enough—to carry me."[6]

Babe generally lived a long life but not necessarily a happy one. Her average life span was fifty years. Once she lived to seventy. When she died, she died of both natural and unnatural causes. They euthanized her several times but never for bad behavior, even though once she killed a man.[7] Mostly they put her down for debilitating diseases such as arthritis, tuberculosis, and twice for "an infarction of the uterus."

Of all Babe's lives, however, one stood out in particular.

She was Hebe, the Greek goddess of youth, although no one called her that. They called her Babe. A stock name for animals larger than a man, at one time or another Babe was a horse, baboon, hippopotamus, giraffe, or an elephant. Their name locked them into Peter Pan's Never-Never Land of perpetual juvenility.

Babe was a good girl, mostly. She understood English and could carry on a conversation with a human being. When someone asked Jim Smith, Babe's keeper, if she really knew her name, he replied, *"Know her name? Well, I should say she did, don't you, Babe?"*

Babe winked, nodded, and then opened her mouth wide.

"It's her way of telling you she understands what you're talking about," Smith said.[8]

Babe led two lives: one public, one private. Her public life was to prove that God had given man dominion over all the animals, even the largest. Dressed as human beings, elephants played *La Condition Humaine* from lust, greed, and vanity to love, loyalty, and sacrifice. They painted in oils, danced the minuet, and played the tuba and the glockenspiel. Nor did they begrudge domination the way big cats instinctively resisted it. The belief—or at least the feeling—was that elephants understood the value of civilization and aspired to join it.

The private life of Babe, however, was the antithesis of her public life. Rather than a child, in her private life she was a mate, a mother, a nurse, and as she aged, a matriarch. The difference was between Child and Queen Mother. In one role she couldn't take care of herself; in the other, she took care of everyone.

Late in the nineteenth century, Barnum's herd sometimes grew as large forty elephants, which gave them an opportunity to salvage a semblance of social order. Sexually mature males took harems of sexually mature females as lesser males jostled for position as the next lead contender. But there were no children, and their society remained fragmented and unschooled.

In 1903 Barnum imported eight calves into his herd. Captured in the wild, they suffered the trauma of a violent separation from their mothers and their native families of aunts and older brothers and sisters. The same Babe that had picked up her newborn Columbia and tried to throw him away in 1880 gradually mellowed into a surrogate mother of eight calves. She soothed and petted them "and talked to them in the elephant language, telling them doubtless, that it wasn't so bad as it seemed, and if they would only be good babies and stop crying everybody would be kind and they would be happy again."[9] And they listened and they grew up under her care and control, and she ruled with an iron trunk.

By 1903 some keepers had developed a better sense of the social abilities of elephant elders, and they found it expedient to allow a matriarch like Babe to take care of the herd. Harry Mooney, the keeper and trainer of the elephant corps of the Greatest Show on Earth (and the coach of Mooney's Giants, the first elephant baseball team) was talking to a reporter from the *New York Times* after the season's first performance at Madison Square Garden in 1913 about how he liked to "let nurse Babe deal with the rowdies." The elephants were behind them as they left the arena in single file. Babe was bringing up the rear. Suddenly a troublemaker named Topsy butted one of the other elephants and then went off on a toot, trumpeting as loud as she could. The rest of the elephants tensed up with the commotion and Coco, the star pitcher of the Giants, bolted out of line and started running to the rear, where Babe was standing.

Babe knocked Coco so hard she fell to her knees. "Topsy and Coco have reached a state where they want to break away from what I might call parental restraint," Mooney explained to the reporter. "Talk about bringing up a family, it ain't nothing to the task we have down here."

Out of respect Mooney called Babe "the real Circus Queen." He deferred to her when the herd grew restless or agitated or one of the other younger elephants balked at loading into a car or performing in the ring. She lent assurance with a gentle touch of her trunk, and when that didn't work, she'd give a resounding swat. According to Mooney, after fifty-seven years in show business, Babe took "a personal interest" in the show and insisted on discipline in the ranks.[10] Together he and Babe held the herd together.

But Babe was aging. In 1916, the circus celebrated her 108th birthday. It was an election year, and both Woodrow Wilson and Republican contender Charles Evans Hughes had ignored the prohibitionist movement in their campaigns (both had "wet" and "dry" platforms), but popular sentiment for banning alcohol was galloping to a finish. Within months of Babe's birthday party in Philadelphia, a resolution calling for a constitutional amendment to prohibit the manufacture, sale, or consumption of alcohol in America passed both houses of Congress.

Elephants, as avid imbibers of spirits, objected strenuously to the prohibition of alcohol, as did the clowns who played "How Dry I Am" while they mimed John Barleycorn's funeral. The madcap jesters, fools, wags, buffoons, jokers, harlequins, pickle-herrings, holy frights of sky larkers, chumps, and cutups, Simple Simons, and Charlie Chaplins of the circus proved it was still possible to have fun.[11]

In 1916, Babe celebrated her fifty-seventh year of service, one year more than Barnum. If she really had been born in 1808, then she would have been alive when the Welshman was walking the Crowninshield elephant up and down the east coast, and before Hachaliah Bailey led Old Bet from the ferry on the Hudson to his farm in Somers, New York. She'd have been in the circus since before the Civil War or the California Gold Rush or even the Battle of 1812, when Uncle Sam appeared for the first time. As the oldest surviving American, Babe had lived through almost the entire course of her country's history. Like Old John (formerly John L. Sullivan, the boxing elephant), Babe settled to the margins of the herd as she aged, but she remained proud as younger females wore her down.[12]

Babe was really born a year before the start of the Civil War. She was fifty-six, not 108. She served Barnum, Bailey, and the Ringlings for forty-three years, which made her, in anyone's book, Queen.

On August 23, 1919, Babe attended a ceremony at the Rock River fairgrounds in Rockford, Illinois, at the start of the Winnebago County fair. The local newspaper remarked she was "beyond the flapper age" but still young enough "to carry her coy cognomen without seeming absurd."[13] She was celebrating her 106th birthday, even though she'd already celebrated her 108th birthday three years earlier.

A local citizen wrote a poem to commemorate her arrival, a stanza of which read:

> On her huge old frame so lank, and lean
> The marks of time are plainly seen.
> Her five score years, and then some more,
> Tell us her useful days are o'er.[14]

Officials made speeches about how grateful they were to the Ringlings for donating Babe as the first animal in the new zoo planned for Rockford, at Black Hawk Park. The city welcomed her with "a freshly threshed peck of oats" and the finest timothy money could buy. No more catching trains in the middle of the night or pushing circus wagons through the mud. She'd spend the last fifty or sixty years of her life in the lap of luxury as Rockford's own.[15] Soon a buffalo named Gus and a tiger named Lily joined her.[16]

Twenty months later Babe got on a train bound for Eagle Pass, Texas, where she changed trains for Mexico City. "Great regret was expressed to lose the elephant," opined the *Rockford Morning Star*, "but the Zoological association could no longer afford to pay her big board bill."[17]

On April 12, 1921, Babe vanished from history.

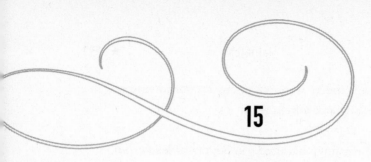

15

AC/DC

◆

from the St. Louis *Republic,* December 12, 1896

AN ELEPHANT TO BE ELECTROCUTED

GYPSY, THE RAMPAGEOUS MANKILLER,
MUST EXPIATE HER CRIMES IN CHICAGO

TROLLEY WIRES ARE TO BE TAPPED AND
SHE WILL GO OVER THE GREAT DIVIDE BY
RAPID TRANSIT

Chicago, Dec. 11—Gypsy, the famous old circus elephant which has killed four keepers, is soon to suffer for its terrible past at the hands of the executioner. The monster, which for the past several years has been running the Harris Nickel Plate Circus to suit itself, will be wiped off the face of the earth with a streak of lightning.

Mr. Harris believes that Gypsy will be of more use to humanity when made over into soap, so the elephant will be electrocuted at Tattersall's as soon as a date can be decided upon. Gypsy is well known all over the United States, and is considered the most dangerous elephant in the country.

Last winter the animal escaped from its home and caused great excitement on the West Side by running through the streets, damaging everything she came in contact with. Before she was captured, Frank Scott, her keeper, was killed, the elephant stepping on him and crushing out his life.

Manager Wills, of the Harris show, applied yesterday to the collector for a permit to electrocute the brute, providing the city authorities thought there was enough electricity in the sky. If there is not, he declares he will tap all the trolley wires in the city and send her to her fathers on the rapid-transit plan.

The execution will be public, and every man, woman or child, who has the necessary admission fee will be given an opportunity of seeing the first pachyderm going over the great divide by bolted lightning.

On a pleasant midsummer's day in 1888, electrician Harold P. Brown put on a public demonstration at Columbia College in New York City that addressed the dangers of electricity. Although Brown had no standing either in the academic or the professional community of electrical engineers—he was a self-educated citizen concerned about the electrification of America—Brown wanted to show once and for all that alternating current, the alternative model to Edison's much-vaunted direct current, was unsafe for human beings. He intended to prove this point by electrocuting two dogs in front of an audience of seventy-five professionals who'd come unaware of his plans to kill the dogs.[1] "It is safe to assume that had the revolting nature of the experiments been known," opined the *Electrical Engineer*, "the attendance would have been very slim."[2]

Brown, perhaps wittingly, stepped into the middle of a feud between Thomas Edison and George Westinghouse over the future of electricity in America.[3] Edison had installed a power grid in a fifty-block section of lower Manhattan in 1882. It took fourteen miles of heavy copper cable to power eight hundred lights.[4] In spite of its success, Edison's direct current had two obvious limitations: first, it could only travel short distances before losing strength—electrifying New York would require a coal-fired station every square mile—and second, it required massive amounts of copper at a time when the price of copper was high.

Westinghouse's current had its deficiencies, too. Foremost among them, at least in Harold Brown's eyes, was that his system required lethal levels of electricity to operate. Indeed, citizens were already dying of electrical shock. After Edison's initial success in New York City, dozens of entrepreneurs saw an opening to make money in the electricity business. Small transmission companies sprouted up with virtually no regulation and laid hundreds of miles of poorly insulated lines in massive overhead tangles in the street. Newspapers regularly reported the electrocutions of people who had come into contact with the wires. ANOTHER LINEMAN ROASTED TO DEATH, read one headline, and AGAIN A CORPSE IN THE WIRE, another read. The papers decried "the arch destroyer hovering about their heads" as it burned down homes and businesses, crippled adults, and orphaned children.[5]

Harold Brown cursed Westinghouse's "damnable" current. It put everyone "in constant danger from sudden death," a point he intended to make graphically when he wrapped bare copper leads in cotton rags soaked with water around the front and hind legs of what was in Brown's words a "large mongrel Newfoundland, with a vicious eye and ready tooth."[6]

Brown then proceeded to give the dog a series of shocks of Edison's direct current, starting at 300 volts and ending with a thousand. The point of the "experiment," as Brown called it, was to show that the dog could withstand levels of current far exceeding the 300 volts that were necessary to pressure Edison's system, but they wouldn't survive Westinghouse's system, which would cause them agonizing deaths.[7]

After the first jolt, Brown's dog cried out so pitifully

that many in the audience left the room in disgust, "unable to endure the revolting exhibition."[8] Crazed by the successive shocks, the dog frantically tried to escape his cage and managed to get his head through the wire mesh, when Brown shocked him again. At 700 volts the dog tore off his muzzle and tried desperately to escape. Brown's assistants retied the dog, and then Brown administered a shock of 1,000 volts that so violently contorted the dog's body with pain that outraged members of the audience demanded the wretched dog be put out of its misery.

Brown, who'd already experimented on dozens of dogs, was hardened to their suffering. His notebooks dispassionately record their deaths with terse statements such as "dog howled for about 1 minute & struggled violently," and "dog yelped and groaned. Died in 90 seconds."[9] Brown had planned to electrocute a second dog that day in order to demonstrate it would only take 300 volts of Westinghouse's current to kill it, when Agent Haukinson of the Society for the Prevention of Cruelty to Animals put an end to it. "If it was necessary to torture animals in the interest of science," Haukinson declared, "it should be done by the colleges or institutes and not by rival inventors."[10]

Brown tried to calm his distressed audience by claiming, rather archly, that he'd have no trouble killing the dog with Westinghouse's current. "As the gentlemen say," he told them, "we shall make him feel better." He then switched to alternating current and gave the dog a charge of 330 volts at unknown amperage that killed him instantly.[11] One disgusted witness said the experiment made a Spanish bullfight seem moral by comparison. Nonetheless, Brown made his point when he declared that the only places alternating current ought to be allowed should be the dog pound, the slaughterhouse, and the state prison.[12]

Brown's reference to capital punishment was calculated. The New York State legislature had established a commission two years earlier to investigate a humane alternative to hanging. (Several hangings had gone off poorly in recent history; either the noose was too loose and the prisoner strangled slowly, or it was too tight and ripped off his head.) Since being appointed, the commission polled two hundred people, mostly judges, lawyers, sheriffs, and doctors, and asked what form of death they found more humane: the noose, poison, the garrote, the guillotine, or electrocution. Eighty-one of the two hundred thought hanging was still the best form of execution, but 119 disagreed, and although they couldn't agree entirely on a method of choice, a two-thirds majority favored electrocution.[13] Five voted for the guillotine and four for the garrote.[14]

Edison, who was a more shrewd and calculating adversary than Westinghouse, seized upon the opportunity to be an advisor to the commission and campaigned to make alternating current "the executioner's current" in order to emphasize its lethality.[15] Edison knew the costs of his system were too high and that cost would likely decide the winner. Still, he intended to sabotage Westinghouse as best he could by connecting Westinghouse and death.

As people batted names for this new form of execution, Edison saw an easy way to link Westinghouse's name with the electric chair, much in the same way that Dr. Joseph-Ignace Guillotin's name became associated with the guillotine.[16] Edison came up with "ampermort," "dynamort," and "electromort" as candidates for a name; however, when one of Edison's associates asked a New York attorney who was well versed in Latin to suggest a name, he suggested *electricide*.[17] He also felt it appropriate to name this method of execution after the man who'd invented it: George Westinghouse.

Westinghouse became both a verb (*to westinghouse*) and a noun (the death chamber, as in "the judge ordered the murderer to the Westinghouse"). *Electrocution* won the day in the end, however, even though the *New York Times* pooh-poohed the word, "which pretentious ignoramuses seem to be trying to push into use."[18]

Brown's critics attacked his methods. While it was true alternating current had killed the dog, hadn't it already been weakened by the series of successive shocks of direct current? (Brown's methods were so imprecise, his extensive notes yielded little useful information from his experiments.) Then there was the matter of scale: one couldn't draw the conclusion that what worked on a seventy-six-pound dog would have the same effect on a two-hundred-pound man.

Brown electrocuted consecutively larger dogs with the goal in mind of proving that AC would be just as effective killing human beings as it was killing animals.

Three days after the disaster at Columbia College, Brown resumed his experiments until he finally executed two calves and a horse in December 1888. "If this sort of thing goes on, with the accidental killing of men and the experimental killing of dogs," wrote the *Electrician,* "the public will soon become familiar with the idea that electricity is death as with the old superstition that it is life."[19]

A month later the New York legislature enacted a law that permitted the execution of condemned prisoners by electrical current. On August 6, 1890, August Kemmler became the first man in America to die in the electric chair.

In spite of Brown's attempts to discredit Westinghouse, Edison's technology nonetheless proved itself unwieldy, inefficient, and expensive. The battle between giants ended on April 16, 1895, when Nikola Tesla and George Westinghouse threw the switch to start the world's first hydroelectric power plant, at Niagara Falls, New York. But eight years later, when the owners of a delinquent elephant asked Edison if he could electrocute a ten-thousand-pound beast, he couldn't resist taking a parting shot at Westinghouse.

Topsy, named after a "pickaninny" in *Uncle Tom's Cabin*, first shows up in a quarter-page advertisement for the

Cooper, Bailey & Company's Great International 10 Allied Shows in May 1876.[20] She's mentioned in passing in small type at the end of the ad, as "the living Elephant, Topsy, only 38-inches high." Based upon her height and weight (250 pounds), she would have been less than a year old.[21] Too young to train, her only job was to stand at the top of the thirty-foot-tall *Moving Temple of Juno* like a cherry on top of a gilt sundae.[22]

She traveled as Forepaugh's "original Baby Elephant" until she outgrew the role. After that, she blurred into the crowd of performing elephants. For twenty-six years she traveled in endless spaghetti loops that covered every state and territory in the Union. She performed as a trick elephant, walking a "high wire" and performing with other animals such as a clown bear and seals that smoked tobacco. Topsy might have disappeared into total anonymity—as many elephants did—if she hadn't stepped out of character in 1897 and tried to kill her handler.

The circus glorified animal violence. For an audience the vicious beast that resisted human authority was far more exciting than an animal that performed selflessly in a chorus line. The elephants that rose to the level of stars were usually the ones that behaved badly. Once a "good" natured animal turned "bad," it gained a reputation, and an elephant with a reputation made good box office, particularly if he had a reputation as a man-killer. The press kept tabs on the number of victims an elephant had, although these numbers were often exaggerated because circus barkers liked to jack up the dramatic potential for violence. The charisma of man-killer became part of the organic histories of rogue elephant stars such as Raja, Hannibal, Mandarin, and Black Diamond. An elephant that came into town with a reputation for having killed humans was, for those who stared at him, a vengeful force of nature.

These reputations were reserved largely for the bulls. If a female killed, it was because she was clumsy or stupid or over-emotional. Generally females were gentle, obedient, and nondescript. If they played in a starring role, it was to complement Romeo or Caesar. For the most part, they endured their suffering at the hands of their trainers. But not always.

In 1897 Topsy picked up her keeper, John Howard, and flung him against the ground so hard that his arm had to be amputated.[23] The keepers and handlers knew, although they wouldn't have admitted it outside their own circle, that Howard had done something to set her off. Females didn't snap like males but they did hold grudges.

Topsy grew intolerant of her abuse. In October 1901 in Paris, Texas, she threw down another keeper and stepped on his head. The newspaper reported that Topsy's trainer had just whipped her for some infraction and "not being able to get at the trainer," she took revenge on her keeper instead.[24]

The following May, Topsy picked up her keeper in Brooklyn, New York, and "with awful force slammed him to the earth several times, breaking every bone in his body and beating his brains out."[25] New York papers speculated for days what might have triggered Topsy's attack on Mr. Joseph Fielding Blount of Fort Wayne, Indiana. In one unlikely version of the story, Topsy kills Blount because he rebuffed her morning greeting, which was a ritual between them. In another, equally unlikely version, she kills him because he reneges on an offer for whiskey. The most realistic version is that Topsy killed Blount after he deliberately burned her with his cigar.[26] In the end, however, it didn't matter whether Blount was responsible for his own death: Topsy had killed a man.

A few days after killing Blount, she attacked another man who was trying to scratch her ear with a stick. Lewis Sells, the co-owner of Forepaugh & Sells Brothers circus, got rid of Topsy within the week. "[She] has not been a bad elephant except when teased by people," he said. "I have decided to sell her because she has now gained a bad reputation."[27]

Enter Elmer "Skip" Dundy and Frederic Thompson, who were building a twenty-two-acre amusement park on Coney Island to rival Steeplechase Park. On the look-out for good draft animals, they felt they could use Topsy to do the "work of horses, capstans and cable," by hauling construction supplies and lifting beams into place.

Coney Island was the heart of Victorian counter-culture in New York. Its outlandish appeal drew huge crowds of people looking for relief not just from the cramped, hot confines of New York City but also from the restrictive mores that pressed upon them equally hard. Coney Island provided access to the ocean and the beach;

it also provided access to craps and card games, drugs, and prostitutes in every price range. Coney Island was Sodom-by-the-Sea.

Steeplechase Park, which opened in 1897, was an electric array of sights, sounds, and smells that captivated the senses; beer gardens and brass bands, baseball, ice-cream hokie pokies, carousels, and coneys with mustard and sauerkraut. You could go for a ride on a roller coaster in the shape of a wooden horse, shoot the water chutes, and visit the "original Turkish Harem."

Dundy and Thompson planned to make Luna Park equally intoxicating.

Spun in 1.3 million electric lights, at night the park turned into a white city that blended the minarets of Ali Baba with the palaces of Louis XVI.[28]

An obelisk called the Electric Tower stood at the edge of a lagoon in the center of the park. Each side of the tower was adorned with eighteen concrete rosettes and an elephant spraying water from a raised trunk. The obelisk looked like a vanilla ice-cream cone turned upside down. Topsy worked diligently all summer and into the fall, and as Luna Park gradually realized its shape late in 1902, she gave no sign she was unhappy about her arrangement. "Such is the effect of honest hard work upon a perverted nature," the *New York Journal* noted in an editorial proclaiming the moral value of hard work.[29]

Topsy's keeper at Luna Park was Frederick "Whitey" Ault, or, as he was sometimes called, "Cocktails," because of his excessive fondness for alcohol. On a blustery Decem-

ber afternoon, with snow flying through the air, a drunken
Ault climbed on top of Topsy and lumbered out of Luna
Park on a spree down Surf Avenue. Waving a pitchfork, he
whooped it up in the street like a drunken cowboy while
police on horseback tried to keep up with him.

Topsy ran for half a mile and then stopped. Ault
goaded her on, but she refused to budge. Frustrated,
Whitey jumped off and goaded Topsy with his pitchfork,
and still she wouldn't move. When a cop named Conlon
finally caught up with them, he tried to arrest Ault.

"Get out," Ault threatened Conlon with his pitchfork.
"If you don't go away, I'll sic the elephant on you."

Conlon pulled his revolver. "Say a word to that brute,"
he replied, "I'll blow your brains out."

Ault surrendered.

Conlon took Ault and Topsy to the police station at
gunpoint. When they arrived, Conlon told Ault to tie up
Topsy. "Tie him yourself," he sneered.

Conlon left the elephant in the street and took Whitey
into the station house to be booked. Topsy followed.

Conlon told Whitey to stop her, but still he refused.
She walked up to the door and, not being able to fit
through, reached into station house and began to trumpet,
frightening everyone in the building. She splintered the
door frame as she strained to get past it, and the front wall
of the station house shuddered. Alarmed for the safety of
the building, the commanding captain told Whitey he
wouldn't press charges if he'd just take his elephant and
go away.

Ault agreed. But instead of leaving, he had Topsy perform for the crowd that had gathered at the station house. Police pleaded with Ault for thirty minutes before he stopped. And even then he led his own parade back to Luna Park, followed by a squad of anxious police officers and dozens of men, women, and children who delighted in the escapade.

The police arrested Whitey as soon as he got Topsy inside Luna Park. In all the hullabaloo, no one noticed Topsy was loose until she showed up at the construction site where she'd been working the last several months and started throwing axes and hammers at the workers.

Her aim was deadly and men scattered for cover. When Topsy picked up a heavy timber and threw it at the carpenters, they went on strike and refused to go back to work until Topsy was gone.

Fred Thompson went back to the police station and pleaded with the police to let Whitey go. The police made him post a five-hundred-dollar bail bond.[30] "It has cost Dundy & Thompson as much for 'Cocktails' fines as for Topsy's keep," observed the *Boston Globe*.

The next day Thompson fired Whitey Ault.

Without anyone to control her, Topsy's fate was sealed. Thompson tried to give her away, first to Princeton University, which said no, thank you, and then to the city of New York, which said the same. No one wanted a man-killer.

In January 1903, as the cold, damp winds buffeted Coney Island, Thompson and Dundy announced that on the fourth they would hang Topsy from the park's Electric Tower and Fountain, a building that looked like a cross between a white frosted French pastry and a brass Russian samovar. Topsy would pay for her crimes against humanity, hoisted by her neck to the top of Electric Tower, where she'd hang above the park lagoon.

The ASPCA denounced the execution, although it didn't argue the right to kill Topsy, just the method. Modern men used modern methods, like electrocution. So Thompson and Dundy turned to Edison and offered Topsy "as a target for a million volts and a thousand amperes."

In March 1896, W. H. Harris of the Harris Nickel Plate Shows had proposed electrocuting an elephant after Gypsy stomped Frank Scott to death after jabbing her in the ribs with a bullhook. Scott was Gyp's third victim.

A Cook County deputy coroner held an inquest on the death of Frank Scott on the following day and returned the verdict that Gypsy was alone culpable for his death.[31] Harris then pledged to electrocute her, tapping into Chicago's electric trolley lines if necessary.

As the star of his show, Harris was in no hurry to execute Gyp. Eight months later Harris announced he'd sent a telegram to General Máximo Gómez, the rebel military commander in Cuba, offering to send Gyp to Cuba "to trample down the ranks of the Spaniards." She'd also be useful for maneuvering artillery pieces. "If Hannibal found elephants useful in battle," Harris wrote in his cable, "why should not Gómez conquer with Gypsy."[32]

Gypsy was neither electrocuted nor sent to Cuba. She continued to perform with Harris Nickel Plate until 1902, when she killed another trainer while in Georgia.

Harris shot her in a swamp, where she was left to rot. Several in the crowd who watched her execution cut off parts of her body to keep as souvenirs.[33]

The year before Gypsy was executed, Frank C. Bostock, an Englishman known as "the Animal King," staged the execution of Jumbo II at the 1901 Pan-American Exposition in Buffalo, not sixty days after Leon Czolgosz gunned down President McKinley in a receiving line at the fair's Temple of Music.

Five days after Czolgosz's execution at Auburn, New York, Jumbo picked up Henry Mullen, an assistant keeper who was mucking out his stall, and "lifted [him] high over his head and brought him down with terrific force against the floor."[34] Bostock was so fed up with Jumbo's perennial bad behavior he decided to kill him, so he booked the Exhibition Stadium at the Pan-American Exposition and sold tickets to an execution.

Thompson and Dundy ran the most popular ride at the Pan-American Exposition that year, a cyclorama show called "A Trip to the Moon," in which voyagers sat in a green and white rocket with flapping wings called Luna and flew to the moon and back. They and a thousand others paid fifty cents apiece to watch an elephant "hanged, or choked to death with chains." But the mayor of Buffalo pleaded with Bostock not to hang Jumbo. At least not publicly. Buffalo already had a black eye with McKinley's death and didn't need another with a spectacle that belonged in the Roman Coliseum, not the Pan-American Exposition.

Wilson S. Bissell also made a pitch not to kill Jumbo. Arguing on behalf of the ASPCA, the former postmaster general of the United States threatened to charge Bostock with excessive cruelty if he went ahead with the hanging. He pointed out that the state of New York had condemned the practice as barbaric and replaced it with electrocution, which was quick and safe. Some had just seen how easily Czolgosz passed into the next world in Edison's film *Execution of Czolgosz with Panorama of Auburn Prison*, a docudrama that passed as documentary footage of Czolgosz's death.[35] (Edison's version shows Czolgosz stiffening and then slumping after three shocks in twelve seconds, when, in fact, he received two intense jolts of one minute each.[36]) The ease with which the Edison actor dies in the film reinforced the popular idea that electrocution was fast and painless.[37]

Bostock conceded. He refunded the admission fees to a crowd that denounced him as a fake and then went ahead with plans to electrocute rather than hang Jumbo. Five days after Leon Czolgosz became the fiftieth man to die in the electric chair, an electrician attached bare copper wires wrapped in wet rags behind Jumbo's ears and flanks and submitted the elephant to 4,000 volts of alternating current from Westinghouse's hydroelectric plant at Niagara Falls.[38]

TOO STRONG FOR ELECTRICITY, ran a headline in the *Philadelphia Inquirer* the next day. COULDN'T KILL THE ELEPHANT, read the *Kansas City Star*, which claimed that the electricity "merely tickled the beast."[39] Certain that the current was on and the circuit was closed, observers concluded that Jumbo's hide had the insulating properties of rubber, and that he was impervious to electricity. So when Edison was presented with the task of electrocuting Topsy at Luna Park fourteen months later, no one really knew what would happen when he switched on the current.[40]

Edison assigned two of his best men to the job. The first was D. P. Sharkey, an electrician who built a pair of elephant sandals made out of wood and copper. The sandals—each "about the size of a small tabletop"—were attached to electrodes that would deliver 6,600 volts through the bottoms of Topsy's feet.

The plan called first for feeding Topsy a pound of cyanide in a loaf of bread in order to incapacitate her, and then hang her. If for some reason that plan didn't work, then a man with an elephant gun would stand by ready to "shoot express bullets into her just abaft the nigh foreleg, so as to cleave her heart."[41] Dundy and Thompson were practical men. If people came to Coney Island in the middle of winter to see an elephant die, then that elephant had better die. With the park opening in a few months, they couldn't afford a big snafu.

The other man was Edwin S. Porter, the head of Edison's motion picture studios, who was in the middle of filming America's first western, *The Great Train Robbery*, which starred America's first movie cowboy star, Broncho Billy Anderson. On January 4, Porter took his moving picture camera and tripod and went to Luna Park to film the elephant sequel to *The Electrocution of Czolgosz*.

By 1:30, fifteen hundred people packed the perimeter of the lagoon next to Electric Tower. The gallows was still rigged with nine hundred feet of inch-and-a-half hawser threaded through four sheaved blocks that ran to the donkey engine in Electric Tower. Halfway across the bridge, Topsy stopped and refused to go farther, the same way she had balked the night she and Whitey Ault went on their wild ride down Surf Avenue.

She wouldn't budge. Desperate, Thompson sent word to Ault that he could have his job back plus a bonus of twenty-five dollars if he could get Topsy to move, but Whitey said he wouldn't do it for twice the money. As the crowd grew restless, Thompson told Sharkey to electrocute Topsy where he stood.

While Sharkey and his men reran the electric lines and set up the sandals, a veterinarian fed Topsy carrots laced with cyanide. While she ate the carrots, Sharkey strapped her right front leg and her left rear leg into the copper sandals. She crushed them as soon as she put her weight on them, but the electrodes maintained contact. At 2:45, long before the cyanide had a chance to take effect, Sharkey closed the electrical circuit and Porter started cranking his camera.[42]

The *New York Times* called it an "inglorious affair" that lacked dazzle.[43] In Porter's film, Topsy lurches only slightly when the electricity hits her. She curls up her trunk toward her mouth as a huge billows of steam rise from her feet and envelop her. She quivers for five seconds and then falls, snapping the rope hawser that was supposed to have hanged her. Behind her, a sign reads THE HEART OF CONEY ISLAND.

Two minutes later the veterinarian pronounced Topsy dead. Her remains were legally conveyed to Herbert H. Vogelsang of New York City, who spent the rest of the afternoon dismembering her. Vogelsang had bought Topsy's remains based upon the residual value of her hide, her skeleton, the oil derived from her fat, and her skull. He cut off her feet to make into umbrella stands.[44]

Edison Electrocutes an Elephant, 1903.

In the long run, the intrigue between Westinghouse and Edison didn't matter. Westinghouse prevailed, and, ironically, won the Edison Medal in 1911 for "his meritorious achievements." Both men went on to make their millions. Luna Park burned down in 1944. But two technologies converged on Topsy on January 4, 1903: the electric dynamo and the motion picture camera. One destroyed her and the other preserved her.

Topsy's ghost returned a year later. Described as "an astral body of huge dimensions," she trod the windswept streets

of Luna Park at midnight clanking her chains and bellowing. One worker fainted when Topsy spewed a shower of
sparks from her trunk. The hot dog man fell to his knees
in fright. And another laborer, after drinking two bottles
of Chianti, saw Topsy doing a trapeze act on the tight
wire between the top of the water chutes and the Electric
Tower.[45]

The following summer, one of the handlers noticed
that the elephants behaved strangely when they came to
a certain place in the park. When the trainer told Fred
Thompson about the elephants' behavior, he sent for men
with shovels to dig at the spot. Six feet below the surface
they found Topsy's skull.[46] As they pulled it out of the
earth, the elephants who had been watching the excava-
tion "trumpeted mournfully . . . and walked silently to
their quarters."[47]

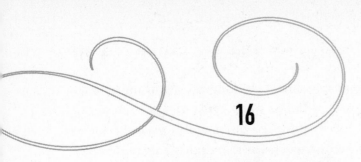

16

Circus Day, Butte, Montana, August 23, 1900

♦

from the *Duluth News-Tribune*, July 23, 1899

ELEPHANT BRASS BAND

RINGLING BROS.' REMARKABLE TROUPE
OF PACHYDERMS

An elephant brass band—a musical organization composed entirely of proboscidians—this is the latest trained animal sensation introduced by the famous Ringling Brothers, sole proprietors and managers of the Worlds' Greatest Shows. There are five of the big, unwieldy elephantine windjabbers, and the way they blow great, blue blasts out of their long helicon horns is a caution to the musical fraternity.

Their repertoire is not an extensive one, but they have so far mastered the intricacies of musical notation as to render "Coming Through the Rye" with such a thunderous volume of sound as to rattle neighboring windows and cause the lions and tigers to roar a protest in deep feline bass.

But the real point the act illustrates and which in itself excites wonder, is the fact that elephants can play music, and, incidentally, that their lung power is several hundred times greater than that of the largest circus band, even when playing double fortissimo passages.

On August 5, 1900, "Plain" Patrick Murphy, age twenty-eight, died instantly when a blasting charge blew up at the nine-hundred-foot level underground in the Diamond Mine in Butte, Montana.[1] The news shocked no one except Plain Patrick's friends and family, who grieved for him in the Irish tradition. Accidents happened all the time in the mines. Men were blown up, fell down shafts, were jerked from hoist cages, or crushed beneath slabs of unstable rock called Duggans, named after a funeral parlor in town. Plain Patrick was one of thousands of men who worked rotating shifts around the clock in mines with names like the Clear Grit, the Orphan Girl, and the Neversweat. Many who were young and unmarried lived in rough boardinghouses "unrestrained by the elevating influences" of civilization, while others like Plain Patrick had families and lived in shantytowns with names like

Walkerville, Corkville, and Dublin Gulch. Ten hours a day, six days a week, Plain Patrick and thirteen thousand of his brothers mined the richest hill on earth.

Butte arrived out of the hill full-blown after the first big metal strike in 1875. The first union strike came three years later, during which time Morgan Earp, brother of Wyatt Earp, was deputy marshal. By 1884 Butte had three hundred mines, nine quartz mills, and four smelters. Five thousand men worked underground. By 1900, the year Plain Patrick died, Butte's population had swelled to 48,000, making it the seventieth-largest city in America.[2] A third of its citizens worked underground.

Even though the unions fought to make conditions safer and cleaner, men came out of the mines after years of inhaling quartz dust with chronic bronchitis, emphysema, silicosis, which the miner's called black lung, and tuberculosis, called miner's con, short for miner's consumption. Those who stayed in the mines lived to an average age of forty-seven. There were a hundred reasons why they didn't live longer: they drank and stumbled onto the tracks and got hit by trains; they brawled with knives and guns in saloons, brothels, and gambling parlors; and they were infected with gonorrhea, typhoid, and smallpox.[3] At work, they dug ever deeper into the ground, where they died in fires, explosions, wall and ceiling collapses, and clouds of poison gas.

Their children died, too. Sixteen percent of Butte's children died before their first birthday from scarlet fever, rheumatic fever, measles, meningitis, pneumonia, and typhoid. Typhoid was pernicious. Bacteria transmitted through contaminated food, drink, or water traveled to the intestines, causing piercing abdominal pain and explosive diarrhea. The bacteria then entered the bloodstream and attacked the lymph nodes, the spleen, and the liver. It took months to get over the fever, if you were lucky. Of Plain Patrick's five children, two were dead from typhoid. He buried his boys in the same grave in a section of the Holy Cross graveyard that became known as Babyland because it contained so many children.

Some resorted to drugs and alcohol as a means to deaden their physical and psychic pain. The coroner's inquests for August 1900 record the investigations into the deaths of men and women who died by their own hand. The men used guns and ropes mainly. Some drank themselves to death, some jumped off buildings or rim-rocks, and some drowned. Women were more inclined to poisoning—laudanum if they could afford it, and if not, carbolic acid.[4] The churches lamented the loss of their souls, and their families buried them. If no one claimed the body, the city buried it in a field with others who'd lost their names.

The majority of working men and women lived along general ethnic and racial lines. The miners and their wives and mothers and fathers came from Wales, Cornwall, London, Edinburgh, and County Cork. They also came from continental Europe, Scandinavia, the Middle East, and the Orient. They brought their languages, their customs, their food, and their music, which they celebrated in their neighborhoods. Butte was made up of a multiethnic citizenry that fondly (and not so fondly) called one another "bohunks, sheep shaggers, wops, krauts, chinks, kikes, and mossheads." It had so many Irish the city declared itself the Fifth Province of Ireland. There were at least a hundred Sullivans in Butte in 1900. But death was a common denominator: a mother's grief was the same no matter what country she came from. Babyland did not have ethnic sections.

Distractions kept their minds off their troubles. Brawling was popular in Butte and it didn't matter if a fight was in a ring, a saloon, or the street. Professional brawlers came to Butte to take on all comers in halls and bars. In August 1900, the *Police Gazette* boxing champion and self-declared "Strongest Man Who Ever Lived," Louis Cyr, offered one thousand dollars to anyone still standing after three rounds. One of the Sullivans took Cyr up on the challenge, but Cyr knocked the wind out of him before he could throw a punch. As soon as he left the ring, another man stepped forward to take his place.

Butte also had horse racing, dog racing, and cockfighting, but baseball was king. The *Butte Smoke Eaters* was one of four teams in the Montana Baseball League in 1900. The *Senators* played out of Helena, the state capital, and the *Indians* played out of Great Falls. The *Smoke Eaters'* fiercest rivals were the *Serpents*, from Anaconda, a few miles to the west.[5] Their games pitted miners of Butte against the chalciners of Anaconda. During the season the *Butte Miner* and the *Anaconda Standard* detailed the state of their teams and adjusted the league standings. Fans obsessed about everything from the quality of pitching and hitting to the uneven quality of umpiring. A thousand people or more showed up for games, especially late in the season when the league title was up for grabs.

In August 1900 the *Smoke Eaters* played the first of a three-game series against the *Serpents* with the Montana league championship at stake. The *Serpents* were in first place by one game going in, but Butte's Bill Hammond was batting a solid .403 and Bob Perham was batting a sizzling .491.

McDonough played first base, Donahue played second, and Dunleavy played third for the *Smoke Eaters*. Schmeer played shortstop. Other teammates included Schnabble, Merkel, O'Connor, and an Italian named Steffani—thirty men of Irish, German, English, and Italian extraction.[6]

On August 11, Claude Schmeer came down with typhoid. Two days later third baseman Bill Dunleavy came down with it. It spread through the ranks of Montana's baseball teams. TYPHOID FEVER IS RAISING HAVOC AMONG THE PLAYERS OF THE MONTANA BASEBALL LEAGUE, ran a local headline. Within a week the league lost so many of its players that it had to draft new rules that let a man walk on three balls instead of four or counted any foul ball a strike in order to keep the game moving. The new rules never came into play even as the teams kept playing and more of their teammates got sick.[7] Dreams for a championship season died. Then, early on a Thursday morning in the middle of summer, the Ringling Brothers' *World's Greatest Show* rolled into town.

In the 1870s, before he changed the title of his circus to the *Greatest Show on Earth*, Barnum called it the *Great Moral and Instructive Exhibition*. Most circuses tried to conform at least superficially to the Victorian ideal that moral entertainment should instruct the viewer in the traditional values of God and country. As a result, circuses presented an odd mélange of religious and political parables without regard for spatial or temporal continuity that swept through Greece, Rome, Egypt, the temples of the Orient, and the castles of Europe, mixing founding fathers with pharaohs and Caesars at whim. Whatever idiosyncratic course through history these shows took, however, they ended up celebrating the overthrow of the tyranny of nations and nature.

In 1898 the United States engaged in rampant acts of adventurism under the guise of throwing off the chains of Spanish oppression in Cuba, Puerto Rico, and the Philippines. Story-papers and dime novels made heroes of the cavalry on San Juan Hill and the U.S. Navy in Manila Bay. For a little while, Leonard Wood, Theodore Roosevelt, and America's admiral, George Dewey, replaced George Armstrong Custer and Buffalo Bill Cody as American icons.

The bigger circuses garnished this patriotic smorgasbord with figures such as Uncle Sam, the man of the people, who walked around the hippodrome in his red and white striped trousers and a blue waistcoat pulled tightly over a white shirt with a red bow tie. As the band played stalwart marches, he'd tip his great blue top hat emblazoned with white tumbling stars and with a sweeping gesture welcome a shapely young woman who played variously the role of Columbia, Liberty, or Virgin West. Dressed in diaphanous, flowing robes, she stood atop a pedestal and looked west as armed colonials stood shoulder to shoulder with their brothers dressed in blue and gray and the Rough Riders in their blue and white polka-dot bandannas. The public loved this kaleidoscopic tumble of history. So did the newspapers, one of which went so far to say, "Barnum tells the truth. All the world says so."[8]

In 1900 the Ringlings' show was called the *Patriotic Spectacle of the Last Days of the Century (or, The Light of Liberty!)*, which consisted of a series of vignettes that celebrated Old Glory. While the band played "The Star Spangled Banner," a squad of American rebels took position against the British redcoats, while another band played "God Save the Queen," followed by French soldiers playing "La Marseillaise," Irish soldiers playing "The Wearing of the Green," and Japanese soldiers playing what was "purported to be the Japanese national air, whatever it may be called." (What role the Japanese played in the American Revolution remains unclear.)[9]

The Liberty Bell rang, Paul Revere rode, and the Minutemen acted out morality plays about progress and the white race.

In the scheme of things, God had placed man a little lower than angels so he might have dominion *over every creeping thing that creepeth upon the earth*. He placed the white man over other less "fortunate" races of men such as the Cubans, the Puerto Ricans, and the Filipinos, who were, in poet Rudyard Kipling's words, "new-caught, sullen peoples, half devil and half child."[10] The "White Man's Burden," he wrote, was to herd the savage and the barbarian into the thrall of empire. Theodore Roosevelt was even bolder. "The world would have halted," he wrote in 1897, "had it not been for the Teutonic conquests in alien lands."[11]

Roosevelt and other sober-minded men like the senator from Massachusetts, Henry Cabot Lodge, and the father of yellow journalism, William Randolph Hearst, argued that Yankee grit and ingenuity had prevailed over nature as Western settlements turned into towns and towns into cities. The Indians were put down, the wolves, bears, and lions were mostly gone, and the railroads brought uninterrupted supplies of timber to the mills and coal and ore to the smelters. Nature was in chains.

Victory was proof of God's intention for Man to subdue the earth, a point Roosevelt liked to make clear when he went hunting. Twice a day the circus celebrated the conquest of the world's largest, meanest, and strongest beasts such as rhinoceros, hippopotamus, hyena, cats with fangs the size of a man's fist, orangutan, and, of course, Job's Behemoth, *the chief of the ways of God*.

P. T. Barnum observed during his stint as a store clerk in rural Connecticut that people might be rubes but they weren't stupid. They knew burlesque when they saw it. The circus performers who played David and Goliath, Jehu and Jezebel, and Samson and Delilah for the crowds were dwarfs, giants, strong men, and hootchy-kootchy girls. The audience hissed at Delilah while the strong man who played Samson winked at the ladies in the audience and flexed his chest. Sometimes the ladies winked back. Not ten minutes after David slew Goliath, he turned into Jack in *Jack and the Beanstalk* and Goliath turned into an ogre who ate Englishmen. *Fee-Fi-Fo-Fum.*

If the elephant straddled God and Beast, then he also straddled Man. The people who came to see the Behemoth also came to see him dance the polka and drink beer. They cheered when he stood up on his hind legs and waved the American flag, and they listened raptly to stories of love spurned and love earned as elephants fell in love, defended their honor, got married, had children, and cheated on their wives.

The Ringling Brothers came to Butte for the first time in 1897, in early June, when the weather was more inclined toward winter than spring. The snow on Homestake Pass, atop the Continental Divide, was knee deep and the edges of the lakes had only begun to thaw. "Cloudy, rainy and dismal," the official biographer for the circus wrote in the route book, a company diary of the daily events in the circus. Then he added: "Business great."

The circus biographer wasn't Samuel Pepys recounting the fine details of the life of Dr. Samuel Johnson; rather, he roughed out the cogent points of the day in a few sentences. In 1897 he joked that Butte was "a beautiful city—called the Venice of the West because there isn't a drop of water within miles of it." He talked about the colorful, lush tropical plants that grew in the city and then admitted he was making it up.

But he didn't make up the scenes of life in a booming western mining town. "Everyone has money and spends it freely," he wrote. "And everyone carries a gun." The people of Butte were a feisty sort, he wrote, as "every native asks 'Why the h— didn't you t'row 'em fer a dollar?' "[12]

Butte was raw and raucous. The month of the circus a sheriff from Wood County, Wisconsin, served a warrant to arrest Jacob Schwartzrock for running away from Wisconsin with Mr. Sitz's wife; someone robbed a train in "true Western style"; and Annie Jones, alias May Jewel, robbed P. Mahoney of $195. During a campaign to kick out the city's "hoboes and footpads," Miles O'Reilly, described by the law as "a secretary of the badlands," found himself standing before the judge answering the charge he was "living upon the earnings of lewd women."

Twenty thousand people went to the circus on opening day.[13] EVERY PROMISE KEPT, boasted one local headline. "No circus ever traveled that did not advertise elephants standing on their heads or daring aerialists standing erect in a flying trapeze with nothing to stay them from falling but their own agility in balancing," wrote the paper, "but there are few circuses where either is ever actually seen." Ringling was the first to deliver on the handbills, the newspaper ads, and the posters that were plastered to every barn and storefront in Silver Bow County.[14]

The Ringlings gave a show worth remembering. "Whether it be the boxing elephants, the elephants that wine and dine themselves, the wonderfully skilled horses, the daring leaping, the skill on trapeze and bars, the fascinating performers from foreign lands, or the immense menagerie," read the paper, "there is in the circus— Ringlings'—a perennial source of delight, of genuine enjoyment."[15] The police were surprised, too. In spite of its reputation for being a breeding ground for crime, the police didn't make a single arrest.

The Ringlings came back in June 1899. "The air is sulphuric today," the biographer groused. But the show was bigger and better than it ever had been. Forty-five railroad cars filled with more performers, bigger tents, and fifteen elephants. "The ponderous beasts did everything but talk," wrote the *Anaconda Standard*. "They stood on their heads, sat up, formed pyramids, tooted horns and beat drums in imitation of a band, sat up to a table and ate and one big fellow left the ring walking on his hind legs.

One could scarcely conceive of an elephant possessing so much intelligence as they displayed."[16]

The Ringlings came back in August 1900, eighteen days after Patrick Murphy died in the Diamond Mine. "Most disagreeable and cold," the biographer griped. The thermometer registered zero at dawn, but the people of Butte didn't care what temperature it was. "[The weather] had no apparent effect on the crowds that usually wait for the coming of the elephant," wrote the biographer.

City stores celebrated with sales and specials. Symons ("Economists for the People") offered a pair of boy's cheviot knee pants for nineteen cents; Hennessy's offered a lady's corset made of French *coutille* for four dollars; and a brothel called the Dumas (pronounced *Do-miss*) gave a freebie to the elephant with the longest trunk.

Schools as far away as sixty-eight miles shut down; the streetcars ran every minute to the show grounds; and the police readied themselves for the onslaught of rowdies and flimflammers that worked the crowd.[17] August 23 was shaping up as a perfect circus day.

In 1900 the Ringlings' circus had expanded to include a thousand people, five hundred horses, twenty-five elephants, and a hundred magnificently carved floats, tableaux wagons, and painted dens and cages.[18] The *Grand Patriotic Spectacle* was so large it contained seventeen coordinated multi-platform presentations called "displays," each consisting of a variety of acts that took place simultaneously either within one of the three rings or on a raised stage.

In one display the circus band played military marches and operatic overtures while Miss Nettie Carroll performed *Deft and Dexterous Exercises on a Frail and Swinging Wire Thread* and Signor Brodaldi walked the high wire in Ring One. In Ring Two, the Yamamoto Brothers from Tokyo sat upon their *Vibrating Bamboo Perch*, and in Ring Three Miss Jessie Leon and Miss Belle Carmen balanced on a high wire. Meanwhile, the Great Setro gave a *Marvelous Display of Strength and Ambidextrous Balancing Feats* while a tumbler called the *European Hand Leaper* vaulted over elephants.

Then there was the hippodrome, the quarter-mile track crowded with animals, jockeys, chariots, and clowns. Men rode the backs of camels and ostriches, and monkeys rode the backs of ponies. No person who went to the circus that day could take it all in.

Al Ringling, the eldest of seven brothers, provided the narration for the *Majestic, Imposing, Ideal, Patriotic Spectacle* that concluded with Uncle Sam freeing a pretty Cuban girl from Spanish chains while the band roused patriots with Sousa's "Stars and Stripes Forever." As the ringmaster, he was the clock by which the circus ran. With a wave of his hand George Washington turned into a singing pig. And when it came to John O'Brien, Ringling made everything under the tent stop so everyone could watch his *Grand Carousel.*

"In one ring, at one time, performed by one man," Ringling announced as O'Brien streamed sixty-one black stallions into the ring so they formed a circle, head to tail, around him. He then urged them into a lope, their hooves churning dirt, manes and tails flying, nostrils flaring, picking up speed with each lap until suddenly all sixty-one stallions reversed direction without a hint of hesitation or loss of coordination.[19] Men jumped out of their seats and whooped while the rest of the crowd cheered and whistled.

O'Brien then split the horses like Moses dividing the sea, one group running clockwise and the other counterclockwise until they threaded together into a fine tapestry woven with thirty-five tons of raw animal fabric. No one had ever seen horses—or any animal—mastered so finely.

Unlike horses, however, elephants bolted at the drop of a hat. It didn't matter if they were staked out in the lot, in rehearsal, or in front of a full house when a blowing piece of paper or a screech from the calliope or something in the wind set them off. Unlike horses that ran around things, elephants ran through them. They trampled wagons, tents, animals, and people in their way. Not even Ringling could stop them.

Al Ringing told the six circus bands to keep playing when things went crazy because music reassured the audience everything was under control even when it obviously wasn't. In 1883, an elephant stampeded during the grand entry during a Barnum show in Chicago. An elephant who was pulling a Roman chariot spooked and started smashing other chariots in her way, which set off a chain reaction of elephants bellowing through the procession.

The audience didn't realize the danger until the elephants were nearly upon them. People panicked and ran for the exits, and suddenly there were two stampedes— one elephant, one human. "For a few moments a general panic and a fearful loss of life seemed inevitable," wrote the *New York Times*, "but the continued playing of the band reassured the frightened multitude. . . ."[20] While the trainers got their animals under control, the clowns smoothed the ruffled feathers of the crowd, and the show went on.

For the most part, elephants behaved. In 1900, the Ringling Brothers divided the elephants into three troupes: Edouard "Perl" Souder's "proboscidian musicians" of the Twenty-Ton Brass Band, "[p]resenting beyond a doubt the biggest band in weight, lung-power and laugh-making extant"; Professor Lockhart's "quintette" of elephant comedians "in a medley of unquestioned funny, ludicrous, button-busting terpsichorean, athletic, musical and Bacchanalian revels"; and Jean Marchand's boxing elephants, who wore striped boxing shorts and threw gloved punches with their trunks.

Lockhart's elephantine comedians dressed in kilts and tam-o'-shanters and danced to a Highland hornpipe, and the Twenty-Ton Brass Band battled with the circus clowns for the title of best clown band.

Ringlings' elephant trainer was Samuel Lockhart, an Englishman who had toured Europe with a trio of elephants he called "the Three Graces."[21] The act was so famous Queen Victoria commanded a performance.

In 1869, Ringling made Lockhart an offer to come to America he couldn't refuse.

Lockhart thought of Asian elephants as "Teutons," compared to their "Negro" cousins because they were easier to train than Africans. The Africans were every bit as smart as the Teutons, just wilder.[22]

First Lockhart taught the elephants how to dance, sit, seesaw, and ride a tricycle. During the years the act got increasingly complex as elephants learned how to play Shakespeare or how to bowl and keep score.[23] They acted in restaurant scenes and barbershop scenes and dressed up as clowns, debutantes, and bankers waving delinquent mortgages.[24]

Lockhart produced a scene about two drunken elephants in straw hats who get into a tussle in a bar. A policeman wearing a bobby's hat and blue shorts waves a billy club in his trunk as he hauls the drunks before an elephant judge, who sends them to the clink.

All this comic mayhem disguised the rigorous discipline of the circus, which by 1900 was a business model of efficiency. Commercial success meant keeping everything in place on time, and the Ringling Brothers, Barnum & Bailey, Forepaugh, Stonehouse Barnes, and many others were brilliant at executing complex plans for moving people, animals, and their business from place to place, nonstop from May to November.

The circus had perfected the model so much that in 1899, Elihu Root, President McKinley's secretary of war (and later Teddy Roosevelt's secretary of state), embedded army officers into the circus so they might learn how to pack and unpack large numbers of people, animals, and matériel quickly and efficiently. The officers bunked on the trains, ate in food tents, and from time to time rolled up a sleeve and swung a sledge. They lived life on the ground as they watched the complex choreography unfold and refold virtually every day.

The army, on the other hand, had a lousy track record when it came to running a war. An overabundance of enthusiasm coupled with gratuitous circumstances resulted in a quick victory in Cuba, and Americans were flush with pride as they turned Teddy Roosevelt and his Rough Riders into an instant icon. But one of the major lessons learned from the war was that the United States had lacked experience mounting a war.

After the war Roosevelt campaigned for the Congressional Medal of Honor because he claimed his bravery was all the more exceptional given that he'd succeeded in spite of the army's failure to provide competent leadership. He complained the senior staff had bobbled the war, an incompetence that was, in his estimation, the result of a country that lacked experience conducting international warfare. When Roosevelt didn't get the Medal of Honor, he complained he was denied the honor because the army resented his criticism. It was a brilliant claim for Roosevelt to make because it solidified his image as a reformer, and it carried him to the presidency in three years.

Roosevelt's criticism was valid, however. Command had indeed failed to provide adequate supplies, transportation, food, medicine, and ammunition on time, and some feared the United States would not have endured a protracted war because of this critical deficiency. But in 1899, a win was a win, however awkward.

Root understood the significance of Roosevelt's criticism and turned to the circus to seek both short-term remedies and long-term strategies to improve the logistical capabilities of the U.S. Army. To the casual observer the circus moved with simple mechanical efficiency, but to a trained eye, the circus was a precise orchestration of time, speed, and distance. A finely tuned hierarchy of power made certain everyone understood the relationship between the whole and its parts, which in turn clarified what needed to be done and when. The day before Butte Ringling had played Bozeman; the day after it would jump to Anaconda, then Missoula on Saturday, and on Monday it would be in Spokane, Washington. Secretary Root admired the efficiency of a command structure that could move battalions of men and their mounts *161 times* in 210 days over a course of fifteen thousand miles.[25]

"When you do sleep?" rubes asked the men who unloaded the trains every morning by six and every evening by midnight.

"In winter," they'd reply.

The circus was structured into four interlocking segments, starting with the arrival, which mirrored the last segment, the departure. The two middle segments consisted of a street parade, which began upon arrival, and the tented performances, given once in the afternoon and again in the evening. The circus didn't unpack as much as it unfolded, and as each act finished it refolded according to schedule that had everyone and everything back on the train by midnight.

At dawn, 6:15 a.m. on August 23, 1900, the engineer of the Ringling Brothers train blew his five-chime whistle as he braked down the steep grade over the Continental Divide. He was miles from sight of the crowds that awaited him at the depot, but the rock canyons delivered the message loud and clear to anyone with his ear cocked to the east. He played the whistle like an organ with five pipes, raising and lowering the pitch, sharpening and flattening notes to announce the coming of the *Ringling Brothers United Monster Shows, Great Double Circus, Royal European Menagerie, Museum, Caravan, and Congress of Trained Animals.*

The temperature was near zero at dawn, yet the streets and sidings at the depot were crammed with people craning their necks to see the yellow train. Plain Patrick Murphy and his family likely would have been at the depot if he hadn't died in the Diamond Mine earlier that month. He would have worked ten hours to make enough money to buy tickets for his family, and like thousands of other citizens, his family would have gone to the depot before dawn in order to get a good spot to see the trains arrive.

The circus train was an impressive sight with sixty-five cars. The number of cars in a train was always in multiples of five because railroads charged for the use of their rails by the total number of cars rounded up to the nearest five. A circus train fifty-six cars long got charged for sixty. With space at such a premium, the circus designed its wagons and cages to make use of every square inch of space available to them. It even stored gear beneath the cars in contraptions called "possum bellies." From the moment someone jumped off the train in morning to the moment the last person jumped on at night, the circus followed a well-practiced script that decided the order of people, animals, and property on and off the train. Before the train even came to a complete halt, the doors of the stock cars slid open. Razorbacks put down gangplanks for the keepers to offload the baggage stock—the working teams of horses and elephants—and then put down metal plates called runs between flatcars so the polers and snubbers could guide the wagons off them. As soon as the wagons rolled off, they were hitched to a team of horses that pulled them away. The wagon that carried the tent poles was so large it took ten horses to pull it.

The wagons containing the poles, stakes, and canvas and crew left immediately for the lot where they'd put up a tent big enough to seat thirteen thousand people. By the time the street parade reached them two hours later, the tents would be set up and the candy butchers would be hawking lemonade and cracker jack.

The second section of the train contained the ring stock—lions, tigers, a polar bear, leopards, hyenas, camels, zebra, and a hippopotamus named Pete.

Unlike the horses and elephants of the baggage stock that were stacked into cars flank to flank, the ring stock cars had individual stalls for its stars, except for the elephants, which were wedged in twelve to a car.

The elephant cars were easy to spot because they had windows or at least ventilators to protect them from cold weather or drafts. The first time the Ringlings came to Butte they brought a "Royal White" Asian elephant named Keddah, who had his own padded car. He was so big he had to wriggle off the car "like a dog squirms under a low gate." Keddah died in a train fire a year later.

The last section of the train carried the performers, who hurried off the train in costume. The ones riding animals in the street parade climbed onto their mounts. If they were pulling a wagon or a float, they'd check the harness and the hitch and then pull into the parade queue waiting for the signal to roll.

Bull men sat astride their elephants. A tuba blurted from a bandwagon and clowns stretched their hamstrings. A few animal wagons took the panels off the cages so people could see the wild animals inside and other wagons remained shuttered but were painted with snarling cats or chest-pounding apes with glowering eyes. The performers then took their places on or beside the chariots, floats, and tableau wagons and waited for the signal for the parade to begin, a screech so pitiful it made the hair on everyone's neck stand up.

The last wagon in the parade was a steam calliope, a thirty two-note pipe organ that traveled in a wagon with its own boiler.[26] Originally made of locomotive whistles, the steam organ was mounted on a painted, gilded, and beautifully carved wagon pulled by horses that were immune to its shriek. Without provision for varying tone or loudness, the circus calliope (pronounced in the circus "CAL-ee-ope") created music by the timing and the length of the notes and couldn't vary pitch or intensity. The temperature of the steam in the pipes determined the quality of the note, so calliopes were famously out of tune, especially in the upper registers, until the metal whistles warmed up. The discordant pipes resonated for miles, and so the first notes alerted everyone in the valley that the grand procession had begun.

The street parade was a matter of pride and honor and a source of endless competition between circuses. They promoted reputation and for decades Ringling, Forepaugh, and Barnum jousted for the honor of the *Biggest and Best*. The Butte parade stretched out for two miles. Thousands of people lined the route to the circus lot for a glimpse of Romans in their chariots or the clowns on their donkeys or Pete the hippopotamus. Four camels pulled a float with a Turkish orchestra on it. Six other bands, including a military band, a jazz band, and Spaderowski Johnsonicola's beloved clown band followed, as did the buskers who juggled and tumbled, and a fire-eater who belched flame. Banners painted with images of the three-legged boy, the living skeleton, and the bird-headed dwarf spoke of wonders inside the tent.

Then the elephants came in grand procession. Caparisoned in Oriental silks, they carried howdahs on their backs from which faux-rajahs waved to the crowd with jeweled hands. The brightly colored drivers, called mahouts, sat on the necks of the elephants and swung their bullhooks. The elephants lumbered along, snorting and snuffling, and sometimes, to the delight of the crowd, blaring like a section of trombones.

The ringing of their chains on the road was the overture to the red and gold Bell Wagon, which contained a gallery of nine cast-bronze cathedral bells weighing more than two tons. Pulled by a team of six matched Percherons, the wagon was adorned at the front corners by two bare-breasted goddesses, their wings outstretched. At the center of the wagon, above the bells, a turbaned god blew wind; and at the back corners Athena's owls puffed up their chests and unfolded their wings.

The wheel spokes of the Bell Wagon were painted white and outlined in red on a blue background, and they spun kaleidoscopically when the wagon rolled. Other magnificently carved, gaudily colored wagons followed with tableaux that included Cinderella stepping into her glass slipper before the handsome Prince, and Pocahontas pleading for Captain John Smith's life. Suddenly Greek Muses, fiery dragons, and heroes of the American Empire crowded the streets of Butte while the city echoed with cathedral bells, a calliope, and the beat of big drums. They entered like Alexander's conquering army, a spectacle that overwhelmed Butte.

Twelve hours later, the army decamped and moved on.

The circus comes to Main Street, USA, ca. 1919.

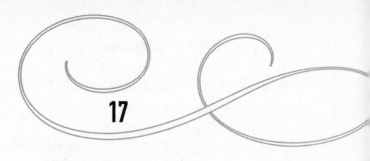

17

Elephant Baseball

◆

Based upon the press release issued by World Elephant Polo
Association (WEPA), December 6, 2009

SCOTLAND TAKES GOLD IN ELEPHANT POLO WORLD OLYMPIC QUAICH[1]

Twelve teams from Nepal, Thailand, Cambodia, Scotland, England, Austria, the United Arab Emirates, and the United States competed in the 28th World Elephant Polo Association's Championships at Kamali Jungle Lodge in Nepal.

Defending world champion team *Chivas Regal* Scotland won the Olympic Quaich in a tremendous battle with *Fosroc Sepoys* United Arab Emirates that ended in a final score of 5–4.

The 13th Duke of Argyle was delighted with his team's performance and said, "There are not many sports in which Scotland enjoys global leadership and with our present record, no one can deny that

Scotland is now one of the world's true sporting heavyweights." Scotland won the Quaich in 2001, 2004, and 2005.

New York Blue United States unsuccessfully defended the titles it won in 2008 for "Best Dressed Team," and the highly coveted "Dominick Moynahan Oscar Award for the Best Off-Field Performance," awarded to Ricky Smith from Wisconsin. Previous to their first championship none of the team members of *New York Blue* had ever ridden an elephant; they practiced by riding on top of automobiles in a Queens, New York, parking lot.[2] "We are excited to represent our country," said a member of *New York Blue*, "even though our country has no idea it's being represented."

In the professional category, *National Parks* Nepal played *Anantara* Thailand in a well-spirited but very hard fought final that resulted in Nepal's first World Cup victory as a republic.

Jumbo reached the big leagues when the world champion St. Louis Browns played the Philadelphia Athletics on October 5, 1886. Browns pitcher George Washington "Jumbo" McGinnis threw to Edward "Jumbo" Harting, and the Browns won, 9–4. Jumbo McGinnis's career lasted five years; Jumbo Harting's, one game. For one glorious game, Jumbo pitched and Jumbo caught.

In 1912, Ty Cobb led the league with the highest batting average, his fifth year in a row. His lifetime batting average remains the highest in the history of the game. In 1912 Honus Wagner was playing his fourteenth season for the Pittsburgh Pirates. (Cobb called Wagner "maybe the greatest star ever to take the diamond.") Grover Cleveland Alexander ("Old Pete") was pitching for the Philadelphia Phillies, and Walter "the Big Train" Johnson for the Washington Senators. The World Series between the Boston Red Sox and the New York Giants went eight games (4-3-1). Five Hall of Famers—two from Boston and three from New York—played in the 1912 World Series, and even though New York lost in the last out of the last game, baseball aficionados still consider the 1912 New York Giants one of the best teams of all time.

Nineteen twelve was also a banner year for Mooney's Giants, the world's first elephant baseball team. Harry J. Mooney, the chief elephant trainer for Barnum & Bailey, knew elephants were agile when it came to swatting and throwing things, so he taught a bull named Pilot how to hold a bat and swing at a ball. Then he taught Bessie how to catch a ball in a mitt harnessed to her trunk.

The hard part was teaching Coco how to pitch. Elephants have excellent aim and a strong "arm," but teaching pitching discipline to an elephant proved a challenge. "It was impossible for me take hold of her trunk and show her how to toss the ball," Mooney explained. "It couldn't have been done that way. What I did was talk to her. I urged her and explained what I wanted just as I would do

Coco pitching to Bessie (note Bessie's mask and chest guard).
Circus poster, 1913.

to a child. When she would make some little progress I would praise her and encourage her, and she would try harder next time." It took Mooney two years to teach Coco how to pitch a decent game, but when she finally took the mound to pitch on opening day, 1912, the stands were filled to overflowing.

Coco was as big a pitching star as Christy Mathewson or Smoky Joe Wood.

Since Pilot was the Giants' only batter, Coco never struck him out because she kept pitching to Pilot until he hit the ball. Sometimes Coco would bean Pilot, who'd then throw his bat at Coco. Sometimes Pilot would smack Coco's pitch so hard the ball went flying over her head.

Coco would chase down the ball and throw it to Bessie at home plate. Since there were no bases for Pilot to run around, he stood at the plate until Coach Mooney gave him the signal to drop to the ground as though he were sliding home. Bessie would tag Pilot and then the elephant umpire would make the call. Photographs of Bessie tagging Pilot at home plate in Madison Square Garden appeared in papers all over the country. The caption read OUT, AT HOME![3]

The Giants played to full houses as they toured the country in 1912 and 1913. Elephant baseball became so popular the Ringlings started their own team, which had nine players instead of the three who played for Barnum & Bailey. Playing all positions "in accordance with the rules of the game," there were now four bases instead of one, and an outfield, where elephants played right, left, and center field. Baldy was their power hitter. They played two games a day in dozens of counties in dozens of states.[4]

When a reporter asked Mooney why he thought elephants loved baseball, he said they did it for the attention. "Elephants love applause as much as a chorus girl does," he said.[5] Indeed, they seemed to play with the same passion as people. They'd wave their ears, snort, and kick at the ground. They even chattered to their teammates as when the first baseman would trumpet a note and the others would return it. Sometimes the pitcher took a time-out to confer with his catcher, the two of them "whispering into each other's ears" as though discussing the next pitch,[6] and when things didn't move along fast enough, the outfielders would grow impatient and throw grass or dirt at the batter.

When the batter did hit a ball—whether fair or foul—he'd run for first base. Sometimes he'd forget and run toward third base. The fielders sometimes got their bases mixed up, too, and threw to the wrong place. The crowds loved it. Baseball was an American cultural taproot and watching elephants play the game was as much fun as watching Mathewson throw against Heinie Zimmerman's blazing .372.

The Gentry Brothers put together their own team in 1915, and Robinson's Circus in 1916. The pitcher for Robinson's Circus was famous for his spitball. "It is often said there is nothing new under the sun," wrote the Springfield, Massachusetts, *Union* about Mooney's Giants in 1914, "but these feats are certainly new and demonstrate as well as anything that might be cited the progress in the development of examples of man's mastery over matter, animate and inanimate."[7]

New York Giants manager John "Little Napoleon" Mc-Graw was a feisty man. "He ate gunpowder every morning and washed it down with warm blood," said one umpire of him. His sandpaper personality rubbed everyone the wrong way. His 1905 Giants are still on *Sports Illustrated*'s list of "Most Hated Teams of All Time."[8]

In July 1902, McGraw trashed the American League president, Bancroft "Ban" Johnson, for expanding the franchise to include a second-rate team from Philadelphia called the Athletics. "The Philadelphia Athletic club is not making any money," he scoffed. "[The league] has a big white elephant on its hands."[9]

The owner and manager of the Philadelphia Athletics, then in its second season, was Cornelius McGillicuddy. The fans called him Connie Mack for short. Mack bet McGraw a thousand dollars that the A's were making money and lots of it. McGraw backed down. Defiantly, Mack raised a flag over Columbia Park with a white elephant on it, and the Athletics became "The White Elephants."

In 1905, McGraw's Giants played in the World Series against Mack's Athletics. Before the game, Mack presented McGraw with a stuffed white elephant. McGraw laughed and promised in return to give the Athletics a good whooping. New York beat Philadelphia four games to one. The Giants' future Hall of Fame pitcher Christy Mathewson pitched three of four shutouts.

After a disastrous season in 1908, Philadelphia sewed a white elephant onto the team's sweaters. The team turned around the next year, and the Mackmen then went on to play in the 1910, 1911, 1913, and 1914 World Series. They won title three times, once against the Chicago Cubs (1910) and twice against McGraw's Giants (1911 and 1913).

After winning the world championship in 1910, Philadelphia citizens presented Mack with a live, whitewashed elephant. Mack was grateful but baffled about what to do with an elephant that was eating thirty-five pounds of hay per hour. "He does not know what he is going to do with the beast," wrote one columnist, "especially when he is away from home on his wedding tour next week."[10] The Chicago *Daily Herald* jeered, recalling the lessons of the Unfortunate Man Who Won an Elephant in a Raffle, as Mack "cursed his lot / that ever he got / an elephant on his hands."[11]

The elephant appeared on the A's jersey sleeve from 1918 until 1963, when owner Charlie Finley traded him for a mule (supposedly to curry favor with Missouri Democrats while the Athletics were based in Kansas City, from 1955 to 1967). The elephant returned as the official team mascot in the 1980s, first as "Harry Elephante" (an allusion to the calypso singer Harry Belafonte) and in 1997 as the team's current mascot, Stomper, while based in Oakland, California.

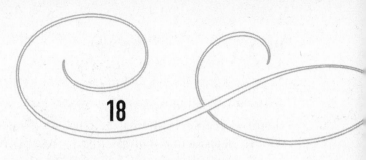

A Lynching in Tennessee

from the *Baltimore Sun*, August 16, 1894

It is a well-known fact that a negro has never tamed an elephant or any other wild animal.

On March 5, 1916, Will Whitley opened the front door of his home in Lebanon, Tennessee, to find the chief of police and his deputy standing on the front porch with their guns drawn. Chief Robert Nolen told Whitley he was under arrest for bootlegging.

Whitley asked for permission to get his hat and returned with a gun hidden inside its crown; he shot Chief Nolen twice, once in the arm and once in the gut.

The deputy returned fire, wounding Whitley, who surrendered.

Chief Nolen died in surgery later in the day.

Citizens marched to the jail, overpowered the sheriff,

and seized Whitley. They hung him from a box elder tree in the town square across from Bradshaw Drug while a thousand people, including the chief's widow, watched.[1] The newspaper reported laconically, "No violence was shown the negro before death, nor was his body mutilated. He hanged for an hour before being cut down by the coroner. Indications are that no effort will be made to punish the lynchers." Whitley was the 154th known African American to be lynched in Tennessee.[2] On March 23, William Thomas became the 155th. Later that year, in September, citizens of Erwin, Tennessee, hung an elephant from a railroad crane for killing a man.

Big Mary was the big star in Sparks World-Famous Shows. She'd come to John Sparks at the age of eighteen months in 1896, and over twenty years he and his son Charlie had trained her to become one of the most famous (and valuable) performing elephants in America. "Mary shows an intelligence that is all but human," Georgia's *Augusta Chronicle* marveled at her performance, "and after becoming acquainted with her it is not hard to believe that animals really think."

Sparks billed her as the "Largest Living Land Animal on Earth, 3 inches taller than Jumbo and weighing over 5 tons." In spite of her imposing size, she made her keen intelligence apparent by thoughtful action. When she was twelve, for example, she decided on a quiet evening in Georgia that she'd go to another tent for a midnight snack. She untied herself from her stake and ambled over to the horse tent, where she knew she'd find the oats.

The horses, which performed every day with Mary, ordinarily didn't object to her presence but Sparks had just brought in a new string of horses, which were startled by the sudden appearance of an elephant in their tent. The horses started "rearing, plunging, kicking and breaking their halters," and causing a stir. "[Mary] knew she was to blame for the trouble," continued the *Chronicle*, "and decided it was up to her to do something." She ran back to her tent, woke up her keeper with "a couple of slaps from her trunk," pulled him out of bed, and "fairly dragged him to the stables, at the same time uttering little squeaks, which the keeper recognized as concern."

The keeper quickly settled the panicky horses "and quiet again reigned over the grounds at the corner of Kollock and Fenwick streets" of Augusta.[3]

Mary was also a major-league baseball player. She batted .490 in the elephant leagues the year she was hung. She was as big a star as Coco, Pilot, or Bessie, who played for Mooney's *Giants*. A home-run queen, she belted the ball so far she had time to run the bases and slide home before the outfield returned the ball. Mary would also sometimes throw down her bat and get into "an animated argument over the next ball to be served by the pitcher." The foofaraw consisted of the two elephants standing trunk to trunk, trumpeting into each other's ear while the audience hooted.[4]

The 1916 season started out like any other. In March, the trainers took the elephants out of winter storage and prepared them for the route. Part of the spring ritual including bathing the elephants and then coating them with cocoa butter and neatsfoot oil. After a winter in cramped confinement, the elephants' skin was usually so cracked and dingy the circus had to soak them with gallons of the emollient. It took six gallons of neatsfoot oil to make Mary look presentable.

The season opened in April in Salisbury, North Carolina. In May they played New York, then traveled up New England to Maine, where they made seventeen stands. They went as far north as Fort Kent on the border with Quebec and then made the 268-mile run south from Rumford Falls to Houlton on the Bangor & Aroostook. By Labor Day, the circus was in Huntington, West Virginia.[5]

On September 9, in St. Paul, Virginia, the circus connected with the Carolina, Clinchfield, & Ohio Railway, which took them to Tennessee. Called the "Costliest Railroad in America," the CC&O connected the coalfields of southwestern Virginia and eastern Kentucky to the cotton mills of South Carolina. Sparks played many of the raw industrial towns east of the Allegheny Mountains and relied on the CC&O to reach the mountain hideaways of eastern Tennessee.[6] The route for 1916 included St. Paul, Virginia, and then traveled across the state line to Kingsport, Erwin, Johnson City, and Rogersville in Tennessee.

While in St. Paul, Paul Jacoby took on an extra elephant hand. Jacoby was the assistant elephant trainer under Louis Reed, who'd just walked away from his job a few weeks before. Now in charge, Jacoby hired Red Eldridge as an "under-keeper," a more or less invented position for someone with no experience.

Walter "Red" Eldridge was a drifter, who would, over the next forty-eight hours, go from obscurity to national notoriety. He showed up in St. Paul looking for work and the Riverside Hotel hired him for thirty cents a day to do odd jobs. No one knew who he was or where he came from, nor cared. Mechanization in the mines was displacing workers and St. Paul was awash in unemployed. The city was more concerned with its own than with men and women on the margins who were running from or to something. No one could say for sure if Walter Eldridge was called Red because of his hair or his cheeks or something else. No one knew how old he was, either: some said twenties, other said thirties. Red Eldridge was so nondescript he would have dissolved effortlessly into the past if Big Mary hadn't squashed his head like a melon.

As Sparks readied for the parade through St. Paul to the show grounds, Red went to Jacoby and asked if he had any work. Jacoby hired him on the spot, handed him a bullhook, and told him to take care of Mabel, a sedate female, while he tended to Shadrack, who had gotten twitchy since Reed had quit. Before he knew it, Red was walking down the streets of St. Paul in a parade, holding Mabel in line with four other elephants, including Big Mary and Shadrack. At the tent grounds he watched the performance from the sidelines while clowns covered him in white greasepaint and put a red ball on his nose.

That evening Red quit his job at the hotel and joined the circus.

On Tuesday, September 12, the Sparks World-Famous reached Kingsport, Tennessee. Unlike St. Paul, Kingsport was a factory town and business was booming. The mood was upbeat and the people there were excited to see the circus.

Jacoby graduated Red from Mabel to Shadrack on the parade to the show grounds in Kingsport with no trouble. There he tethered Shadrack to a stake next to Mary, who was browsing on the hay. Nearby, three boys stared wide-eyed at the elephants. "See that one?" Red pointed at Mary. "She killed a dozen men. She killed her trainer last week up in Roanoke." Later the newspapers would claim Mary had killed at least eight men, but the truth was that Mary had never killed anyone until she killed Red Eldridge.

The bleachers in Kingsport were full as Mary, Shadrack, Mabel, Ollie, and Topsy marched around the ring in a long mount, the forelegs of each elephant resting on the back of the elephant before it. They sat on their haunches, raised their legs and trunks, trumpeted, and stood on their heads. Everything went well until after the performances, when they took the elephants to bathe in a nearby pond as a treat for a good performance.

Red sat on Big Mary's shoulders as she sauntered down the street toward the watering hole. She and the other elephants walked through Kingsport in orderly fashion, undistracted by the enthusiastic people who lined Center Street to watch them pass. Some were eating treats they'd bought at the show—such as watermelon and molasses balls—and they pointed at Mary, the "Largest Living Land Animal on Earth," and shouted hurrah.

The last building on Center Street housed the blacksmith Hench Cox. As Big Mary passed in front of Cox's forge, two hogs squabbled over a piece of watermelon rind in the street. Mary, like most elephants, was fond of watermelon and made a detour toward the hogs.

Red Eldridge jabbed Mary with his bullhook and she twitched her withers but didn't return into line. He jabbed her harder the second time and still Mary ignored him. The hogs scattered as Mary reached for the rind with her trunk, when Red Eldridge smacked her hard on the side of the head with the bullhook.

According to one account, Mary ripped Red off her back with her trunk, "lifted him 10 feet in the air, then dashed him with fury to the ground . . . and with full force of her biestly [sic] fury . . . sunk her giant tusks entirely through his body. [She] then trampled the dying form of Eldridge as if seeking a murderous triumph, then with a sudden . . . swing of her massive foot hurled his body into the crowd."[7]

In another version Mary throws Eldridge against a soda stand and then stomps on his head while the crowd on the street scatters in panic.[8] The smithy Hench Cox ran out of his forge and shot Big Mary five times with his Colt single-action .32-20 pistol; she shuddered with each shot but none of the bullets seriously harmed her.

In spite of the tumult around her, Mary remained

curiously calm. The source of her agitation now lying in a lifeless heap, she simply stood in place as if awaiting further direction. Sparks people quickly surrounded her in order to cordon her from the crowd that was re-gathering.

The crowd in the street swelled to hundreds when word got out that one of the Sparks elephants had gored a man to death in front of Cox's forge. Most were curious; some were angry. Then someone shouted "Kill her!" and Hench Cox ran back into the forge for more bullets.

As soon as Charlie Sparks got wind of something gone wrong, he mounted his horse and forced his way through the crowd to Big Mary, which only made things worse because his horse was skittish around elephants. When his horse suddenly found himself in the midst of five elephants hemmed in by a surging wave of people, he threw off Sparks and bolted through the crowd.

Again, someone shouted "Kill him!" Here and there voices called for immediate retribution. Sparks got to his feet and held up his arms to address the crowd. He agreed to the call for justice but said a mob couldn't kill an elephant no matter how hard it tried. Guns weren't powerful enough—witness Hench Cox's failed attempts to stop her—and they couldn't electrocute her because Kingsport couldn't muster the amount of electricity necessary to kill an elephant. (Neither claim was true.) The crowd backed down when it realized it couldn't throw a rope over a tree branch and lynch Mary, so it settled for Sparks's implicit promise of an orderly execution.

Sparks didn't plan to honor his pledge. Given the chance he'd argue the town had no claim to retribution. If a grievance was to be made against the elephant, that right belonged to the circus, not Kingsport. From experience Charlie Sparks knew that cooler heads would prevail with time, and that he had to create that space before something ugly happened.

Sparks also knew he needed only a few hours to get the circus out of town and on its way to the next stop. In the middle of a run of one-day stands, the schedule called for him to be in Erwin the next day, Johnson City on Thursday, and then Rogersville on Friday. Unfortunately, all three towns were within forty miles of Kingsport, and word was already spreading like wildfire up and down the line that a circus elephant had killed a man there.

The people of Kingsport sought an injunction to keep the circus from leaving town while it filed legal charges against Big Mary. They argued premeditation to a magistrate: because Big Mary *conspired* to kill Walter Eldridge, she was guilty of first-degree murder and should not be allowed to flee the jurisdiction.

John Sparks was shrewd enough to realize that if he left town without putting on a second performance, he'd open himself to charges of fraud and larceny. Sparks had built a reputation for itself as "the Show That Has Never Broken a Promise." Its advertising touted, "Never exaggerating advertising, advertising only what it exhibits— giving so much for so little." John and his son Charlie had built their business on the idea of "honest entertainment" and offered a thousand dollars to anyone who could show the circus "tolerates, harbors, or carries any form of graft, gambling devices, games of chance, or any other scheme whereby the public is cheated in any manner what-so-ever."[9] To violate this trust was to undermine the credibility and the reputation of everything they'd built. Fearing that accusations of fraud and theft would mortally wound the circus, Charlie Sparks decided to stay in Kingsport and put on a full performance at eight o'clock that evening as scheduled, aware that the sheriff could show up at any minute waving papers in his fist.

But the injunction didn't come in time, and by midnight the train was loaded and on its way to Erwin.

The next morning the people in Erwin read a headline story in the *Johnson City Staff* about "Murderous Mary," who'd killed a man in Kingsport. The paper reported she was a vicious man-killer and that Walter Eldridge had been her eighth victim.[10]

The mayors of Johnson City and Rogersville immediately banned Murderous Mary from their towns, which presented Sparks with a dilemma: either let Erwin kill Mary—which would cost the circus its star attraction and cripple it financially—or finish out the season with her, risking forfeitures on the schedule. Whether Big Mary was executed or spared in the next few hours didn't matter: the fate of Sparks World-Famous Shows had already been decided.

Erwin became even more agitated when it learned that a magistrate in Kingsport had issued an order of execution on Murderous Mary but could not enforce it because the elephant had left its jurisdiction. Under Tennessee law, Murderous Mary had forfeited her right to live, and so the magistrate had sentenced her to "hang by the neck until you are dead."[11] Now it fell to Erwin to carry out the sentence, not as a point of law, but as a point of honor.

Once Sparks agreed Mary would die, the task of deciding how to kill her prompted three proposals. The first suggested using field artillery. In fact, men were already on their way from Kingsport with a Civil War cannon and they intended to put a cannonball through her. The second proposal had more support. Murderous Mary should be taken to the railroad yards and chained between opposing engines that would then pull her head off. The third proposal met with the greatest approval. Since the magistrate in Kingsport had specifically ordered the elephant to hang, so should she die.

The question of how to hang an elephant was answered easily: the CC&O had a hundred-ton railroad derrick car in Johnson City they could get to Erwin in a few hours. Its crane could easily lift Mary off the ground.

The men of Erwin talked to the men of the railroad, and the CC&O agreed to send for the crane from Johnson City. It would arrive some time around three, during the matinee performance. Erwin's first lynching was under way.

The weather in Erwin was dismal. It had rained heavily the night before and the hard-packed dirt of the roads had turned into muck. At dawn, a steady drizzle kept the air wet and cold while crowds converged on the side of the muddy road.

Charlie Sparks knew the people lined up on the street hadn't come to see his snarling cats or the tumbling clowns or the horses caparisoned in silver: they'd come to see Murderous Mary on her death march. He'd seen the story in the *Staff* and had heard about the proposals to kill her. Reluctantly, he consented to the demand for immediate justice, and, given the choices of her being shot by a cannon, or drawn and quartered by locomotives, perhaps hanging from a chain noose seemed somehow less cruel.

Big Mary was fine with her day as it was going. She'd just finishing unloading wagons from the train and had assembled for the parade, which began at 10:30. Everything went according to schedule as she followed the line through town to the show grounds, where she helped set the tents, the same routine she'd followed for twenty years. Standing at her stake, she contentedly showered herself with hay.

The matinee began at two. The bleachers, which seated five thousand people, held three thousand, a thousand more than the entire population of Erwin. People came from Kingsport, Johnson City, Okolona, and Flag Pond to see Mary give her final performance.

During the matinee, Derrick No. 1400 arrived from Johnson City. Designed to unload railroad ties, generators, and other heavy equipment onto the track, the squat crane extended barely high enough to lift an elephant off the ground by its neck. The crane operator, Sam "One-Eyed" Harvey, calculated the elephant would clear the ground by about two feet but no more. He was told to ready his crane for a lynching.

While the steam boiler to No. 1400 fired up, One-Eyed Harvey attached a length of seven-eighths-inch chain to the hook of the crane arm. It was so heavy it took two men to lift the end of the chain high enough to slip onto the winch hook.

If any had come with the expectation of seeing a rogue, they were disappointed. Big Mary gave no hint of an aberrant personality as she played a variety of tunes on her horn, stood on her head, and pitched a baseball. She performed so well that the *Johnson City Staff* remarked the next day that she'd played "with almost human intelligence."[12]

Nonetheless, as soon as the matinee was over Charlie Sparks led Mary out of the tent and toward the rail yard.

Carolina, Clinchfield & Ohio Railway Derrick Car No. 1400.

Shadrack, Mabel, Topsy, and Ollie followed. Part of the crowd went ahead to make sure they got a good spot to see the hanging while others followed Mary as she made her way toward No. 1400.

Mary balked in view of No. 1400 and sat down. When she refused to get up, it seemed to some she sensed something was wrong. Jacoby used Shadrack to bully her back to feet. When she still refused to budge, Jacoby put Ollie and Topsy on her flanks and Mabel at the rear to escort her to the gallows.

They left Murderous Mary beneath the crane arm of No. 1400. Three thousand people watched breathlessly as two men cinched the chain around her neck and One-Eyed Harvey engaged the winch and drew up the chain around Mary's neck so that she dangled with her hind feet still on the ground.

Mary gasped for air as she danced in a circle. Slowly the crane continued to raise her until finally she dangled just inches from the ground. The crane groaned under the weight, but the cable continued to wind around the drum, lifting her three feet off the ground.

Only Harvey hadn't snatched the cable up fast enough, and so instead of breaking her neck, he was strangling her. She struggled as much as her weight would allow. The crowd, struck dumb by fascination and horror, watched as she swung in small arcs beneath the iron hanging tree. And then the chain broke.

The crowd panicked when it saw Murderous Mary trying to get to her feet. Fearing a stampede, people turned and ran away—creating their own stampede—which crushed a blind banjo player who'd come to hear the hanging.

But Mary had split her pelvis and couldn't get up. At first she was too dazed to feel her pain, but as oxygen returned to her lungs and her brain, she began to moan. It

Execution of "Murderous Mary," Sparks' Man-Killing Elephant at Erwin, Tennessee, September 13, 1916.

took eighty minutes for men to find another chain heavy enough to hang her. The second time Harvey hung Mary, he jerked her more forcibly into the air.

She barely contested.

Sparks World-Famous Shows put on the second show at 8 p.m. People, aroused by the day's events, filled the bleachers, screaming and laughing with delight as the clowns and acrobats went through their routines. Shadrack, Mabel, Ollie, and Topsy also performed, this time without Big Mary leading the way.

Meanwhile, an engine pushed No. 1400 down the track to a pit half the size of a boxcar near the track. The crane swung Big Mary over the hole and then dropped her into it as roustabouts quickly covered her with dirt. The exact location of her grave was to be a secret.

As Big Mary fell into her grave, Shadrack went crazy inside the circus tent and charged into the reserved seats and tried to overturn the bleachers. "Someone yelled 'The Elephants are loose,'" wrote the *Johnson City Staff* the next day, "but this was superfluous as [Shadrack's] angry snort had already warned the people, who arose as if a chunk of dynamite had been fired beneath them and broke into a mob, yelling, screaming, fighting their way to the middle of the tent seeking an exit. Women tumbled over, men were knocked down in the wild scramble, hats were smashed, skirts were torn in the effort to get away."[13]

Jacoby, who was practiced in elephant behavior, took decisive control of Shadrack, the way Red Eldridge might have done with Big Mary the day before if he'd known how. After the initial fright, the audience cautiously returned to its seats while the roustabouts in the train yard smoothed gravel atop Big Mary's grave.

A few days after her death, the Associated Press called the CC&O and asked the railroad if it would exhume Big Mary so they could reenact and photograph the hanging. The people at Clinchfield declined the offer.

Sparks went on to play Johnson City and Rogersville and finished the season in Georgia and North Carolina. He eventually replaced Big Mary with Zulu, whom he billed exactly the same as he had Mary, as "the Largest Living Land Animal on Earth, 3 inches taller than Jumbo and weighing over 5 tons."[14] The circus survived fifteen more years.

The blind banjo picker the crowd trampled was buried in Evergreen Cemetery in Erwin, along with One-Eyed Harvey, who died years later. Mary's body still rests in an unmarked grave in the old Clinchfield yard.

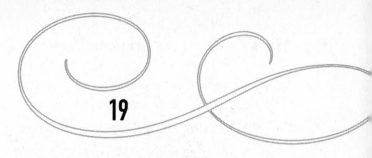

19

How Jumbo Got His Shnozz

---◆---

from the *Trenton Evening Times*, January 6, 1918

HOUDINI TO MAKE ELEPHANT VANISH

Harry Houdini, who escapes from everything except the income tax, retired from vaudeville this season, but has been engaged by Charles B. Dillingham to provide a big novelty in "Cheer Up!" the Hippodrome show, in New York, beginning tomorrow.

The magician has evolved a new trick to mystify the public. He calls it the "Vanishing Elephant," and has been working on it four years. An elephant weighing 6,000 pounds will walk out on the stage and suddenly disappear.

The elephant actually vanishes in full glare of the light, without the use of traps, as the tank of water under the Hippodrome prevents any such camouflage. Houdini has constructed a gigantic

cylinder-shaped container of such dimensions that
the largest elephant obtainable can enter with ease.
It walks through this mystic tube and vanishes.

———————————— ◆ ————————————

Nineteen twelve was a big year for the movie industry in
America. A lot had happened during the thirty years
since the Frenchman Étienne-Jules Marey's camera shot
the first frames of animal locomotion. In 1912, the first
film version of *The Charge of the Light Brigade* appeared,
as did the first *Dr. Jekyll and Mr. Hyde*. D. W. Griffith
released the first gangster film, *The Musketeers of Pig Alley*, and Dorothy Gibson, a survivor of the disaster of the
RMS *Titanic*, starred in what is arguably the first reality
disaster movie, *Saved from the Titanic*, which was released
to theaters within weeks of the ship's sinking. In 1912
Paul Rainey's *African Hunt* became the first jungle adventure and the cowboy film officially became the Western. A film company that specialized in making Westerns
and was tired of making movies in Bayonne, New Jersey,
opened the first film studio in Hollywood.[1]

Nineteen twelve was also the year of the first elephant
comedy.

Elephants had traveled through the media landscape
since the invention of the motion picture camera. As the
camera explored the immediate world around it—such
as shots of the traffic circling the roundabout in London's Piccadilly Circus or the Kaiser riding in his gilded

carriage down a Berlin boulevard—it also instinctively turned to the beasts in the zoo, thus capturing the first moving images of lions, bears, and, of course, elephants.

When the novelty of motion pictures wore off, however, people craved more excitement than dazed animals staring at the camera. As the camera ventured abroad, it came back with movies that showed elephants festooned in jewels and silks riding with maharajahs sitting in solid silver howdahs, and they saw holy men in robes festoon elephants with flowers and wash them in the sacred waters of the Ganges.

In 1899, a part-time silversmith and maker of novelties named Gottfried Wilhelm Bitzer remade himself into a motion picture cameraman named Billy Bitzer when he filmed a race between an elephant, a horse, a bicycle, and an automobile on the streets of New York City (*A Unique Race*).[2] By 1903 Bitzer was shooting films with names like *New York Fire Department Returning* and *Opening the Williamsburg Bridge*. He invented the fade-out, the iris shot, and soft focus. He shot hundreds of short films before D. W. Griffith picked him to shoot *Birth of a Nation* in 1913, *Intolerance* in 1916, and *Way Down East* in 1920.[3] Billy Bitzer was, arguably, America's first big-picture cameraman.

At the same time, another man who at one time had been an exhibition skater, a sign painter, and a telegraph operator also picked up the camera. Edwin S. Porter, the man Edison chose to film Topsy's electrocution in 1903, went back to Luna Park a year later to shoot another film about an elephant that rode the park's giant water slide.

Apparently the elephant liked the water slide so much he wouldn't get out of the pool. He hits "the water with a tremendous splash [and] remains under the water for a short time, enjoying his cool bath," reads Edison's catalog description. "It takes considerable coaxing on the part of his Arabian keeper to get him to come out of the water."

As film turned away from films about the coronation of the king of Norway to stories of the Queen of the Nile, elephants went from objects of curiosity to vaudeville actors. They costarred in skits and theatrical bits, usually alive but on at least one occasion, dead.

In 1911 the Warwick Trading Company made *Light and Shades of the Bostock Circus Farm*, a short that superimposes the real death of an elephant over a melodrama about a keeper who is distraught by the death of his companion.[4] The seams between fiction and nonfiction are rarely so obviously—or so grotesquely—apparent.

The film was shot over winter, as the Bostock Circus wound down from six months on the road. It was meant to be a peek behind the canvas to see what a circus did during the off-season. Circumstances, however, collided to create a Victorian morality play that takes place over the corpse of a dead elephant.

The story is four minutes long and is divided into three acts. The first act is in the style of *the curious eye*, and shows clips of life during the off-season, such as men with their teams of horses, the trainer with the bear, and the keeper with his elephant.

The keeper prods the elephant to stand for the camera.

Then in a series of shots he washes her, trims her nails, and walks her back to her shed for a nap. "This wonderful, great, loving chap works hard all day," reads the title card.

Until now the sequences play like a series of disconnected snapshots into the lives of the Bostock circus people and animals. The performances are ingenuous and the representation feels harmlessly mediated by the camera. But the film undergoes a radical transformation in the second act, when the keeper returns to the shed to find his beloved elephant dead.

The viewer either presumes the elephant is alive and pretending to be dead, or the elephant is really dead. When the keeper finds the elephant dead in the doorway of the shed, he throws up his hands to signal his shock and then runs to his friends, who throw up their hands in equally melodramatic fashion when they hear the news. The men run back to the shed like Keystone Kops and upon seeing his dead comrade again, the keeper turns inconsolable.

His friends try to pull him away, but he pushes them out of the way, and the men again throw up their hands. The emotional and physical movements of the actors reflect the conventions of the Victorian stage, which to the modern eye look hopelessly contrived.

The actors mug for the camera for forty seconds and then the last act is starkly existential as it reverts to the same documentary style of the first act. The same men who paraded teams of horses past the camera in the first act now skid a dead elephant across a muddy field on a bleak day. The elephant's body is deflated and misshapen, an inanimate lump of flesh.

The next shot reveals men stacking brush onto the elephant's body and setting him on fire. The title card reads *The End* and finishes with a shot of the elephant's smoldering corpse.

A few months later, the first elephant comedy arrived.

The elephant comedy is a retelling of *The Unfortunate Man Who Won an Elephant in a Raffle*, the literary forebear of what later became known as the White Elephant. The plotline is simple: a man who by good fortune inherits an elephant, which turns out to be much more trouble than he's worth. The juxtaposition of an elephant at large in the middle of American middle-class society provided lots of opportunities for laughs as the protagonists of the story struggle to solve the problem of what to do with an elephant. At least seventeen elephant-on-the-loose comedies appeared between 1912 and 1920, with names such as *Elephant on His Hands* (1913), *Come 'Round an' Take That Elephant Away* (1915), and *Too Much Elephant* (1917).

In *Elephant on His Hands* (1913), a young Lon Chaney (in a very early performance) plays Eddie, who finds himself the hapless owner of an elephant when his uncle's circus goes broke. When Eddie can't find a place to put the elephant, he brings him home, with ruinous consequences. Slapstick comedian Hughie Mack reprised the role in 1920 in what film historian Cole Johnson calls "the *Citizen Kane* of berserk elephant movies" as a pair of inherited elephants ran ramshackle through town. In the film, they run into the showers at a girls' gym and scare up a bevy of young women wrapped in towels. Comedian Bill Murray reprised the role in *Larger than Life* in 1996.

Buster Keaton (*Three Ages*, 1923) and Laurel and Hardy (*Flying Elephants*, 1928) worked elephants into their comic routines. In *Smith's Family Candy Shop* (1927), an elephant gives a shave, complete with talc, to an unsuspecting man in a barbershop, and in *Elephant on His Hands* (1920), an elephant disarms a hotel detective and shoots Hughie Mack in the butt.

Elephants played their shtick deadpan, like Jimmy Durante in the Broadway musical *Jumbo*, which opened in the theater district of midtown Manhattan in 1935. Durante played Pop Wonder, the owner and manager of the Wonder Circus, whose most prized possession is his elephant. But Pop's gambling puts the circus in jeopardy as creditors angle to force Pop to settle his debt by selling Jumbo.

Both Jumbo and Jimmy Durante had enormous noses. Durante called his "the Shnozzola," an Italianization of a Yiddish word for a very big nose. Durante's shnozz looked at least as big as Jumbo's and their physical resemblance created a physical and emotional connection between Pop Wonder and Jumbo. Pop so trusted his pal Jumbo that Durante allowed Rosie, the elephant that played the part of Jumbo, to step on Jimmy Durante's head 223 times during the run of the show.

One of Durante's signature jokes came from a gag in *Jumbo*. When Pop's creditors squeeze him for money, he tries to skip town with Jumbo when a process server catches them.

"What are you doing with that elephant?" he demands.

"Elephant?" Durante deadpans in rubbery style, with Rosie standing behind him, *"What elephant?"*

Produced in 1935 by the impresario Billy Rose, *Jumbo* ran in the Hippodrome in New York City, a theater with 5,300 seats and which was putatively "the Largest Theater on Earth." In 1918, Harry Houdini had made a ten-thousand-pound elephant disappear from the expansive stage of the Hippodrome, and only the Hippodrome could have accommodated the staggering array of *Jumbo's* fire eaters, jugglers, acrobats, chorus girls, educated dogs, educated parrots, and a whipsnapper, who snatched cigarettes from a pretty girl's red lips with a bullwhip.[5] A man balanced a cement block on his head while another man pounded it with a sledgehammer; an iron woman drove nails with her fist; and an axe-thrower cleaved an apple perched on his daughter's head.

Richard Rodgers and Lorenz Hart wrote the music and lyrics for *Jumbo*.

Together Rodgers and Hart wrote thirty-six Broadway shows, including most famously, *Pal Joey*. The Paul Whiteman Orchestra, the most popular band of the 1920s, performed the music for the play. *Jumbo* included ten numbers by Rodgers and Hart, including the memorable "The Most Beautiful Girl in the World" and the eminently forgettable "The Circus Isn't Under Canvas; It's in Your Heart."[6]

The band was as much about performance as it was about music. Sometimes Whiteman would lead his orchestra from the saddle of a white horse while camels, zebras, and ostriches trotted across the stage. *Jumbo's* over-the-top style was a great, loud, colorful celebration of life, a welcome oasis in the great desert of the Depression, but the show closed after five months. By 1938, the real estate beneath the Hippodrome became too valuable to squander so frivolously, so the Hippodrome gave way for an office building.

Jumbo reappeared twenty-seven years later as an MGM studio production, still starring Jimmy Durante as Pop Wonder. And again an elephant steps on his head.

The same year Billy Rose premiered *Jumbo* at the Hippodrome, Walt Disney announced he was going forward on the first feature-length animated production of *Snow White and the Seven Dwarfs*. The financial success of *Snow White* notwithstanding, Disney's second and third animated features—*Fantasia* and *Pinocchio* in 1940—disappointed at the box office and left the Disney studio strapped for cash, so Roy and Walt Disney started production on a less ambitious and substantially shorter animated feature about a flying elephant named

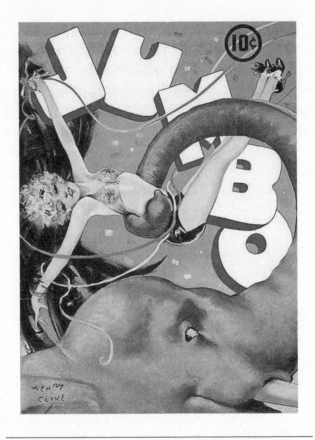

Henry Clive's poster of Billy Rose's Jumbo, *1935.*

Dumbo, which they hoped would backfill the studio's coffers. The same year as Billy Rose premiered *Jumbo*, Disney released *Elmer Elephant* as part of the "Silly Symphony" series of cartoon tour-de-forces that won seven of the thirteen Academy Awards the studio garnered between 1932 and 1943, including such landmark works as Mickey Mouse (1932), *Three Little Pigs* (1934), *Snow White* (1937), and *Fantasia* (1941).

The story line of *Elmer Elephant* was charming yet familiar: at a birthday party for Tillie the Tiger, other child-animals mock Elmer for having a big shnozz, but Elmer turns out the hero of the day when he saves the shapely Miss Tiger from her burning house by dousing the fire with water from his ample trunk. Disney re-employed the theme five years later, when he created Dumbo.

Instead of a big nose, Dumbo has ears so big he can fly, and like Elmer he saves the day. Disney returned to the formula a third time in 1960 in another elephant cartoon, *Goliath II*, in which the undersized son of a great elephant (no bigger than "one of his father's toenails") shows that his mettle is as big as his father's.

The Disney elephant turned out to be an ideal vehicle to convey the Protestant values of middle America. Whereas most other animals were known by a singular virtue—the hare was fast and the tortoise slow, for example—the elephant embodied the same values—and foibles—as humans.

Colonel Hathi in Disney's *Jungle Book* (1967) lampoons Alec Guinness's portrayal of Colonel Nicholson in *Bridge Over the River Kwai* (1957). In "Colonel Hathi's March" (a reference to the "Colonel Bogey March" from the *River Kwai*), the pretentious cartoon bull and his herd stomp through the jungle singing,

Oh, the aim of our patrol
is a question rather droll;
For to march and drill
over field and hill,
is a military goal!
A military goal!

Disney's cartoon elephants were much more popular than the real elephants in live-action adventures such as *Toby Tyler* (1960), *Runaway on the Rogue River* (1974), *Something Wicked This Way Comes* (1983), and *Operation Dumbo Drop* (1995). In 2000, Disney released *Whispers: An Elephant's Tale*, about a baby elephant who is orphaned after poachers kill his mother. The *New York Times* called *Whispers* "a custard of cloying anthropomorphism under the Walt Disney Pictures label compounded out of extraordinary nature film bonded to a layer of inane dialogue."[7] The film went barely noticed.[8]

Live elephants lacked the charisma of animated ones, so they ended up as jungle wallpaper in dozens of melodramas about Africa and Asia. A herd of elephants flatten a Laotian village in *Chang* (1928), and Bomba the Jungle Boy in *Elephant Stampede* (1951) calls upon elephants to trample ivory poachers. Since Elmo Lincoln starred as the first Ape Man in 1918, elephants have been a staple of the Tarzan movie franchise, which includes more than three hundred titles.[9] Although elephants appear in the Tarzan movies frequently, their expressiveness was too subtle to be captured by the optics of the day, as opposed to the over-the-top expressiveness of a chimpanzee, Tarzan's chief animal sidekick. Producers created a stereotype of elephants as "Nervous Nellies" who were quick to raise the alarm and just as quick to stampede.

Disney's animated elephants, on the other hand, were anything but the plodding beasts of jungle melodramas. In *Fantasia* an elephant named Elephanchine (a pun on ballet master George Balanchine) and an elephant chorus line dance in pink ballet slippers to the music of Ponchielli's *Dance of the Hours*. When Hyacinth Hippo, still in her tutu, falls asleep, elephants surround her like graces celebrating her dream, painted in salmons and lemon meringue. Many felt the power of animation came from the easy way it nullified the laws of physics. As Hyacinth Hippo deepens her dream, elephants blow fountains of bubbles that lift her effortlessly into the sky.

The possibility of a bubble of gas lifting an elephant into space wasn't as surreal as it seemed. In 1913, a fellow at the Royal Astronomical Society, Professor H. Krauss Nield, discovered an element called coronium. The Russian chemist Dmitri Mendeleyev had predicted the existence of two inert chemical elements with a lower atomic weight than hydrogen, which he called newtonium and coronium. Nield, who discovered coronium in the corona of the sun, calculated the gas was exponentially lighter than hydrogen—the gas that filled airships—and that a volume of it the size of a baseball could lift any elephant into the sky. In enough quantity, he wrote, coronium would power manned spaceflight.

Nield took the green emission line of wavelength 530.2 nanometers as proof of the existence of coronium. However, scientists working on the principle of Occam's razor in the 1930s concluded a simpler explanation: the color at that point in the spectral wavelength wasn't coronoium but highly ionized iron. Coronium ceased to exist except in the mind of Disney, where the laws of physics did not matter, and where hippos and elephants in the land of Coronium could dance on their toes, float, and even fly.

A year after the release of *Fantasia*, elephants and bubbles returned when Dumbo and Timothy Mouse got drunk on water spiked with champagne. They hallucinated "Pink Elephants on Parade," a five-minute sequence that looks more like a product of the drug counterculture of the 1960s than the year immediately prior to World War II. In the squash and recoil world of the cartoon, elephants contort themselves into everything from a hissing cobra to a hootchy-kootchy girl. They march in plaid and polka dot, their trunks blaring trumpets as a chorus sings in a manic register: "Pink elephants on parade / What'll I do? What'll I do? / What an unusual view! / I could stand the sight of worms / And look at microscopic germs / But technicolor pachyderms / Is really too much for me."[10] Self-inventing neon pink elephants pinwheel across a Jackson Pollock universe for a few minutes before they melt into harmless clouds at sunrise as Dumbo and Timothy Mouse awake in the top of a tree, dazed by their drunk.

Disney's Winnie the Pooh has a similarly fantasti-
cal dream about elephants—called Heffalumps—in *The
Many Adventures of Winnie the Pooh* (1968).[11] "Heffalumps
and Woozles," a juvenile corruption of Elephants and
Weasels, are out to steal Pooh's honey. "They're extraordinary so be wary," advises the chorus. "If honey is what
you covet, you'll find that they love it / Because they
guzzle up the thing you prize."

And while Pooh and Dumbo dreamt of plaid and
polka-dotted elephants, two scientists gave gargantuan
doses of LSD to elephants from the Tulsa Zoo.

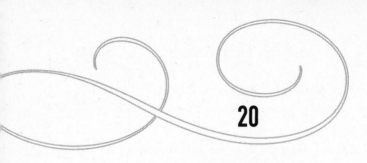

20

Secret Agents

◆

from the *Dallas Morning News*, September 27, 1963

ELEPHANT FLEES CARNIVAL, BREAKS WINDOW, HURTS MAN

LANSING, Mich. (AP)—A 3,000 pound elephant broke away from a carnival Thursday night, smashed through a store window and seriously injured one person in a panicky run down city streets.

A detective shot and killed the animal after a 12-block chase.

Police said the 12-year-old elephant rumbled out of the carnival grounds at the Logan Shopping Center on Lansing's southwest side shortly after 7:30 p.m.

The animal shattered a window in Arlan's Department Store, roamed around inside and finally left. A woman clerk called police and shouted, "An elephant got loose and smashed its way into the store."

Police said the elephant, owned by King Bros.
Carnival, injured Asa Schiedel, 67, near his home.
He was reported in fair condition at Ingham Medical Hospital. A hospital spokesman said Schiedel
suffered multiple fractures of the pelvis.

In 1953, the Central Intelligence Agency launched a
closely held operation that funded projects regarding human behavioral modification, or, as some called it, mind
control. The CIA's Office of Technical Services created
a program called MKULTRA, which tested the effects
of hallucinogens on a variety of subjects, including unsuspecting hospital patients, prison inmates, prostitutes
and their johns, soldiers, and elephants. Researchers even
dosed their own colleagues. In 1953, a civilian employee
of the army killed himself after jumping from a motel
room window during a meeting of LSD researchers in
New York City after he was given the drug without
knowing it.

The mission of MKULTRA was to develop and test
"biological agents and delivery systems against humans
as well as animals." Researchers studied the physiological
and psychological effects of heroin, morphine, mescaline,
psilocybin, marijuana, alcohol, and its darling drug, lysergic acid diethylamide-25, LSD.

LSD is a powerful psychotropic drug that affects the
central nervous system by altering behavior and percep-

tion. Albert Hofmann, a Swiss chemist working for the pharmaceutical giant Sandoz, first synthesized and tested LSD in 1938. Related to a grain fungus that grows on rye, LSD was used by early researchers as a tool in experimental psychiatry years before the counterculture of the 1960s discovered it as a recreational drug.

LSD affects the brain principally in the cerebral cortex, which is the seat of mood, cognition, and perception, and the locus ceruleus, which receives sensory signals from the body. The drug dramatically intensifies colors, smells, sounds, and other sensations. A person's emotions may swing wildly from fear to euphoria so rapidly as to experience both emotions at the same time. The perception of time ribbons out endlessly, unfolding exquisite—or horrific—detail. A dose can last as long as twelve hours, during which time a subject can bask in extended elation or wallow in nightmarish visions of insanity and death. MKULTRA sponsored 149 research projects in eleven years, many of which focused on LSD.[1]

In 1962 an article appeared in *Science*, arguably the most distinguished and influential periodical in science, titled "Lysergic Acid Diethylamide: Its Effects on a Male Asiatic Elephant." Written by Louis Jolyon "Jolly" West, Chester M. Pierce, and Warren D. Thomas, the report describes the result of administering a massive dose of LSD to a fourteen-year-old elephant from the Oklahoma City Zoo named Tusko, one of a handful of male elephants left living in America.[2]

In their paper, Drs. West and Pierce of the University of Oklahoma School of Medicine's Department of Psychiatry, Neurology, and Behavioral Sciences laid out the rationale for their experiment and then related the events that followed. (As the director of the Oklahoma City Zoo, Warren Thomas played no significant part in the design and execution of the experiment other than to volunteer Tusko for the experiment.) "There is a now a growing interest in this animal on the part of the psychiatrist," the authors wrote in their introduction. In their view, desirable traits specific to the elephant, such as intelligence, a long life, highly organized social behavior, and an "extraordinary psychobiology in general," made the animal an ideal mental corollary for human beings.

West and Pierce argued that musth was a form of transient madness. "The male elephant's periodic madness is an almost unique phenomenon in nature," they wrote, "and it provides an interesting opportunity for psychiatric research." So they designed an experiment to incite musth in Tusko by giving him LSD.

With the majority of MKULTRA's records since destroyed, one can only infer a link between the CIA and Jolly West's interest in creating and studying model psychosis in an elephant. Their interests and their histories certainly overlapped. The purpose of West's study was to determine, if possible, if the temporal gland secretions that ran down the elephant's head to his mouth at the start of musth actually triggered aggression or if it reflected "a more profound inner periodic hormonal thunderstorm which also disrupts his brain and behavior." In other words, they intended to induce aggression "madness" in Tusko.

On August 3, 1962, West and Pierce administered nearly a third of a gram of LSD in a dart they fired into Tusko's rump. They then turned on a camera to document what would become the second recording of the death of an elephant since Edwin Porter had filmed Topsy's electrocution in 1903.

Clinical detail buffers the drama of the event. "Five minutes after the injection he trumpeted, collapsed, fell heavily onto his right side, defecated, and went into *status epilepticus*," West wrote tersely as he transcribed Tusko's behavior after injecting a dose of LSD three thousand times greater than an average human dose. The doctors calculated (for reasons undisclosed) an elephant would have an innate resistance to the drug. A dose extrapolated for weight, suggested West and Pierce, "would at best be of borderline effectiveness," so they increased the dose by a factor of thirty.[3]

The dart startled Tusko, who trumpeted and then ran around his pen, not so much angry as anxious. Over the next three minutes his restlessness turned into agitation, as he tried to shake off the drug. Suddenly Tusko stopped running and began to sway. His hindquarters buckled, and he fell over.

Judy, a companion elephant, urged Tusko to get up, but his throat was closing and he gasped to breathe. His legs went rigid and he bit his tongue, which turned blue.

West tried to mitigate Tusko's respiratory distress

with 2.8 grams of an antipsychotic called chlorpromazine (well-known as Thorazine), and when that didn't work he administered a massive dose of pentobarbital sodium, a tranquilizer. Tusko took one hundred minutes to die.

"It appears that the elephant is highly sensitive to the effects of LSD," West and Pierce concluded in *Science*, "—a finding which may prove to be valuable in elephant-control work in Africa."

Only West and Pierce weren't interested in elephant control in Africa; they were interested in the value of LSD as a drug that could model psychosis. They sacrificed one of ten male elephants in America at the time in order to reach the conclusion that "a male elephant whose temporal glands had been surgically removed early in life might grow up to be a sexually capable but behaviorally tractable animal, one that never went on musth."[4]

The experiment would have gone largely unnoticed if it hadn't been for the Church of Scientology, which publicly accused West of being high on acid during the experiment.

The church's accusation stemmed from either an accidental or intentional misreading of a newspaper story that reported Dr. West had taken LSD "before" the experiment, leaving open to interpretation the conclusion that he'd taken the drug immediately prior to the experiment rather than at a more distant past. Like other researchers of his time, West admitted testing LSD on himself in order to better relate to a subject's symptoms.

West denied the accusation, but the church said it had proof. "[West] was evidently under its influence," the church rebuffed, "at the time *he sloshed through the beast's entrails*, performing an 'autopsy' which he recorded on film" (emphasis added).

The peculiarity of the charges raised eyebrows. What interest did the Church of Scientology have in Jolly West and his LSD research? What was really on the film? Information was quick to emerge that West had recently criticized the Church of Scientology in the press as a cult that manipulated its congregants with mind control, and so, West claimed, the church manufactured the charges in an attempt to discredit him. The footage the church claimed to show him prancing about in an elephant gut pile didn't exist, West pointed out, because he'd recorded the experiment, not the autopsy, which was a day later.

Confronted with this information, the Church of Scientology issued new allegations that West was really a federal drug agent who had penetrated the "LSD-using subculture" by pretending to be one of them. In a transcript of a conversation Jolly West supposedly had with his superiors at the drug agency, Jolly West told them hippies "loved me and trusted me after I told them that I was . . . the famous guy who had killed an elephant with LSD."[5]

While West wasn't a spy for the government, the CIA did fund his research in experimental psychology through front organizations such as the Foundations Fund for Research in Psychiatry, Inc., and the United States Public Heath Service, although West may not have known of the connection between his work and the interests of MKULTRA.

In 1969, Jolly West left Oklahoma for the University of California, Los Angeles, where he met Dr. Ronald K. Siegel, a colleague who became interested in West and Pierce's original research question: *could LSD precipitate aggression in elephants?* A psychopharmocologist "engaged in the research and study of the effects of drugs on human behavior," Siegel had already published articles on the effect of pot on pigeons and the effect of LSD on blind monkeys; he'd also studied alcoholism and opium addiction in elephants.[6]

Siegel developed a working hypothesis that Tusko hadn't died of an overdose of LSD in West's experiment, but from toxic doses of chlorpromazine and pentobarbital, the cocktail of drugs West had used to try to resuscitate him. Then Siegel announced his intention to repeat West's work. "[I cannot] let the obvious mistakes and procedural errors of [West's] 'experiment' remain uncorrected," he declared.

Twenty years after the disaster in Oklahoma, Siegel gave alternatively high and low doses of LSD to a young male adult and a female sub-adult elephant. Over the next twenty-five hours, he calculated the mean percentages of behaviors such as swaying, chirping, rocking, ear flapping and head shaking, and "inappropriate" behavior such as shallow respiration, falling over, and aggression.[7] Both elephants adopted in a "sawhorse posture," an uncoordinated stance with spread legs, characteristic of animals under the influence of hallucinogens. Early on the young male turned aggressive, snorted, and charged Siegel, but then they became dyskinetic and fell down. He then showered himself with hay.[8]

Neither elephant suffered any long-term ill effects from the LSD, lending credence to Siegel's hypothesis that the chlorpromazine and barbiturates, not the LSD, had killed Tusko. "It is concluded," Siegel wrote in a paper for the *Bulletin of the Psychonomic Society* in 1984, "that elephants can tolerate high doses of LSD but that the resultant behavior provides an unsatisfactory model for the natural aggression and behavior disorders associated with musth or temporal gland secretions."[9]

After CIA director Richard Helms ordered the destruction of all documents related to MKULTRA in 1975, the demarcation between the national intelligence effort and the national scientific effort blurred.[10] While no one has proved a connection between the CIA and the University of Oklahoma School of Medicine, Jolly West and Chester Pierce's research was consistent with other animal trials the CIA did fund, ranging from pigeons to primates to man.

And elephants. But the lessons learned from administering a gargantuan dose of LSD to an elephant didn't warrant killing an elephant and then putting two more at risk in order to test the claim that elephants were highly susceptible to LSD. Tusko died with his body and his mind racing out of control, a victim of the LSD culture of the 1960s.

The film that documents Tusko's death is in the UCLA archives but is unavailable for viewing.

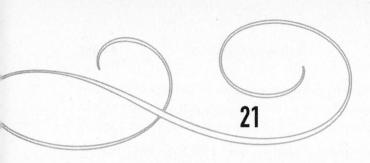

21

Seeing the Digital Elephant

◆

from the *Daily Oklahoman*, Oklahoma City, June 6, 1927

ELEPHANT COMMITS SUICIDE

Cumberland, Wis., June 26—Queen, an elephant which headed the Yankee Robinson herd, committed suicide by jumping into Beaver Dam Lake and drowning herself. It took fourteen horses to drag the carcass from the river.

◆

The Al G. Kelly & Miller Brothers Wild Animal Circus of Hugo, Oklahoma, once the king of truck circuses, bought eleven elephants between 1946 and 1950. Its first elephant, Tena, lived twenty-two years, until a bus hit her. The others, like Daisy and Anna May, shuffled in and out of the chorus line of elephant showgirls, replaceable parts in the assembly line called the circus.[1]

In 1955, Kelly-Miller bought a female—all their elephants were females—named Shirley, who'd been snatched from her family in Sumatra at the age of five, old compared to most elephant abductions. She was Kelly-Miller's sixteenth elephant, and like the others, she figured into the scheme of things more or less anonymously.

Nonetheless, Shirley managed to surface into public attention a few times over her twenty-eight years in the circus. During the Cuban Revolution in 1958, Fidel Castro's army seized her while she was touring with the circus on the island. Likely the absurdity or the impracticality of keeping an elephant hostage induced the rebels to let her go after a few days.

Shirley made the news again five years later when she was stranded aboard a burning freighter off the coast of Nova Scotia. For the 1963 season Kelly-Miller leased a ramshackle steamer so it could tour the Atlantic coast bottom to top. Its first stand in Nova Scotia was Yarmouth, on the southern tip of the province, east of the Bay of Fundy.

The *Fleurus* took four days to cross the rough seas of the bay. The bilge pumps couldn't keep up with water rushing belowdecks, so by the time the ship pulled into Yarmouth Harbor she was listing so badly the three elephants chained to the deck were struggling to stay on their feet.

The crew hoisted the animals in their crates off the ship and walked the elephants over a gangplank onto the dock. Determined to stay on schedule, Kelly-Miller put on its performance in town while the *Fleurus* pumped seawater out of its hold. By the time the show was over, the ship had been righted; the crew loaded the animals on board and made ready to sail.

As they prepared to make way, the ship's boiler over-heated and a fire broke out, spreading quickly to the deck, where the elephants were chained. Animals on board screamed and bucked as they tried desperately to escape their cages.

Frantic, the crew unloaded the animals while flames engulfed the ship. With the help of the Yarmouth Fire Department, they saved all the animals except a zebra, which burned to death. The fire scorched Shirley's leg, side, and back, and burned away half her ear.

Kelly-Miller insisted the show go on, either by truck or by rail, but it didn't go any farther than Yarmouth because the logistics of moving a circus through the Canadian Maritime Provinces quickly proved quixotic. Kelly-Miller's 1963 season was over. It rented trucks, loaded its people and stock, and left Yarmouth on a caravan down the continent.

The bull men loaded all three elephants on one truck. Ordinarily they would have chained the elephants together and to the walls and floor of the box to stabilize it, but rental trailers didn't have wall and floor anchors to hold three-quarter-inch thick chains, so they chained the elephants together and then packed them together as tightly as possible.

Two days later word came back that the trailer had turned over on a highway in New England, killing all the elephants except Shirley. She survived the truck wreck—just as she survived the shipwreck in Yarmouth and capture by rebels in Cuba—only to have Kelly-Miller decide she was bad luck, not because she was trouble, but because trouble followed her. After she served Kelly-Miller for eleven years, they sold her to another circus, one of the great elephant circuses in America: Carson & Barnes.

Carson & Barnes calls itself *Real Circus*. In 2012, it performed seven hundred shows in 250 communities in fifteen states spread across the continent. It has been home to sixty-nine elephants over the past seventy-six years. At one time it had so many elephants the keepers had to stencil their names on their foreheads to tell them apart.

Carson & Barnes was famous for being home to elephant bad girls such as Barbara, the Harry Houdini of the Elephant World, who'd run away three times in two years, twice in Wisconsin and once in the Ozarks. In Sauk City, Wisconsin, in 1977, the residents of the Maplewood Nursing Home watched incredulously as Barbara crashed through the front plate glass window and then ran out the back door, carrying the door and the jamb with her.[2] "All my life I had to travel to get to the circus," beamed one resident. "Today it finally came to me."[3]

Isa and Lily also became famous when they ran off *Thelma & Louise*–style in Choctaw County, Oklahoma. The sheriff and his posse poked around in the poison oak and bois d'arc for six days without finding them. "You could be within 25 feet of them and not see them," the sheriff said after coming up empty-handed. He'd even tried to track them with hounds, but the dogs were as befuddled as anyone.

Folks speculated about a sheriff who couldn't find two elephants in his own backyard; after all, Oklahoma was hardly a good hideout for elephants. A wiseacre put a sign on the highway that read CAUTION ELEPHANT CROSSING, and another drew a picture of a steer with big floppy ears and a trunk on the form cattlemen used to report lost or stolen cattle and sent it to the Cattlemen's Association in Oklahoma City. "It is definitely the first missing-elephant report we have ever received," said an association spokesman.[4]

Isa (pronounced "eye-za") and Lily gave birth to what must have been the first elephant knock-knock joke.

Knock, knock.
Who's there?
Isa.
Isa who?
Isa never comin' home.

On the seventh day of the search for Lily and Isa, a convict bolted from the county prison farm. "That gave the deputies something else to search for and the townspeople something else to talk about," a local newspaper noted.[5]

To keep the search going, Carson & Barnes put a $150 bounty on the errant pair and for a while the woods buzzed with motorized bikes and still they couldn't find them. The ticks and chiggers were so thick in the woods that people more or less stopped looking for them after a few days. Besides, vacation Bible school at First Baptist was starting up. People said the runaways would show up sooner or later no worse for the wear. After all, this was Oklahoma, not the Congo.

True enough, after a month of rambling around Choctaw County, Lily and Isa peacefully surrendered themselves, no worse for the wear.

Not all Carson & Barnes elephants were divas, however. Like Shirley, they lived their lives more or less to the expectations of their masters, which meant hitting their marks on time and keeping their fuss to a minimum.

Some of Carson & Barnes's elephants established emotional relationships with one another in spite of being captive. In 1973 Shirley met a traumatized calf named Jenny, who'd just been taken from her family, also in Sumatra. Frantic, she looked for her mother or her grandmothers; and instead found Shirley.

Perhaps because Shirley hadn't been abducted until she was five, she had a better-developed sense of family than calves like Jenny did. Shirley tried to fill the emotional void in Jenny's life by becoming a surrogate mother, and what she couldn't offer in terms of maternal skills, she made up for with devotion.

Sadly, the bond between them wasn't powerful enough to overcome Jenny's emotional distress, and she became so troubled that Carson & Barnes declared her a nuisance and pulled her from the circus. In a last-ditch effort to get some value from her, it sent her to the Hawthorn Corporation in Illinois to be used as a breeder.

The Hawthorn Corporation was in the business of leasing tigers and elephants to occasional users such as a community chest program that needed a live tiger for its annual gala or a county fair that wanted to give elephant rides. It also sold tigers to the pet and breeder's trade, notorious for their lack of ethical practices. Hawthorn's corporate interests were rarely for the good of their cats or elephants. (In March 2004, John Cuneo, the chief executive of Hawthorn, pled guilty to nineteen flagrant violations of the Animal Welfare Act, including "a failure to provide adequate food and water; failure to provide adequate veterinary care; failure to provide adequate shelter; and, failure to provide conditions that do not cause physical harm, unnecessary discomfort, behavioral stress, and trauma to the animals." The U.S. Department of Agriculture, charged with enforcing the Animal Welfare Act, fined Hawthorn two hundred thousand dollars and ordered Cuneo to surrender his elephants.)[6]

It was too late for Jenny. While at Hawthorn, the bull they chose to mate with her crushed her rear leg so badly she walked with a bad limp. Now unsuitable for breeding, Hawthorn returned her to Carson & Barnes, who locked her away for two years before selling her to King Royal, a small truck circus run by John "Gopher" Davenport and his wife, Gigi.

The Davenports toured Jenny for three years, living on the edge of catastrophe as they gradually exhausted their capital assets. During the summer of 1997, the USDA cited Gopher Davenport for abuse after it found the body of Heather, an eight-year-old African elephant, stuffed inside a sweltering trailer in Albuquerque, New Mexico.

The story made national headlines and outraged the public, and turned into a public crusade. Celebrities such as Kim Basinger, Ali MacGraw, and Judge Reinhold lobbied to have Davenport's license to operate a circus revoked.[7] Finally, officials in Albuquerque rescued Davenport's elephants, but by then Gopher and Gigi Davenport had abandoned Jenny in Las Vegas with a woman with terminal chronic obstructive pulmonary disease (COPD).

Betty Honn ran Animal Adoptions, a service that found new homes for domestic and wild animals in southern Nevada. She ran the shelter out of a run-down building and relied on the charity of others to donate their time and money to keep her desert ark afloat. She had dogs and cats, tigers and bears, zebras and camels, and when Gopher Davenport gave up Jenny, she had a physically and mentally handicapped elephant. Jenny was malnourished and hobbled badly on her rear leg, which had turned arthritic. She also had chronic foot rot, a major cause of elephant death.

Betty Honn was in the terminal stages of emphysema and had only months to live when she accepted Jenny. During the time she had left, Betty and her daughter nursed Jenny as best they could and looked for a suitable home for her. Weeks before Betty died in January 1997, she decided to send Jenny to Tennessee.

Shirley's later life was a carbon copy of Jenny's. After

nine years with Carson & Barnes, another elephant trampled her, dislocating the femur and tibia of her rear right
leg, causing it to jut out a sharp, awkward angle, as though
completely dislocated.[8] Either Carson & Barnes couldn't or
wouldn't set her leg—a procedure that would have required
considerable expense and time—but in any case they instead withdrew Shirley from the chorus line and sent her
to the midway to show as a freak. Two years later, Carson
& Barnes gave up on Shirley and sold her to the Louisiana
Purchase Gardens & Zoo in Monroe, Louisiana, where she
spent the next two decades in solitary confinement.[9]

Spent physically and emotionally, Shirley turned into
an emotional zombie. The Louisiana zoo was so alarmed
by Shirley's declining mental health that in 1999, it sought
professional help for her. Historically, zoos traded away
animals when they became troublesome.

The administration decided Shirley should be moved
to a sanctuary in order to salvage what was left of her life.
The administration also decided, henceforth, to stay out
of the elephant business.

The North American Regional Studbooks for Asian and African elephants are as close to a genealogy for North
American elephants as is possible. They record—in terse

language—the life histories of elephants in America starting with Jacob Crowninshield in 1796.

Shirley is listed in the Asian studbook as #525 (studbooks aren't exclusive to males). Her sire and dam are recorded as *WILD*, and her life history is condensed to four words and three dates: "SUMATRA 1953," "MILLER (???)," "MONROE 1977," and "HOHENWALD, 1999."

Hohenwald translates from the German as "high forest," although the town of Hohenwald, Tennessee, is less than a thousand feet above sea level. The official census lists the population at 3,615 residents. In 2011, Business-Week.com named Hohenwald the runner-up in Tennessee in the category of *Best Place to Raise Your Kids*.

The Natchez Trace runs by Hohenwald. "Walk in the footsteps of Andrew Jackson, Aaron Burr, Thomas Lincoln and countless other early Americans along the old Natchez Trace," reads the Lewis Country Chamber of Commerce brochure.[10] Lewis County has both Amish and Mennonite settlements, the grave of Meriwether Lewis, a general store, two wineries, and a 1960s-style commune called "the Farm," inspired—and paid for—by Stephen Gaskin from the original Haight-Ashbury scene.[11] The Lewis County Museum of Natural History, which is also located in Hohenwald, was inspired—and paid for—by Dan Maddox, once named Best Hunter in the World by both Winchester and Weatherby. Maddox's trophies—which include elephants—make up the third-largest game mount collection in North America.

The Elephant Sanctuary in Tennessee.

Ten miles northwest of the museum is the Elephant Sanctuary, home to one of the largest herds of elephants in the New World. It's not a zoo or a circus or a wild animal park. It has no water slide, no concession stands, and no performing animals; in fact, the public isn't welcome. Anyone driving by the Elephant Sanctuary wouldn't know fourteen elephants were roaming the loblolly pines nearby.

The Elephant Sanctuary is a refuge for old, sick, and abused elephants. Established in 1995, its mission is to let elephants live as free of human domination as possible. They no longer have to work as performers or act as objects of curiosity; instead, they can spend their days bathing in the ponds, foraging the meadows, and roaming unfettered except for the fence that encloses the 2,700-acre refuge.

Shirley arrived in Hohenwald on July 6, 1999, with Solomon James, Jr., who had been her keeper in Louisiana for twenty-two years. Solomon James's relationship to Shirley was much like Matthew Scott's relationship to Jumbo: he was emotionally invested in her and had mixed feelings about letting go. His emotional farewell to Shirley is documented in *The Urban Elephant*, a film produced by Allison Argo for the PBS series *Nature* in 2001, clips of which are available on YouTube.[12] "I don't know who's [*sic*] the first to put a chain on her," says James wistfully as he lets Shirley go, "but I'm glad to know . . . that I'll be the last to take it off."

Upon her arrival in Hohenwald, Shirley ate a watermelon, took a shower, and rested while Carol Buckley, the cofounder of the Elephant Sanctuary, brought in Tarra to introduce to Shirley. She was the first elephant Shirley had seen in nearly a quarter century.

Buckley had used Tarra to greet Jenny when she came to Tennessee. She had calmed her as she "gently stroked Jenny's head with her trunk and finally coaxed her to entwine trunks." The moment was so moving, wrote Buckley, that everyone "watched through tears of relief and joy at this obvious display of comfort and love."[13]

Now Buckley wanted Tarra to reach out to Shirley so she could finally reconnect with her species. The twenty-five-year-old, herself a veteran of multiple circuses, zoos, and a safari park, walked to the gate separating her from

Shirley and reached between the bars with her trunk. Shirley joined Tarra at the gate, intertwining her trunk with Tarra's. Their connection was immediate and intimate as Shirley took Tarra's trunk and guided it to the wounds on her body as though she were relating her personal history.[14] Tarra "purred" as she gently rubbed her trunk against them. Solomon James wept.

All hell broke loose that evening when Jenny returned to the barn. Even after two decades, she recognized Shirley on the spot. "Jenny wanted to get into the stall with Shirley desperately," wrote Buckley. "She became agitated, banging on the gate and trying to climb through and over. After several minutes of touching and exploring each other, Shirley started to ROAR and I mean ROAR—Jenny joined in immediately. The interaction was dramatic, to say the least, with both elephants trying to climb in with each other and frantically touching each other through the bars. I have never experienced anything even close to this depth of emotion."[15] Shirley and Jenny bent the gate so badly the staff barely managed to open it so the girls could join one another. "They are as one bonded physically together," Buckley said. "One moves, and the other moves in unison."

The next day Shirley and Jenny spent the day side by side. "[A]nd when Jenny lay down, Shirley straddled her in the most obvious protective manner and shaded her body from the sun and harm."[16] The two spent the next six years together, until Jenny died of bacterial sepsis at the age of thirty-four, in what should have been the prime of her life.[17]

Shirley at age sixty-five, her ear burned away from the shipwreck fire and her right rear leg damaged from a botched attempt to breed her.

The Elephant Sanctuary is divided into three parts: Asia, Africa, and Q. The Asians are separated from the Africans because they don't mix well socially. Circuses and zoos threw them together even though the species speak and act in very different ways. For example, Asians are typically more taciturn than Africans, who do crazy things like knock down trees for the fun of it. The Asians mistake the Africans' physical exuberance for aggression and it makes them uncomfortable, so the Africans live in Africa and the Asians live in Asia.

Q stands for *Quarantine*. Between 1994 and 2010, fifty elephants—about one in eight of all elephants in America—tested positive for tuberculosis.[18] The disease usually expresses itself through the lungs but sometimes it infects the spine, the kidneys, or the lymph glands. Tuberculosis wastes the life force, making breathing and moving increasingly difficult. Elephants catch tuberculosis from people. Then they spread the disease to each other, and sometimes they give it back to humans.[19]

Free to range unchecked in a population, tuberculosis can turn endemic or even pandemic, a "hyper-disease" that can threaten the existence of an entire species. In 2006, biologists Bruce Rothschild and Richard Laub discovered TB bone lesions in more than half of the mastodon skeletons in North America and concluded that "virtually every late Ice Age mastodon in North America had tuberculosis," and that it likely contributed to their extinction.[20]

When the USDA's Animal and Plant Health Inspection Service (APHIS) ordered the Hawthorn Corporation to surrender its elephants in 2006, all sixteen had been exposed to *Mycobacterium tuberculosis*. Two died before they could even get on a truck to leave; of the remaining fourteen, one went to Oklahoma, one to Texas, two to California, and ten to Tennessee. Of the ten who went to Tennessee, three died, one was pronounced cured, and the six others are still in Q.[21]

As unlikely a person as you would expect to meet in rural Tennessee, Rob Atkinson was the CEO, or as the staff calls it, the Chief Elephant Officer of the Elephant Sanctuary. A Brit, he quit as the head of wildlife for the Royal Society for the Prevention of Cruelty to Animals to head the largest elephant sanctuary in North America. A large, tall man, he stands out in a crowd, and his English accent makes him seem out of synch with what you'd expect in Hohenwald. Raised in the West Midlands of Herefordshire, he can talk farming and livestock as well as anyone.

But Hohenwald had long since grown tolerant if not accepting of the Chinese, Mexicans, hippies, and winemakers who've moved there, so Atkinson's arrival hardly ruffled a feather.

In 2010 the Elephant Sanctuary moved into a restored crumbling brick building in downtown Hohenwald that now houses offices, an operations center, a store, and a large public space to give talks, show films, and put on shows about elephants for schoolchildren who come by the busload from the counties. The walls inside the Elephant Sanctuary on West Main are lined with crayoned portraits of orange and purple elephants, bursting with flowers and fireworks. Rob Atkinson is like one of those

Rob Atkinson.

elephants, large, endearing, a bit off-color, and the focus of the lives of a lot of local people.

Atkinson and his people practice a management style that not only protects elephants from humans, but also humans from elephants. Actuarial studies reveal that the profession of elephant keeper is more dangerous than deep-sea trawler fishing. Using the same research method as Stephen Roberts in his study of the most dangerous oc-

cupations in Great Britain, Atkinson, who holds a doctorate in zoology from Oxford, found elephant keeping 48.6
times more hazardous than the average job.[22] Another research team reached the same conclusion with its finding
that an elephant handler was three times more likely to
die on the job than someone in the next most dangerous
occupation, coal mining. "If you don't like those kind of
odds," the authors comment, "you could reduce your risk
by joining the police force or fire department."[23]

To mitigate this danger, the Elephant Sanctuary employs a method of interaction with elephants called Protected Contact. The core philosophy of PC, as the system
is known, is to minimize human contact with elephants
by giving them the space and the freedom to act as they
choose and still provide them critical care. By minimizing control over the elephants, they are free to live as
normal life as circumstances allow, circumstances that are
in many cases no less deficient than the spaces available to
them on African or Asian reserves and parks.

The alternative method to Protected Contact is Free
Contact, or FC. FC employs the model of dominance
through the use of a master (a bull man or a mahout) and
a bullhook or an electric prod, devices that foster violence in both people and elephants. Circuses still use Free
Contact, as do many zoos, although Protected Contact
has been gaining managerial sway. With a mandate to
develop techniques that rely on positive rather than negative reinforcement, the Elephant Sanctuary broke from
Free Contact altogether in 2006 after Winkie knocked

Protected Contact.

down caregiver Joanna Burke and stepped on her, killing her instantly.

Today, no one works with elephants without insuperable barriers between them. The chain link that surrounds the perimeter of more than four square miles of the sanctuary doesn't betray the fortress-sized defenses that cross the property. Steel girders and cable strong enough to stand up to the full force of an agitated elephant separate humans from elephants, but not in a way that stops the animals from interacting with each other through voice and touch.

Steve Smith, the director of Animal Husbandry at the Elephant Sanctuary and one of a contingent of thirteen caregivers, spends his days either with the elephants or preparing for them, such as fixing their individually formulated meals.

In spite of plentiful grazing, the elephants rarely miss a meal at the barns. The lure of grains, fresh fruits and vegetables, and an occasional molasses ball is too strong to resist. And each time an elephant returns to the barn, she reopens the discussion about what's going on in her physical and emotional life.

It also gives the caregivers time to tend to their physical needs, especially their feet and their teeth, which are particularly susceptible to disease. Instead of using a bullhook to position the elephants for care, however, Smith uses a device that looks like an eight-foot Q-tip called a target pole, which is as soft as the bullhook is hard and as blunted as the bullhook is sharp. A target pole doesn't demand an elephant do a thing by jabbing or poking, but rather asks politely (and repeatedly when necessary). If she complies, the caregivers shower her with praise and generous helpings of fresh fruits and vegetables, and while she munches happily on her bounty, her caregiver smears salve on her sores, tends her feet, and periodically takes blood to check for tuberculosis. This style has dramatically reduced stress and injuries in both elephants and humans.

However much Hohenwald may be "high forest," it isn't heaven. The Elephant Sanctuary in Tennessee consists of fourteen aging spinsters in a retirement home who share similar psychopathologies, including, some argue, PTSD.

Gay A. Bradshaw is a trans-species psychologist who holds two doctorates, one in forest ecology from Oregon State, the other in "depth psychology" from Pacifica Graduate University, where she wrote the dissertation "Elephant Trauma and Recovery: From Human Violence to Trans-Species Psychology." The Kerulos Center, a not-for-profit 501(c)3 in southern Oregon founded by Bradshaw in 2008, defines trans-species psychology as the "science of sentience grounded in the concept of oneness with nature." Her work focuses on elephants she has diagnosed with PTSD.

Originally Bradshaw's poster child was Delhi, #285 in the *AZA Elephant Studbook*. Born in India in 1946, she'd been abducted as an infant and sold to an American circus before the age of one. After serving for twenty-seven years, the Hamid-Morton Circus of Egg Harbor Township, New Jersey, sold Delhi to the Hawthorn Corporation, which for thirty-two years kept her chained inside a windowless barn when she wasn't rented out. She developed advanced osteomyelitis, a life-threatening bone disease that particularly affects the toes and makes standing painful.[24]

The Department of Agriculture finally confiscated Delhi after her Hawthorn keeper chemically burned her feet by submerging them in pure formaldehyde in an ill-advised attempt to treat them. Delhi was nearly dead by the time she reached Tennessee.

The Elephant Sanctuary gave her palliative care so she could spend her final days free of pain, but Delhi remained alive for five years. During that time Gay Bradshaw diagnosed her with PTSD. "We should look at the person Delhi has been," she explains, "a person who went through horrific ordeals, [and] survived. . . . "[25] Bradshaw believes, as do others, that elephants suffer the same symptoms of PTSD as people and that they respond the same way to therapy.

If indeed the two species share similar psychologies when it comes to grief, joy, love, altruism, and other emotions we normally associate with the human condition, then it may be possible—perhaps likely—that our species share similar if not identical clinical pathologies. At a minimum the symptoms of psychopathy express themselves in correlative states, which means a diagnosis of PTSD for a "shell-shocked" elephant might not be so far-fetched.

Today Billy replaces Delhi as the national poster child for PTSD. After coming to the Los Angeles Zoo in 1989 at the age of four, Billy and another four-year-old named Becky were replacements for McClean and Sage, African bush elephants who'd died at the zoo. (McClean died after falling into a moat and Sage died when the zoo put her down after she became crippled.[26]) For seventeen years Billy lived with Becky, Calle, Rosie, Tess, and Ruby, and one by one they disappeared until only Billy was left. For three years Billy stood by himself on a barren half acre as hard as concrete. He had no dirt to kick, no water to splash, and after Ruby left in 2003, no one to keep him company. All Billy could do was stare at the lush foliage just out of reach.

He started to bob his head. He started with two or three quick vertical shakes of the head that turned into ten shakes and a meaningless obsessive behavior. When visitors asked zoo tour leaders why Billy was acting so strangely, they made up explanations such as *Billy is rapping to his iPod*.[27] (Officially, the zoo explained his head bobbing as "a comforting or thumb-sucking behavior" that he exhibited when it was getting close to dinner or when his keepers came by to visit.[28])

Scientists describe this aberrant behavior as stereotypy, a compensating neurosis that expresses itself through obsessive behavior, a frequent reaction to extreme boredom. Confined to sensory-poor environments long enough, elephants rock, weave, bob, nod their heads, or toss their trunks repeatedly. Until recently, the definition of stereotypy was the display of repetitive, unvarying behavior with no *obvious* goal or function. Science has since discovered that the function of stereotypy is to raise the body's production of endogenous opioids and lower the production of cortisol, which in turn slows the heart.[29] In other words, Billy was self-medicating.

In 2006 a variety of Los Angeles citizens banded into action groups to get Billy out of the zoo and up to the

PAWS elephant sanctuary near Sacramento so he could join Ruby. In the spirit of the FREE WILLY campaign of the early nineties, they campaigned to FREE BILLY.

Meanwhile, the Los Angeles Zoo proposed its own solution: expand the elephant exhibit and add more elephants. It presented plans to the City Council for a $42 million world-class elephant facility to be built on 3.5 acres that could house as many as eleven elephants.[30] Supporters of the Pachyderm Forest, as it was to be called, predicted it would become "an important part of the shared vision to make the Los Angeles Zoo a gem among the great cultural attractions in this City." More important, it would serve the important function of creating "memories for the children of Los Angeles, memories upon which an appreciation for wildlife and wild places will be built."[31]

In 2006, in a 13–2 vote, the Los Angeles City Council approved Pachyderm Forest and appropriated $12 million to begin construction. Bob Barker, animal rights activist and the former host of the television daytime show *The Price Is Right*, led the attack against the Pachyderm Forest. "Let's do get Billy out of that zoo," he pledged. "Let's do close the elephant exhibit at the zoo. Zoos . . . all over the world are closing elephant exhibits. Everybody knows that's passé." Other cries went up. "If it's illegal for us to profit from the trade in ivory," proclaimed one, "then it should be illegal for us to profit from the enslavement of elephants."[32]

On October 8, 2008, City Councilman Tony Cardenas reversed his opinion about building the Pachyderm

Forest. "After uncovering information it has come to my attention that many facts were not presented [in 2006]," he said in a press release, "and after reviewing medical records one thing is clear, elephants don't live in zoos, they die in zoos." He felt it was time for Los Angeles to join the other cities in the United States who'd shut down their elephant exhibits. Cardenas called for the council to halt construction of the Pachyderm Forest and instead use the unused funds to build a municipal elephant sanctuary in San Fernando Valley. "If we are going to tout ourselves as one of the most compassionate cities towards animals," he said, "then we can no longer turn a blind eye on the suffering of elephants."[33]

Cardenas's defection sent shock waves through the community. During the public comment phase in January 2009, Hollywood A-list celebrities such as Halle Berry, Cher, Madeleine Stowe, and Lily Tomlin weighed in on the cruel nature of Billy's captivity. "I'm not a fanatic, just an animal lover," Cher told the City Council. "[They say] it's always been done this way, there have always been elephants in the city zoos throughout history . . . and that's what makes it right. It doesn't make it right," she said, and then added, "We've had other things that we're ashamed of. We've had slavery, you know. It wasn't right."[34]

Kenyan author and elephant conservationist Daphne Sheldrick entered the fray from her home in Kenya. "I have spent 50 years of my life working with elephants and have hand-reared more than 90 from infancy," she wrote in the *Los Angeles Times*, "so I feel qualified to offer some advice." She begged the council to "extend compassion" and let Billy join Ruby in San Andreas. "Like humans," she pleaded, "they need the companionship and comfort of friends."[35]

But wild animal television host and former zookeeper Jack Hannah disagreed. "If this small group of activists has its way, Billy will be shipped off to an elite area hundreds of miles from Los Angeles," he said, appealing directly to Angelenos. "There it costs $200 a person to visit Billy, and then only on select days. In Los Angeles, a day at the zoo can be enjoyed year-round for roughly what it costs to see a movie. Billy would become inaccessible to Southern California's working-class families, the 20,000 schoolchildren who visit him at the zoo each month and the millions of future visitors who come to learn about the Earth's largest land mammal." He went on to say the Pachyderm Forest was right for Billy. "I can unequivocally say that if you can find a better home for elephants than the Pachyderm Forest, I'd love to see it." With two pools and a waterfall, and a "roaming area larger than the playing field at Dodger Stadium," it would provide "the kind of nurturing and healthcare elephants at an alternative location simply can't get."[36]

Hector Tovar, a columnist for the *Times*, agreed with Hannah. Moving Billy to a sanctuary "might be good for Billy, but it would be a disaster for the zoo." "A subtraction" of Billy—indeed, any animal—hurt everyone, but most of all it hurt the children. Tovar asked outright, "If a city government can shift direction for the sake of an elephant, I thought, why can't it also bend, shift and compromise for its children?"[37]

Celebrity sweetheart Betty White, a longtime supporter of the zoo, teamed up improbably with Saul Hudson, better known as Slash, former lead guitarist for Guns N' Roses, to make a video urging people to support the Pachyderm Forest. "We're right on the cusp of getting our magnificent elephant exhibit, and there's a group of people who are trying to stop it," says White in her video. "For people to say they're animal lovers and want to shut these animals out of zoos and let them die—as they say, 'die with dignity'—doesn't make sense to me." Slash agrees. "It seems to me that zoos are the one safe haven for animals at this point."[38]

While some pursued the question of humaneness in the court of public opinion, others pursued it in the court of legal opinion. In 2007 actor Robert Culp (costar of the television series *I Spy*) and Los Angeles real estate mogul Aaron Leider sued Los Angeles to halt construction of the exhibit based upon a "taxpayer waste" statute that provided injunctive relief to stop fraud, waste, or injury to public property.[39] Culp and Leider called the Pachyderm Forest "a shameless political boondoggle," and Bob Barker quipped, "The Price is definitely not Right."

Culp and Leider cited the zoo's dismal history with elephants as a wanton waste of life and taxpayers' money. "Since 1975, thirteen (13) elephants have died at the zoo and half of those did not live to the age of 20," their motion reads. "Zoos can not accommodate the basic physical and psychological needs of elephant's [sic] in captivity."[40]

In 2008, Los Angeles Superior Court judge John Shepard Wiley threw the case out of court for lack of legal merit. Leider appealed.

In January 2009, the Los Angeles City Council voted 11–4 to keep Billy and finish construction of the Pachyderm Forest. "Today is a victory for science, zoo visitors, staff, volunteers, donors and most importantly elephant welfare," zoo director John R. Lewis announced. "We eagerly await the completion of the Pachyderm Forest so we may finish a world class habitat for elephants that will educate and inspire over a million zoo visitors a year."[41]

The following year the Second District Court of Appeal reversed Judge Wiley's decision and ordered that *Leider v. Lewis* be tried.[42] But delays kept the trial out of the courtroom for years. The Pachyderm Forest opened in December 2010, renamed Elephants of Asia, home to Billy and two Asian spinsters, Tina and Jewel, whom federal marshals had seized from Maximus Tons of Fun in Leggett, Texas, after charging the Davenport family with nineteen violations of the Animal Welfare Act.

Today Billy, Tina, and Jewel spend their days in the Patti & Stanley Silver Deep Water Pool or by Elephant Lake, a gift from the Winnick Family Foundation. Guests to Elephants of Asia can also travel to the Cardamom Mountains courtesy of the Fritz B. Burns Foundation and learn about the plight of elephants in Cambodia. "When you visit the Elephants of Asia," says the Los Angeles Zoo, "you will have the opportunity to make a contribution towards the conservation of Asian elephants in Cambodia."[43]

This personal appeal to participate in conservation action constitutes one of the foundation blocks of why zoos claim social relevance. People removed from the tragedies of Africa and Asia get involved emotionally when they see Billy, Tina, and Jewel plead for their brethren in Cambodia, and so they give money to help the cause. So far the Los Angeles Zoo has sent fifty thousand dollars over ten years to help the elephants in Cambodia. The money goes to Flora and Fauna International, a charity registered in Great Britain, whose mission is to balance the needs of people with the needs of threatened species.[44] The Cambodian Elephant Conservation Group of Flora and Fauna International works with the Royal Government of Cambodia to create, manage, and develop the needs of the last elephants in Cambodia, most of whom live in the Cardamom Mountains. Estimates of the number of residual elephants in Cambodia range between two hundred and six hundred.[45]

The Association of Zoos and Aquariums is a self-regulating network "of more than 6,000 committed zoo and aquarium professionals, organizations, and suppliers world-wide."[46] To become a member of the AZA, one must comply with the ideology that governs the body and demonstrate compliance by submitting to a rigorous investigation of one's company's financial and performance records. Those who violate the AZA's code of ethics may be reprimanded or sanctioned, and in severe cases, denied certification and ejected from the organization.

In 2011, the AZA sponsored a Harris Interactive Poll, which collects data that "measure, and trend, the knowledge, opinions, behaviors and motivation of the general public."[47] Using "advanced quantitative methods," the poll seeks to demonstrate that elephants are powerful instruments for conservation. The poll finds that 95 percent of people who go to zoos agree with the statement "seeing elephants in zoos helps people appreciate them more." Eighty-six percent of the respondents also agree with the statement "visiting zoos encourages people to donate time and/or money to elephant conservation."[48] Often quoting the poll verbatim, AZA members frequently point to these results as a justification for the animals' captivity.

Four years earlier the AZA published a larger, more comprehensive study, funded by the National Science Foundation, that reached a different conclusion. In contradiction to the Harris Poll, the NSF study of "Why Zoos Matter" found that only 54 percent of visitors to zoos and aquariums said they felt "a stronger sense that they were part of the solution to environmental problems and conservation action" as a result of going to a zoo or aquarium. And, answering a question about the role zoos play in education, only 39 percent of visitors felt zoos played a positive role.[49]

The dramatic difference between studies likely has to do with constitutional flaws in the studies themselves, rather than with the lesson that "advanced quantitative methods" don't always produce definitive results. Ambiguity remains a ghost in the machine that can't be purged. One assumes, in order to give the benefit of doubt, that elephants serve some good by teaching people about their ecological crisis and prompting them to take action. One also assumes, at least implicitly, some turning of the tide in the fight against extinction or at least some gaining of ground. In spite of claims to the contrary, however, the money the Los Angeles Zoo gives to elephant programs in Cambodia isn't enough to create meaningful change.

In fairness, the amount of money needed to fund research, provide security, develop education programs, and recompense the victims of elephant violence is beyond the financial capacity of any zoo. And yet American zoos have $200 million worth of construction upgrades planned for their elephant exhibits over the coming decade. Given that the total habitat of elephants in American zoos is about a third of a square mile—with most living on lots of a half-acre or less—the expenditure averages $445,000 for each elephant in captivity in a population density of 1,200 per square mile. In comparison, the annual budget for the *entire* Kenyan Wildlife Service is about $30 million, only a portion of which goes to manage, research, and monitor the 36,000 elephants who live in the country's forty national parks and reserves. Tsavo National Park alone, which is home to a third of Kenya's elephants, is 18,000 square miles, an area larger than Switzerland, and has a population density of less than one elephant per square mile.[50]

The proposition that zoos spend $200 million to upgrade its exhibits begs the question of how much impact that much money might have on the crisis in Cambodia—or anywhere—but a more appropriate question would be to ask what progress these conservation groups have made with the total amount of dollars that zoos actually contribute.

The North Carolina Zoo provides a case study of partnerships between zoos and an on-the-ground conservation organization. In 1996, the zoo signed a memorandum of agreement with the World Wildlife Fund "to reduce both impacts on the human population (injuries and crop losses) and the killing of elephants" in the West African nation of Cameroon.[51] In 2009, Dr. David Jones, the director of the North Carolina Zoo, made a video called *Saving Earth's Largest Land Mammal*, in which he explains the threats facing elephants in Cameroon today, including meat and ivory poachers and locals killing them in retribution for raiding their crops, tearing up irrigation pipes, and wrecking equipment.[52] By tracking the elephants, managers hope to better manage the volatile interfaces between human and animal ranges.

Whatever incremental progress the program may have

made over the past sixteen years was wiped out in early 2012 when bandits rode six hundred miles on horse and camelback across Sudan and Chad into Cameroon and killed half of the four hundred elephants in the Bouba N'Djida reserve—as much as 20 percent of all elephants in Cameroon.[53] They hacked out their ivory with machetes and left their bodies to rot in the equatorial sun. (The same thing happened in Sierra Leone in 2009 when poachers took advantage of a country in the middle of a civil war and decimated the country's largest elephant herd.) The risk the poachers ran was virtually nil since 80 percent of the elephant range in all of Africa is unprotected, and much of the rest is poorly protected because there isn't enough money to police the elephants adequately.[54]

Elephants once roamed 3.5 million square miles from West Asia along the Iranian coast into the Indian subcontinent, eastward into Southeast Asia and China. Today, they are extinct in West Asia, Java, and most of China. Their habitat has shrunk to 187,000 square miles, broken up across thirteen countries, seven of which have elephant populations smaller than a thousand.

Fifty-one countries host native populations of elephants. Most count their herds in hundreds, not thousands.

The thirteen range nations of West Africa[55] share a total of 7,745 elephants.[56] Half these countries have relict elephant populations numbering less than two hundred. Niger has eighty-five elephants; Togo has four; and Senegal has one.[57]

In other places there are too many elephants to count. Kruger National Park in South Africa estimated in 2012 it had more than thirteen thousand elephants, nearly twice the number the park felt it could carry without harm to other plant and animal species. South Africa outlawed culling as a management practice in 1994, and in the years since then, elephants have swollen to such numbers that officials have knocked down border fences to let the elephants out of the park, renewing the discussion for the need to cull.

In places like Zimbabwe and Kenya, elephants who compete with people for the resources of their ecosystem have been reclassified as pests.[58] The problem became so serious in Kenya that the Kenya Wildlife Service formed a hit squad called Animal Control, which shoots persistent offenders. The Species Survival Commission's African Elephant Specialist Group of the International Union for Conservation of Nature calls human-elephant conflict "a major threat to long-term survival of the species."[59] Charts now routinely map the number of elephant incidents per square kilometer per year as people and elephants overrun each other while politicians and scientists mull what to do.

Aaron Leider's suit finally proceeded to trial in the summer of 2012. Experts testified for six straight days. Attorney for the plaintiff David Casselman showed pictures of Billy's decrepit feet and explained that the painful condition was the result of standing for years on hard-packed dirt. The zoo's low regard for their well-being, he argued, passed the threshold of inhumane.

Deputy City Attorney John Carvalho rebutted Casselman by claiming Billy's foot condition was a sign of age, not abuse. He also defended the zoo's treatment of its elephants and the $42 million it had spent on Elephants of Asia. "The evidence will show," he presented in his opening argument, "that the elephants at the exhibit are pampered, they are protected, they are well cared for and, yes, they are loved." He said the elephants lived privileged lives, with daily pedicures and an animal psychiatrist on call. "If only people were treated so well," Carvalho said.[60]

Generally people don't think a lot about animal rights. For many Christians and Jews the Bible settles the issue definitively in Genesis 1, in which God gives humans the right to exploit "every living thing that moveth upon the earth." More and more, however, people turn to Genesis 2, in which God tasks humanity with the responsibility "to dress and keep" his world. Zoos not only teach about nature by letting people experience it vicariously; they also confirm people's moral obligation to protect it.

People care that animals are treated humanely, and they respond viscerally to accusations of abuse. Every year they contribute countless millions of dollars to rescue everything from dogs and cats to horses, bats, and potbellied pigs. And when the Internet made it possible for hundreds of millions of people to connect with their interests and passions online in real time, they started to chat and blog—creating their own narratives—and launching their own crusades. Citizen watchdog groups reported suspected abuse and expert witnesses testified that the elephants were subject to systematic physical and mental abuse. Some campaigns were sophisticated and were sponsored by political action committees such as the American Humane Association, the ASPCA, World Wildlife Fund, the Wildlife Conservation Society, Defenders of Wildlife, and People for the Ethical Treatment of Animals. More spontaneous campaigns, such as SAVE BILLY, came from the grass roots.

Most people agree animals should be treated humanely, but not everyone agrees what that means. For example, when it came to the question of deciding what constituted a humane amount of space for a captive elephant, the American Zoo Association, although conceding "space may be important for elephants," argued that the assumption that *larger means better* was largely untested, and that until valid scientific studies could confirm the minimum amount of space necessary to fulfill the physical and psychological needs of a captive elephant, the question of space remains open to interpretation.[61] Still, the AZA argues the *quality* of space is more important than its *quantity*. In other words, space doesn't matter provided you have enough distractions to keep the elephants busy and therefore sane.

This point of view is counterintuitive to those who see space as a critical function of quality. In Tsavo National Park, Kenya, an elephant averages 1.5 square miles of range, roughly two thousand times the space available to a captive elephant in America.[62] The U.S. Fish & Wildlife Service estimates an elephant requires "a living space" of eighty square miles.[63] It follows, if only intuitively, that a humane space would have to be larger than a half acre, and at least large enough to give an elephant a semblance of a normal life.

The elephant industry doesn't focus its research on the relevance of space to physical and psychological health, however. Rather, it focuses on improving elephant reproduction. Corporate research centers such as the Endangered Ark Foundation (founded by Carson & Barnes Circus) and the Center for Elephant Conservation (CEC; founded by Ringling Bros., Barnum & Bailey) dedicate themselves to "acquire and save threatened and endangered animals" by developing science to sustain captive and wild populations through artificial insemination.[64] Over the past twenty-two years, the CEC has produced twenty-five live elephant births, which it points to as evidence of progress.[65]

The International Union for Conservation of Nature disagrees. The Asian and African elephant specialist groups in the Species Survival Commission of the IUCN criticize the general failure of breeding programs worldwide, stating bluntly that captive breeding "does not see any contribution to the effective conservation of the species."[66] Artificial insemination, for reasons not clear, produces a heavy predominance of males (83 percent), a figure opposite what circuses and zoos wanted.

On July 23, 2012, at 3:35 p.m., Los Angeles Superior Court judge John L. Segal issued a fifty-six-page, strongly worded ruling regarding Aaron Leider's petition to shut down Los Angeles's Elephants of Asia exhibit for being inhumane and a waste of taxpayer money. "Contrary to what the zoo's representative may have told the Los Angeles City Council in order to get construction of the $42 million exhibit approved and funded," Judge Segal wrote, life for Billy, Tina, and Jewel "is empty, purposeless, boring, and occasionally painful." And if any thought otherwise, he added, they were "delusional."

Judge Segal stopped short of closing down the exhibit because the zoo's mistreatment didn't meet the standard of cruelty "beyond the 'ordinary' circumstance of captivity." In his decision, however, Segal broached the question of "whether the recreational or perhaps educational needs of one intelligent mammal species outweigh the physical and emotional, if not survival, needs of another." Unfortunately, however, Judge Segal decided California law could not provide relief. Given the lack of scientific

evidence to establish the minimum amount of space necessary for a captive elephant, the court couldn't find in
favor of claims of abuse.[67]

However, Segal was emphatic that the elephants
weren't receiving proper care. Rejecting the zoo's senior
elephant keeper's claim that Billy's head-bobbing was
"like a dog wagging its tail when his or her master ar-
rives home," the judge accused her of perpetuating "the
anthropomorphic fantasy that elephants are happy to see
her and live their lives in captivity." Rather, Billy's obsessive head-bobbing was obvious "evidence that Billy is
stressed, frustrated, unanimated, and unhappy, and that
the zoo is not meeting his needs."

He also admonished the zoo for systemic ignorance.
"[The elephants'] lives are supervised, managed, and controlled by zoo employees who appear to be in the dark
about normal and abnormal behavior of elephants, in denial about the physical and emotional difficulties of the
elephants they manage and whose lives they control, and
under the misconception that the elephants prefer to live
their lives in an exhibit with human companions rather
than with other elephants," he wrote in his findings. "The
elephants are hardly, as defendants contend, 'thriving.'"

Segal issued injunctions that prohibit the zoo from
further use of a bullhook or an electric prod, and ordered
the zoo to exercise its elephants at least two hours a day,
weather permitting.[68]

Within hours of his decision, people were leaving
posts on local websites. "Now there is proof," PetPeeves

wrote, "and like the circus we have all been lied to—the AZA hates sanctuaries because sanctuaries prove what the elephants need and no zoo can do that. THIS the AZA does not want people to know."

ZooCares shot back, "Hey PetPeeves, guess what? Your side of this dispute LOST. The exhhibit [*sic*] is staying OPEN. Reading your post makes me wonder—did you even bother to read the article?"

Time2Reflect added two hours later, "There are many issues that were brought up in this trial, but what stands out to me is an overall negative campaign against zoos in general with the LA Zoo playing the role of punching bag for those who say a sanctuary is the only answer."[69]

The hostility between zoos and sanctuaries constantly verged on feud. Each side accused the other of intentionally misleading the public when it came to telling "the truth" about the other. Their mutual antipathy came into sharp focus in 2012 when the Toronto City Council declared that city zoo's elephant exhibit inhumane and ordered it shut down. The council then directed zoo personnel to find homes for Iringa, Toka, and Thika in a warmer climate with more space.[70]

As a member of the Canadian AZA, the zoo tried to adhere to AZA guidelines by finding the elephants homes in other accredited institutions but failed to place them in the time allotted by the City Council, so the council ordered the zoo to send its elephants to the PAWS sanctuary in California, a decision that ignited a firestorm of controversy.

The AZA reacted to the City Council's action by threatening to revoke the zoo's accreditation for not following its code of professional ethics, which included not dealing with unaccredited institutions such as PAWS. When a councilman denounced the AZA's intrusion into city affairs, the *Toronto Star* shot back, "But that's the organization's job. Since in its view it is unacceptable to send elephants to an unaccredited facility, the AZA's action should come as no surprise."

Tension boiled over. The mayor accused the City Council of "making policy on the fly" rather than deferring to experts who cautioned against the consequences of a rash decision, and the *Star* sided with the mayor. "Zoo officials are in the best position to conduct such an analysis, not councilors," it chided under the snide headline "The Toronto Zoo's departing elephants have squashed its accreditation. Thanks, Bob Barker." (Barker had offered to pay the cost of flying the elephants to California in order to deflect the objection that the city should not pay such a large expense.) In its editorial view the council's decision had cost the zoo its professional reputation, which would in turn have negative repercussions for the city.[71]

The Toronto City Council stuck to its guns. "We've had four elephants die at the Toronto Zoo in recent years, primarily from being in captivity," a councilor told the press; the time had come to take action.[72] Iringa, Toka, and Thika were going to California.

The AZA stripped the Toronto Zoo of its accreditation after it had been a member in good standing for thirty-seven years. Pat Derby, the cofounder of PAWS, bristled at the AZA's claim it was maintaining rigorous professional standards. "If the AZA's standards were meaningful," she rebutted, "the zoo would have lost its accreditation years ago for keeping multiple elephants in a barren, confined space with no opportunity to express basic elephant behavior."[73]

Toronto became ground zero of the struggle between the AZA and sanctuaries. Pro-AZA forces argued the zoo should reapply for admission—an exiled member may reapply after a year provided it is in full compliance—which meant the city would have to reverse its decision to send its elephants to a sanctuary and find homes for them in other AZA zoos.

Pro-sanctuary forces argued that the question about PAWS not being accredited was a red herring. It *was* accredited, just not by the AZA. The Global Federation of Animal Sanctuaries (GFAS) is a network of animal sanctuaries, orphanages, rescue centers, and shelters around the world with its own criteria for accreditation. But the AZA does not recognize GFAS accreditation. When seen through a political filter, the question wasn't about accreditation as much as it was about whose accreditation mattered more.

The sniping between factions went on for months while Iringa, Toka, and Thika waited for things to sort out. Slowly, however, it became clear the elephants were going to California. The city took up Bob Barker on his offer to fly the elephants there, and true to his word he rented a Russian cargo jet with a bay big enough to hold three steel transport crates, each the size of a railroad car.[74]

The first of the custom-made crates arrived on February 27, 2012. With a departure date set for August, the zookeepers turned their attention to training the girls to go willingly into their boxes.

In August, two days before the elephants were scheduled to leave for California, the city suffered a "heat wave," with temperatures hovering around 29 degrees Celsius (84.2 Fahrenheit). So rather than expose the elephants to more stress, they decided to wait for cooler weather. September maybe.[75]

That November, the elephants were still in Toronto. The City Council officially reaffirmed its intent to move the elephants to California. "I think it's disappointing," said John Tracogna, the zoo's chief executive officer, of the council's decision, "but we also have to accept the decision of council and move on."[76]

More than a year after the decision in 2012 to transfer the trio of elephants to PAWS, the elephants continue to await transfer to California.[77]

At seventy-one, Lydia is the oldest elephant in America. In summers she gives rides to children at the Wild Kingdom Zoo and Fun Park in York, Maine. The USDA has cited her owner thirty-one times for failing to provide "veterinary care, shelter from the elements, adequate ventilation in the transport trailer, and proper food storage" and for other infractions.[78]

The second-oldest elephant in America lives in "retirement" at the Wild Adventures Animal Park in Valdosta, Georgia. To stay busy, she paints pictures for the theme park's Safari Outfitters and Adventure Emporium, which retails original art by her, a rhinoceros, a peacock, and a porcupine. The Emporium also sells exotic compost called "Zoo Poo."[79]

Born in 1948, Shirley in Tennessee is the third oldest.[80] Her dislocated leg still juts out an awkward angle, but she no longer hobbles as she did when she was with Carson & Barnes. Today she journeys to the farthest reaches of a place in Tennessee called Asia.

Only 2 percent of captive elephants live past the age of fifty. The life expectancy of an African elephant in a zoo is 16.9 years, on average less than half the life span of an elephant in Amboseli National Park, Kenya (35.9 years). Asians fare little better at 18.9 years. Even an elephant who spends her life working in a Burmese labor camp lives, on average, 22.8 years longer than an elephant in captivity. An article published in *Science* on the "Compromised Survivorship" of elephants in captivity concludes frankly, "overall, bringing elephants into zoos profoundly impairs their viability."[81]

They die in accidents, under anesthesia, and by a host

of diseases grossly antagonized by captivity. Some elephants are stillborn; some killed by inexperienced mothers; and others after being attacked by elephants in a rage or a panic. Fewer than 1 percent of elephants in captivity die of old age.[82] Of the forty-seven male elephants in North America, the oldest is only forty-eight.[83]

Captive elephants also suffer a wider and more severe range of immunodeficiency disorders, chronic foot and joint problems, and reproductive instability as well as a wide range of psychopathy, including infanticide and self-mutilation. The question arose in the public conscience: *Is it morally justifiable to sacrifice elephants in order to conserve them?* For a growing minority, the answer is no.

Several major zoos, including those in the Bronx, Chicago, San Francisco, Detroit, and Anchorage, have either closed their elephant exhibits or have pledged to close them. The trend is gradual but persistent. In 2011 the AZA launched an initiative requiring all members to phase out Free Contact and adopt Protected Contact as the preferred method of care. "AZA standards for elephant management recognize that a diversity of approaches exist," reads the AZA's latest *Standards for Elephant Management and Care,* "but encourage members to continue to experiment with the goal of maximizing elephant health and reproduction, and minimizing risk of injury to keeper staff."[84] No more bullhooks and electric prods.

People sense that elephants share the same emotions they do. Prominent elephant researchers such as Iain and Oria Douglas-Hamilton, Joyce Poole, Cynthia Moss, Gay

Bradshaw, and Caitlin O'Connell have written books that endorse the emotional individuality of elephants as passionately as Jane Goodall endorses the emotional lives of her chimpanzees.[85] More than ever, people are interested in the emotional lives of elephants, and more than ever, they have access to them.

The virtual elephant is both a real elephant and a metaphysical torrent of bits that stream onto the Internet. Shirley is a virtual elephant. Even though she roams quietly through the forest outside Hohenwald, she's exposed for anyone to watch at any time. The Elephant Sanctuary in Tennessee has fourteen surveillance cameras, called Elecams, mounted on fifty-foot towers that observe Africa, Asia, and Q. They transmit images to an office ten miles away, where Carol Durham sits in front of a computer terminal and scans the fields and barns. When she sees something interesting, she zooms in for a closer look and streams it onto the Web.

The sanctuary calls these episodes "Elecam-Encounters" and they offer a remarkable level of intimacy with elephants. At will, viewers can toggle between Elecams in Asia, Africa, and Q to follow Shirley or any of the other elephants as they go about their personal lives.

On April 30, 2012, an Elecam, perched high and above, recorded Shirley stopping on the path along the lake and staring intently at something out of frame. Unable to see into the dense foliage at the edge of the trail, and what Shirley is so intent upon, the camera waits. Her tail swishes when suddenly Tarra enters the frame.

With Tennessean songbirds singing in the background, Tarra walks up to Shirley and nudges her with her trunk. Shirley nudges Tarra back. They look like two friends spending a minute to catch up as they stand head to head and trunk to trunk, whisking their tails and flapping their ears. Then, after a minute, they go their separate ways.

"Shirley and Tarra Greet at the Lake" is one page in the electronic archive that makes up the Elephant Diaries.[86] These behind-the-scene glimpses of elephants feel intimate because they feel natural, especially when compared to the unnaturalness of an elephant in a zoo. The Elecams visually supplement the written narratives created in the website's blogs ("Ele-Notes"), photo albums, and memorial pages that make up the biographies of the elephants.

People leave electronic poems, laments, curses, and blessings. After Jenny died, Ms. Campos' fifth graders at Parkview Elementary in Carpentersville, Illinois, wrote, "We're proud that you were able to spend your last years with Shirley at such a great place! We will miss you a lot." And an admirer in Sri Lanka wrote Jenny, "Remember, the noble thing in your life was to be an elephant." Most comments came from mourners who left notes like "I am truly sad sweet little Jenny Jelly Bean had to leave so soon and I'm sure that Shirley must miss her deeply."[87]

The Elephant Sanctuary of Tennessee's website received 8 million hits in May 2012. More than a quarter million hits a day.[88] Additionally, people watch videos on YouTube like "Flora and Tange Have a Mud Party," "Sissie, Winkie, and the Water Wagon," and "Minnie's New Blue Popcorn Toy," and they listen in on their conversations in "Girl Talk."[89] Although the gradients of meaning and feeling between a real and virtual visit are hard to compare, the sheer volume of traffic, however parsed, argues that the virtual elephant is as emotionally powerful as her literal presence.

More people visit Hohenwald on the website in a day than any zoo in the United States. Some are drawn to a technology that streams instantaneous data into the electronic ether; some are drawn out of casual curiosity for elephants; and others come because they care about them. Teachers take their classes on electronic field trips to visit with Shirley and Tarra. Kids, excited to visit elephants virtually, leave cyber-notes like the one a second grader left for Shirley:

> I will give you ice cream on a plate.
> I will give you one motorcycle. ONLY ONE!
> I will kiss you on your ear.
> Love, Cyrus

The strength of a virtual experience lies in its power

to create a sense of intimacy remotely. An emerging generation of digitally savvy people comfortable with technology makes it possible to see the "natural" lives of elephants up close and personal. As people gradually accept virtual reality as a genuine surrogate for actual experience, then the intimacy of watching an elephant real time on the Internet is as emotionally powerful—and perhaps more so—than a fleeting visit to the zoo in real space.

Millions of people visit zoos every year, and millions more will make virtual visits to sanctuaries and reserves not just in the United States but also in Cambodia and Cameroon, where they will see elephants slaughtered for meat and ivory. They will see crops and fences trampled in India and the retributive killings that follow; they will see elephants beaten, shocked, chained, and starved; and they will see the police shoot down Tyke in the streets of Honolulu.[90] They will also listen to the narratives that go with these images.

But as human-elephant conflicts intensify, as the lust for ivory drives up its cost, and as the numbers of people fighting starvation increase, elephants find themselves increasingly marooned on shrinking biological islands. They raid human settlements to find food and sometimes they kill people. In Sri Lanka, villagers poison or shoot on average 120 elephants a year, and elephants kill half as many villagers.[91] As pressure builds between the species, human management intensifies, and in the world of the Internet, that means constant vigilance. Like Big Brother, someone is *always* watching.

Technology makes looking easy. A multiplicity of

electronic eyes survey what they see and stream it around the globe 24/7. Ironically, surveillance frees the virtual elephant to roam the world. Like the man in the retirement home in Sauk City who was pleased the circus had finally come to him, so the elephant now comes to anyone.

Lincoln's emancipation elephant blends man and beast in the 1863 image of an elephant with the head of a black plantation picker. It's easy to miss *The Unfortunate Man Who Won an Elephant in a Raffle* in the lower right-hand corner of the picture as he thrusts out his arms and begs the viewer to tell him what to do with his elephant.

He awaits an answer that might never come. Scrutiny doesn't always provide clarity, so the unsettled question of what it means to be humane floats like dust in the air, subject to the whim of social and political currents that move it around. Meanwhile, elephants live in purgatory, or worse, as they await the final terms of survival.

Notes

1: Seeing the Elephant

1. The sex of the elephant is uncertain but was described more commonly as a female than a male.
2. *New York Argus*, June 22, 1796.
3. *New York Argus*, April 18, 1796.
4. The families of Crowninshield and Hawthorne would cross paths for many more years in both social and literary ways.
5. Boston Handbill, 1797, printed by D. Bowen.
6. The year Bailey bought his elephant is uncertain and has been various reported between 1805 and 1806. There is also dispute to the claim that his elephant was from Africa since there were no apparent trading routes with Africa in the early nineteenth century. Terry Ariano, "Beasts and Ballyhoo: The Menagerie Men of Somers," *Westchester Historian* (Summer 2008), 2. Some have speculated that Crowninshield's elephant was the same elephant Hachaliah Bailey found in the cattle yards in New York.
7. One senses by reading Savage's newspaper advertisements for 1804 that he was struggling to clear his expenses. In June 1804 he reduced the price of admission from fifty to twenty-five cents. "It is hoped," Savage wrote, "the public will embrace the opportunity afforded them of viewing one of the largest animals of the world. . . . " "Elephant," *Independent Chronicle* (Boston), vol. 36, no. 2430, 4.
8. Bailey may have also been a frequenter if not a part owner of the Bull's Head Tavern near the stockyards in the Bowery. The

Bull's Head was the last stage stop before entering or leaving New York City, and so it was a natural meeting place for enterprising ship captains, bankers, ranchers, and other adventurers.

The idea of buying an elephant may have occurred to Bailey as far back as nine years earlier, when Crowninshield showed his elephant at the Bull's Head in the spring of 1796.

9. Hachaliah Bailey was not related to James A. Bailey, who became P. T. Barnum's competitor and finally partner in the circus business.

10. The American circus had many "fathers," such as John Bill Ricketts, Isaac van Amburgh, Victor Pépin and Jean-Baptiste Breschard, Seth Howe, Adam Forepaugh, Hachaliah Bailey, and P. T. Barnum, all of whom either by necessity or inspiration found their way into show business. They were a mix of magicians, educators, entertainers, and master storytellers who offered a patchwork of truths and fictions expertly cobbled together about worlds both hidden and forbidden.

11. There is a suggestion but no proof that Welshaven Owen sold the Crowninshield elephant to Edward Savage, and that Savage sold her to Hachaliah Bailey.

12. Bet was not known as Old Bet until after her death, perhaps as a way to distinguish her from another elephant Bailey later bought that he called Little Bet.

13. *Alexandria, Virginia, Gazette,* April 19, 1814.

14. Stuart Thayer, *Annals of the American Circus, 1793–1829* (Manchester, MI: Rymack, 1976), 55.

15. Quoted in Shana Alexander, "Belle's Baby—225 Pounds and All Elephant," *Life*, May 11, 1962, 106. Another version of this tale is that the farmer was offended because the troupe had crossed his land on the Sabbath.

16. Generally the claim that a musket ball couldn't hurt an elephant was true; many elephants had been shot by muskets over the years and easily survived their wounds, but a well-placed shot to the eye or other key organ could kill.

17. "The Elephant Columbus," *Boston Daily Advertiser,* December 17, 1817, 4.

18. "Another Great One Gone!" *New Orleans Times-Picayune,* March 25, 1837, 2.

19. Alexander, "Belle's Baby," 127; also Stuart Thayer, "The Elephant in America Before 1840," *Bandwagon* 31, no. 1. (1987), 21–22.

20. LaVahn G. Hoh and William H. Rough, *Step Right Up! The Adventure of Circus in America* (White Hall, VA: Betterway Books, 1990).

21. P. T. Barnum, *The Life of P. T. Barnum, Written by Himself* (Buffalo, NY: Courier, 1886), 20.

22. Ibid., 38.

23. Philip B. Kunhardt, Jr., Philip B Kunhardt III, and Peter Kunhardt, *P. T. Barnum: America's Greatest Showman*, New York: Alfred A. Knopf, 1995, 20.

24. Quoted in *The Life of Joice Heth, the Nurse of Gen. George Washington (the Father of Our Country), Now Living at the Astonishing Age of 161 Years, and Weighs Only 46 Pounds* (New York, 1835), 11.

25. Maelzel's Chess-Player, known as the "The Turk" because he was dressed in Oriental clothes, played an equitable game of chess. Invented in 1769 in Hungary, it was considered a "pure machine" and toured in Europe for decades playing chess with the likes of Napoleon before he came to the United States in 1825. Edgar Allan Poe wrote an essay about the Turk that contemplates a mechanical being independent of human inflection. Edgar Allan Poe, "Maelzel's Chess-Player," *Southern Literary Messenger*, April 1836, 2:318–26. The Turk was fake and had a man hidden inside the machine.

26. Barnum, *The Life of P. T. Barnum*, 120.

27. Phineas T. Barnum, *Struggles and Triumphs, or, Sixty years' recollections of P. T. Barnum, Including his Golden Rules for Money Making* (Buffalo, NY: Courier, 1889), 120–21.

28. Ibid., 76.

29. George H. Baker, "Records of a California Residence," *Quarterly of the Society of California Pioneers* 8 (March 1931): 46–47, 48.

30. Catherine Sager, in Joyce Badgely Hunsaker, *Seeing the Elephant: The Many Voices of the Oregon Trail* (Lubbock: Texas Tech University Press, 2003), 111.

31. Kenneth L. Holmes, *Covered Wagon Women,* ed. Kenneth L. Holmes and David C. Duniway, vol. 4, Bison Books ed. (Lincoln: University of Nebraska Press, 1997), 188.

32. Joseph Schafer, ed., *California Letters of Lucius Fairchild* (Madison: State Historical Society of Wisconsin, 1931), 34.

33. Hunsaker, *Seeing the Elephant*, xvi.

34. Ezra Meeker, in ibid., 159.

35. *The Journal of Walter Griffith Pigman*, ed. Ulla Staley Fawkes (Mexico, MO: Walter G. Staley, 1942), 23.

36. Merrill J. Mattes, *The Great Platte River Road* (Lincoln: Nebraska State Historical Society, 1987), 61.

37. J. S. Holliday, *The World Rushed In: The California Gold Rush Experience* (Norman: University of Oklahoma Press, 1981), 165.

2: The Unfortunate Man Who Won an Elephant in a Raffle

1. "Seeing the Elephant," *New York Times*, March 1, 1861.

2. The Civil War Sites Advisory Commission ranking of Civil War battles during 1861 attributes fifteen wins to the Confederacy and fourteen to the Union; six were undecided.

3. Letter, Alonzo D. Bump, May 15, 1863, http://www.encounter-america.org/bump/Bump-Bio-Html-Pg1.html, accessed December 2011.

4. Letter from Hearvey J. Slutts to Noah Slutts, dated January 18, 1863, http://mcquoidg.tripod.com/frm16.html, accessed December 2011.

5. Letter, Abraham Lincoln to the King of Siam, January 3, 1862, http://www.civilwar.org/education/history/primarysources/lincoln-rejects-the-king-of.html, accessed December 2011.

6. Republished from the *New York World* as "The Lincoln Elephant," *Macon, Georgia, Telegraph*, November 25, 1862, p. 2. See also "Lincoln and His South Carolina Elephant," April 10, 1862, 2.

7. *The Correspondence of Walt Whitman*, Gay Wilson Allen and Sculley Bradley, Volume I (New York: New York University Press), Correspondence, 1:323.

8. "An Elephant's Travels," *New York Herald*, November 6, 1875.

9. "A Victim of the Cruel Hoax," *New York Times*, November 21, 1874, 9.

10. "An Awful Calamity," *New York Herald*, November 9, 1874. The story is actually published on page three. The first two pages of *Herald* were just advertising; the actual "news" didn't start until the third page.

11. "Practical Jokes," *New York Times*, November 10, 1874. Bennett's reputation as a playboy infatuated with the toys of power generated its own headlines. He owned a mansion, automobiles, a railroad car fitted as an apartment, and a yacht fast enough for him to cross the Atlantic in thirteen days, twenty-one hours, and fifty-five minutes, winning the first transatlantic yacht race. Once he was so drunk he stood up during dinner, pulled down his pants in front of his fiancée's parents, and urinated into the fireplace.

12. "Wild Beasts," *New York Herald*, November 11, 1874, 3.

13. Carl Sandburg, *Storm Over the Land* (New York: Harcourt, Brace, and Co., 1942) 87.

14. Humorist H. L. Mencken called the *Herald* "journalism for the frankly ignorant and vulgar." *The American Language,* 2nd ed., revised, available at Bartleby.com.

15. "Two things elected me," Grant claimed of his success in 1868 and 1872: "the sword of Sheridan and the pencil of Thomas Nast."

16.   There's been discussion about the timing of the hoax and Nast's cartoon, which predates the publication of the *Herald* stories by two days. It's been suggested Bennett had intended to publish his hoaxes in the November 2 issue (supported by the fact that the newspaper story gives the date of the mayor's order for martial law as November 1). Bennett had wanted the story to run just before the midterm elections on November 3. But Bennett didn't like the story as it was written and ordered it be rewritten for the following week's issue. Nast likely had gotten wind of the story and drew the cartoons in time for the November 7 issue of *Harper's*, two days before the stories appeared in the *Herald*.

17.   William Henry Wyman, *Bibliography of the Bacon-Shakespeare Controversy* (Cincinnati: Peter G. Thompson, 1884), 38.

18.   In 1876, Nast drew an elephant impassively crushing a two-headed Democratic tiger beneath its feet, thus predicting a win for Rutherford Hayes. (*"THE REPUBLICAN VOTE SOLID FOR THE UNION."*) On November 7, 1876, by a margin of a quarter-million votes, the people of the United States voted the Democratic contender Samuel J. Tilden, the governor of New York, its next president. But Tilden was one vote short in the Electoral College, and the Republicans mounted an aggressive campaign to challenge the results in several states, accusing the Democrats of using strong arm tactics and bribery to keep African-Americans from the polls. When the dust settled, Nast's prophecy proved right: a commission assembled for the purpose of deciding the winner voted along party lines and chose Hayes as the country's nineteenth president. The Democrats responded with "Tilden or Blood," raising alarm for the possibility of yet another civil war. Both sides compromised in the end, but the Republican victory was costly. After Hayes's inauguration in early March, Nast published a cartoon later that month that showed a heavily bandaged and lame Republican elephant sitting beside the grave of the recently departed

Tammany Tiger. Nast quotes Pyrrhus: "Another Such Victory, and I am Undone."

3: Race to the White House

1. Taft was more commonly depicted as "Billy Possum," the successor of Roosevelt's teddy bear. Taft's running mate, James S. Sherman, was "Jimmy Possum." The reference likely alludes to a political dinner hosted in Atlanta by southern Republicans before his inauguration during which Taft ate barbecued opossum in persimmon sauce. "Taft Eats 'Possum, Gives Southern Pledge," *New York Times*, January 16, 1909.

2. Taft, who liked to drive himself on occasion, was the first president to be pulled over for speeding and the first president to talk his way out of a ticket.

3. "Persons in the Foreground," *Current Literature* 42, No. 6 (June 1907): 618.

4. Udo Keppler, "Fireman, Save My Child," *Punch*, May 4, 1910, and "Hurry, William, and Hook Me Up," March 16, 1910.

5. Udo Keppler, "The Old Rut," *Punch*, November 10, 1909.

6. When Taft left the White House four years later, he weighed 340 pounds, which prompted a few to comment on his own elephant-ness.

7. Roosevelt actually charged up a smaller, adjoining hill called Kettle Hill.

8. The fourth major candidate for the presidency was Eugene V. Debs, one of the founding fathers of the International Labor Union and the Industrial Workers of the World (IWW). He ran as a socialist whose rallying cry was "Working Men Vote Your Ticket." This was Debs's fourth run at the White House, and he would run a fifth time in 1920, from inside his cell in a federal penitentiary after he'd been charged under the Sedition Act of 1918 for publicly denouncing America's involvement in World War I.

9. Democrats favored free trade, whereas Republicans favored protectionism. The dates 1893–97 next to the Capitol Building mark the last Cleveland administration.

10. "Heat's Scythe Mows Down 56 on Fifth Day," *New-York Tribune,* Friday, July 7, 1911, 1.

11. "Elephant Holding Donkey to a Tie," *New York Times,* July 10, 1911, 7.

12. "Democratic Donkey Quits the Big Race," *New York Times,* July 15, 1911, 14.

13. "Admiring Eyes Gaze at Judy and Jennie," *Philadelphia Inquirer,* July 15, 1911, 2. See also "Both Elephant and Donkey Quit," *Baltimore American,* July 16, 1911, 4.

14. "Donkey-Elephant Race Called Off," *Philadelphia Inquirer,* July 16, 1911, 4.

15. "Elephant's Job," *Time,* November 7, 1932, 13. See also "Elephants Call at White House," *Riverside (Calif.) Daily Press,* October 27, 1932, 6.

16. See also *Carteret (N.J.) Press,* November 4, 1932, 7, http://archive. woodbridgelibrary.org/Archive/CarteretPress/1932/1932-11-04/pg_0007.pdf, accessed March 2013.

17. Speech of Senator John F. Kennedy, Boston Garden, Boston, http://www.presidency.ucsb.edu/ws/index.php?pid=25686 #ixzz1dDtp4P1l. See also http://www.youtube.com/watch? v=GXEkz6ksxdk.

4: The Voyages of Columbus

1. As with most large bulls, his size was likely exaggerated.

2. Anne was sometimes known as Queen Anne.

3. "Elephants, Their Character, Habits and Education," *New York Herald-Tribune,* March 10, 1865, 6.

4. Raymond sold Anne to the Philadelphia Zoological Garden United with New York Institute, a circus that was in business between 1843 and 1845.

5. "Hannibal. The Story of an Elephant," *Illustrated New Age,* June 23, 1865, 4.

6. Wording in an advertisement for Raymond & Waring, *New Hampshire Sentinel,* October 21, 1840, 4.

7. "Sagacity of an Elephant," *Rhode-Island American,* January 15, 1833, 1.

8. "Elephants," *New York Herald-Tribune,* March 10, 1865, 6.

9. "A Circus Reminiscence,"*Cincinnati Chronicle,* December 31, 1870.

10. "The Elephant Columbus," *Alexandria (Va.) Gazette,* March 17, 1841, 2.

11. "An Enraged Elephant," *New London (Conn.) Democrat,* January 1, 1847, 3.

12. "Seeing the Elephant," *Philadelphia Inquirer,* December 23, 1847, 1.

13. "Death of the Two Elephants 'Virginius' and 'Pizarro,'" *Middletown, Conn., Constitution,* April 28, 1847, 1.

14. "Jubilee of Victory," *New York Herald,* March 5, 1865, 5. Also "Hannibal: The Story of an Elephant," *Illustrated New Age,* June 23, 1865, 4.

15. "Death of the Elephant Hannibal," *New York Times,* June 2, 1865.

16. Peggy Samuels and Harold Samuels, *Teddy Roosevelt at San Juan: The Making of a President* (College Station: Texas A&M University Press, 1997), 13.

17. As noted above, Roosevelt did not lead his charge up San Juan Hill, but up a smaller hill known as Kettle Hill; however, the narrative of the charge became a staple in American heroic history.

18. "An Elephant a Defendant," *Logansport Pharos,* February 19, 1897, 8.

19. Advertisement, *Trenton Evening Times,* August 17, 1903, 9, and *Worcester Daily Spy,* July 7, 1903, 7.

20. "Hargreaves Big Railroad Circus (20 Cars) Season of 1904," *Note Sheet,* No. 13, July 15, 1944, 1.

5: Romeo and Juliet, an American Tragedy

1. In Shakespeare's *Troilus and Cressida*, Ulysses says, "The elephant hath joints, but none for courtesy; his legs are legs for necessity, not for flexure."

2. "Dancing Elephants: 4-Paw's Famous Troupe of Almost Human Quadrille Pachyderms," *Kalamazoo Gazette*, June 20, 1889.

3. Work on the bridge began in 1797 but a storm blew it over in 1798. Work on its replacement took five years (1803 to 1809). George Rogers Howell and John H. Munsell, *History of the County of Schenectady, N.Y. from 1662–1886* (New York: Munsell, 1886), 52–53.

4. An advertisement for the menagerie carried in the *Boston Courier*, December 6, 1832, refers to Romeo as "imported by P. Dodge, Esq., in December last."

5. On February 11, nine days before Romeo's arrival in Boston, an abolitionist paper in New York (the *Liberator*) commented that the elephant Caroline was the likely contender for the role of Juliet.

6. "The Elephant in Trouble," *Daily National Intelligencer*, October 1, 1852, 3. In another version of the story, only Juliet falls through the bridge and Romeo catches her with his trunk, only to slip slowly from his grasp.

7. Among her keepers, she always remained Jenny.

8. Jenny Lind was trained by Dan Rice, a clown famous for being the model of Uncle Sam, who started his own circus. He ran for president of the United States in 1868.

9. Jenny, as the tight-knit community of handlers always called her, was so weakened by the forty-five-minute swim in frigid waters that she caught pneumonia. "An Elephant Swimming the Ohio," *Weekly Wisconsin Patriot*, September 1, 1860; *New Albany (Ind.) Daily Ledger*, September 13, 1860.

10. This total doesn't count the thirteen days lost waiting for a replacement tent during the 1864 season.

11. When Lake Delavan was dredged years later, they pulled up a huge bone, which was at first assumed to be a mastodon bone and then recognized as one of Juliet's leg bones.

12. Advertisement, *National Republican*, April 11, 1885.

13. *The Ways of the Circus: Being the Memoirs and Adventures of George Conklin, Tamer of Lions* (New York: Harper & Brothers, 1921), 114.

14. "Conquering an Elephant," *Augusta (Ga.) Chronicle*, April 3, 1866, 4.

15. "Taking an Elephant," *New Philadelphia Ohio Democrat*, December 31, 1869. For years Forepaugh claimed he was the man who broke Romeo.

16. "Conquering an Elephant," *Augusta Chronicle*, April 3, 1866. Articles like these frequently circulated among newspapers for many months after the event.

17. "A Shocking Affair—The Elephant 'Romeo' Crushes His Keeper to Death," *Cleveland Plain Dealer*, December 26, 1867; *Waynesboro Villages Record*, January 3, 1868.

18. Romeo reportedly killed five of his handlers; accounts differ as to who they were. One account gives the chronology of "Long John" Evans in 1852, followed by "Frenchy" Williams in 1855, Stuart Craven in 1860, "Canada Bill" Williams in 1867, and a man named McDevitt in 1869. Other accounts give names such as Nicholas Mick, a man called Moran, and a West Indian named Meeks. The deaths of Long John Evans and Canada Bill Williams are the only ones that have been documented. Dan Rice claims Romeo killed seven people in all, three before coming to the United States and four afterward. Maria Ward Brown, *The Life of Dan Rice* (Long Branch, NJ: Author, 1901), 259.

19. "By Mail and Telegraph," *New York Times*, February 25, 1872, 1.

20. "Death of the Elephant Romeo," *Easton (Md.) Gazette*, June 29, 1872.

21. "Bad Elephant Romeo," *Cleveland Plain Dealer*, March 18, 1895.

22. "A Chicago Ghost Story," *Albany (N.Y.) Evening Journal*, June 17, 1872.

23. Advertisement, *Trenton Evening Times*, June 29, 1890.

24. http://www.circusinamerica.org/cocoon/circus/xml?targ=b10, accessed August 2012.

25. *Rockford (Ill.) Republic,* December 14, 1912. The film opened in October 1912.

6: Amok

1. Lauren Porter, "Widening the Circle: What We Can Learn from the Elephants," Centre for Attachment, http://www .centreforattachment.com/index.php?option=com_content &task=view&id=40&Itemid=53, accessed March 2013.

2. "Kills His Trainer," *Wisconsin Daily Advocate*, June 4, 1898, 8.

3. "Elephant Forgets Not His Murderous Act," *New York Times*, April 28, 1901.

4. "Emotional Insanity in an Elephant," *Portland Oregonian*, August 18, 1874, 1.

5. In 1902, the Great Syndicate Shows was renamed the Great Eastern Shows. In 1903 it was named yet again as Howes Great London. Homer C. Walton, *Bandwagon* 9, No. 2 (March–April 1965), pp. 4–11.

6. Ibid.

7. Alexander, "Belle's Baby," 133.

8. "Milestones, Aug. 3, 1931," *Time,* August 3, 1931, http:// www.time.com/time/magazine/article/0,9171,846966-2,00 .html#ixzz1ATwV7E00, accessed June 2012.

9. Official Route Card, Al. G. Barnes Wild Animal Circus, No. 11, Season 1936. Also Season 1922, 1930.

10. "Elephant Goes on Rampage," *Idaho Statesman*, May 18, 1922, 2.

11. "Tusko, Huge Elephant, Runs Amok," Sedro-Woolley, *Wash.*, *Courier-Times*, May 15 (16), 1922.

12. http://www.skagitriverjournal.com/S-W/Town/QuestionsS -W1.html, accessed March 2013.

13. "Tusko, Huge Elephant, Runs Amok," Sedro-Woolley.

14. "Elephant on Rampage," *New York Times*, May 18, 1922.

15. "Six-Ton Tusko's Career Colorful, Lively," *Portland Oregonian*, December 20, 1931, 27.

16. George Washington Lewis, *I Loved Rogues* (Seattle: Superior, 1978), 120.

17. Black Diamond spent fourteen years of his life with Gentry Circus before it sold him in 1914.

18. "The Story of Black Diamond," *Bandwagon* 3, No. 3 (May–June 1959), 17–18.

19. Al. G. Barnes called Black Diamond "Tusko" and called Tusko "The Mighty Tusko."

20. As many as four human deaths have been attributed to Black Diamond, although there's only evidence to account for two.

21. Al. G. Barnes Official Route, 1929.

22. Mrs. Fred P. Hodge, "Black Diamond," *Navarro County Scroll* 14 (1969).

23. According to Slim Lewis, Pearl tried to kill the trainer so many times he left the circus in fear of his life. Lewis, *I Loved Rogues,* 43.

24. Ibid., 43.

25. Ibid., 45.

26. Hodge, "Black Diamond."

27. "Milestones," *Time*, August 3, 1931, http://www.time.com/ time/magazine/article/0,9171,846966-2,00.html, accessed February 2, 2011.

28. Hodge, "Black Diamond."

29. Lewis, *I Loved Rogues*, 47.

30. "Outlaw Elephant 'Taken for Ride' by his Mates; 'Put on Spot' by Friends," *Corsicana (Texas) Daily Sun*, October 17, 1929, 1.

31. Lewis, *I Loved Rogues*, 48.

32. "Black Diamond," *Time*, October 28, 1929. Black Diamond's skull remained on display at the Houston Museum of Science until 1970, after which a man who'd seen Diamond kill Eva Donohoo bought his remains and returned them to Corsicana, where a taxidermist mounted his facial skin, bullet holes and all. A bust of Hans Nagel, Houston's first zookeeper, was also mounted on one of Black Diamond's feet. It has since gone missing.

33. Gay Bradshaw, *Elephants on the Edge* (New Haven, CT: Yale University Press, 2009), 83.

34. Charles Siebert, "An Elephant Crack-up?," *New York Times*, October 8, 2006, http://www.nytimes.com/2006/10/08/magazine/08elephant.html?pagewanted=all&_r=0, accessed March 2013.

35. Jesse Donahue and Erik Trump, *American Zoos During the Depression* (Jefferson, NC: McFarland, 2010), 161.

36. Lewis, *I Loved Rogues*, 117.

37. "Attempts Started to Stop Walkers," *Portland Oregonian*, May 20, 1931, 3.

38. Advertisement, *Portland Oregonian*, June 13, 1930, 2.

39. Painter surfaced in New Orleans after pulling the same con in New Orleans later that year. As in Lotus Isle, Painter skipped on his debts. "Al Painter Walks Out on Walkathon at New Orleans, Leaving Bad Checks," *Portland Oregonian*, November 28, 1931, 4.

40. There was a third man with Gray and O'Grady, known only as Dougout. He does not appear to be a business partner.

41. Lewis, *I Loved Rogues*, 117.

42. Ibid., 118.

43. http://www.criticalpast.com/video/65675071113_Leon-Pinetzki_wrestles-down-elephant_Rosie_fight-with-elephant, accessed March 2013.

44. The economy had improved slightly by 1932, with an addi-

tional one million people going back to work, but the public gauged Hoover's policies more as an impediment to progress.

45. "Milestones," *Time*, January 4, 1932.

46. Lewis, *I Loved Rogues*, 126.

47. Lewis, O'Grady, and Gray often had help from others such as "Double-Ugly" Red, Dougout, Ben Myers, and George Krueger. Myers and Krueger were local and Red and Dougout were circus hands.

48. Lewis, *I Loved Rogues*, 141.

49. Richard C. Berner, *Seattle 1921–1940: From Boom to Bust* (Seattle: Charles Press, 1992), 298; Lester M. Hunt, "John T. Dore Dead," *Seattle Post-Intelligencer*, 1; "Colorful Career Ended By Mayor Dore's Death," *Seattle Post-Intelligencer,* ibid., p. 2.

50. Donahue and Trump, *American Zoos During the Depression*, 165.

51. Ibid., 164.

52. Lewis, *I Loved Rogues*, 153.

53. http://bellevuecollege.edu/cpsha/esj/tusko.htm, accessed March 2013.

54. Tusko's remains are locked away in the University of Oregon's Museum of Natural and Cultural History.

7: Farming with Elephants

1. *Gleason's Pictorial*, a popular illustrated periodical published in Boston, printed a very similar picture of an elephant plowing a field in India the year before.

2. "A Great Farmer—The 'Elephant,'" *Cleveland Plain Dealer,* April 3, 1855, 2.

3. Barnum, *Struggles and Triumphs*, 132.

4. "Jumbo and Another Barnum Elephant," *Cincinnati Daily Gazette*, March 18, 1882, 10.

5. Barnum, *Struggles and Triumphs*, 133.

8: Jumbo Nation

1. Arstingstall was also referred to as the Colonel, an honorific that fit his job description better than "Professor."

2. "In a Circus Menagerie," *New York Times*, April 30, 1882. The use of the title "Colonel" was strictly honorific. George Arstingstall served during the Civil War as a private in Company D of the Second Kentucky Volunteers.

3. The value of Barnum's elephants in 1860 was a quarter-million dollars.

4. Matthew Scott and Thomas E. Lowe, *The Autobiography of Matthew Scott, Jumbo's Keeper* (Bridgeport, CT: Trow's, 1885), 21.

5. Ibid., 43, 44.

6. A. H. Saxon, *P. T. Barnum: The Legend and the Man* (New York, Columbia University Press, 1989), 295.

7. By most accounts, Barnum never bought the house.

8. Mark Twain, *Following the Equator: A Journey Around the World* (Hartford, CT: American, 1897), 641.

9. Twain despised Barnum and called his museum "one vast peanut stand." The facticity of these stories is questionable.

10. *London Times*, March 9, 1882, quoted in Paul Chambers, *This Being the True Story of Jumbo, the Greatest Elephant in the World* (Hanover, N.H., Steerforth Press, 2008), 114.

11. "A Reminiscence of Jumbo," *New York Times,* May 1, 1887, 11. For Barnum's account of the transaction see Barnum, *The Life of P. T Barnum*, 332.

12. The narrative I've constructed unfortunately minimizes the role that James Bailey and James Hutchinson played in making their circus a success. My emphasis on Barnum does not intentionally downplay their importance. To the contrary, they were crucial to the success of the circus.

13. Alice played the ever-faithful Penelope to Jumbo's Ulysses. "I don't think that Alice ever deceived Jumbo," Scott said in confirming her fidelity. "She certainly never flirted with any other

elephants, although she often had the chance." Jumbo was just as smitten. Scott claimed he "possessed more real affection and love at first sight than most of the young men of the present generation do in a like situation." Scott and Lowe, *The Autobiography of Matthew Scott*, 51.

14. "A Reminiscence of Jumbo," *New York Times*, May 1, 1887, 11.

15. Scott and Lowe, *The Autobiography of Matthew Scott*, 67.

16. Twain attributes this quote to a man he met on board ship whom he calls the Second Class Passenger.

17. M. R. Werner, *Barnum* (New York: Harcourt, Brace, 1923), 337.

18. Advertisement, *New York Sun*, April 17, 1882.

19. "Barnum's Invading Hosts," *New York Times*, March 25, 1883.

20. Werner, *Barnum*, 333.

21. "Jumbo Landed in Safety," *New York Times*, April 10, 1882, 1.

22. "Jumbo on His Travels," *New York Times,* April 23, 1882.

23. Although many of Barnum's claims are suspect, if he exaggerated about Jumbo's rate of return, he didn't exaggerate by much. The *New York Clipper* reported Barnum's receipts for six days in Philadelphia as $80,130.20. He also told a reporter that Jumbo's receipts for six weeks was $336,000, although such a number would have been speculative.

24. "Delaney's Denial," *New York Times*, September 13, 1882.

25. [Unknown], *The Book of Jumbo: The History of the Largest Elephant That Ever Lived*, n.p., 1883.

26. "The Jumbo of Steam-Whistles," *New York Times*, May 26, 1882.

27. Tom Thumb's "German Waiter Routine" was one of the most famous in circus history and copied by other circuses. The act pitted a sniffy German waiter, played by a clown, against Tom Thumb as a drunken diner who cheats the waiter out of several bottles of wine.

28. J. & P. Coats also produced at least two cards showing Jumbo tied up with its "Best Six Cord" thread.

29. "At Barnum's Circus," *New York Times*, March 27, 1883.

9: Jumbo Saves the Brooklyn Bridge

1.   America had many Eighth Wonders of the World. William Jennings Bryan dubbed the Natural Bridge in Virginia one, as did Theodore Roosevelt with Burney Falls in California. Similarly the Grand Canyon, Yellowstone, Yosemite, and other sites of natural awe were all the "Eighth Wonder of the World."

2.   "Brooklyn Bridge," *St. Nicholas* 10, No. 9 (July 1883), 690.

3.   Emma Lazarus, "The Colossus," in *The Poems of Emma Lazarus*, vol. 1 (Boston: Houghton Mifflin, 1889), 2.

4.   Elizabeth Brand Monroe *The Wheeling Bridge Case: Its Significance in American Law and Technology* (Boston: Northeastern University Press, 1992), 3.

5.   The ferry actually crushed Roebling's foot; the actual cause of his death was tetanus, which resulted from his injuries after he refused medical help.

6.   The bridge trains didn't start until September.

7.   David McCullough, *The Great Bridge* (New York: Avon Books, 1972), 542.

8.   Ibid., 531–34.

9.   Ibid., 544.

10. "Dead on the New Bridge," *New York Times,* May 31, 1883, 1.

11. "Bridge Inquest Ended," *New York Times,* June 6, 1883.

12. McCullough, *The Great Bridge*, 545.

13. Architect James B. Eads had already used an elephant to prove the structural integrity of his daring cantilever bridge across the Mississippi River in June 1874. Walt Whitman even commemorated the event with a singularly bad poem, "Song of the How-Come-You-So." It's possible the New York Bridge Company was aware of the success of Eads's publicity stunt and decided to copy it.

14. Saxon, 297.

15. At least one contemporary source suggested that Barnum

agreed to walk Jumbo and the other elephants across the bridge hoping the authorities would refuse to let the herd cross over. "That would give the Barnum people a chance to say that Jumbo was so big that the authorities of the bridge were afraid to let him cross the structure, and the circus people foresaw a splendid advertisement." This assertion is likely not true because Barnum staged the event with and not in spite of the bridge company. *Harper's Round Table*, August 6, 1895, 6.

16. An approximation of the weight of the animals, the people, and the trains and carriages.

17. Scott and Lowe, *The Autobiography of Matthew Scott*, 87.

18. As Barnum told it, Jumbo had grown nearly three feet since arriving in America and now stood thirteen feet, four inches tall. In fact, Jumbo hadn't grown at all.

19. Scott and Lowe, *The Autobiography of Matthew Scott*, 93.

20. "The Elephants Cross the Bridge," *New York Times*, May 18, 1884.

21. "He Met Sam Patch's Death," *New York Sun,* May 20, 1885, 1.

10: The Skeleton and the Manikin

1. "Jumbo the Hero," *Springfield (Mass.) Republican*, September 19, 1885, p. 5.

2. Accounts differ as to how much of the train derailed. The engine derailed for certain, but reports varied as to the number of cars that went off the tracks.

3. In 1875 an elephant named Betsy tried to turn over a parked train in Bridgeport, Connecticut. "Betsy Fights a Locomotive," *Bridgeport, Conn., Morning Telegraph*, November 21, 1875, 1.

4. "Jumbo's Tragic Death," *New York Herald*, September 17, 1885, 5.

5. "The Great Jumbo Killed," *New York Times*, September 17, 1885, 5.

6. "Jumbo Saves a Friend," *Boy's Life*, May 1989, 11.

7. Letter from P. T. Barnum to Henry A. Ward, dated October 9, 1883, Department of Rare Books, Special Collections, and Preservation, River Campus Libraries, University of Rochester, http://www.lib.rochester.edu/index.cfm?PAGE=3599, accessed August 2011.

8. Barnum was a trustee of Tufts, which became Tufts University in 1955.

9. Saxon, 299.

10. Ibid., 406, n. 93.

11. Cornell University studied Jumbo's brain. "Studying an Elephant's Brains," *New York Times*, November 29, 1887, 3. Cornell also bought his heart in 1889 for around thirty dollars.

12. Les Harding, *Elephant Story: Jumbo and P. T. Barnum under the Big Top* (Jefferson, NC: McFarland, 2000), 101.

13. Kunhardt, 188.

14. This scene comes from a circus poster titled *Literal Scenes taken from a Photograph of the 3 Rings, Racing Track and Interior View of the 7 United Monster Shows*, in ibid., 282–83.

15. "Alice and Jumbo," *New York Times*, April 21, 1886, 8.

16. "The Greatest Show on Earth," *New York Magazine* 26, No. 4 (January 25, 1993), 25.

17. Saxon, 406, n. 98.

18. There's an indication Tom Thumb spent his final days at the Central Park Zoo in New York, although there is no record of when or how he died.

11: White Elephants

1. Holder reports a white elephant was exhibited in Holland in 1633. Charles Frederick Holder, *The Ivory King* (New York: Charles Scribner's Sons, 1886), 133.

2. Gaylord may have been accompanied by Thomas H. Davis and another man, although little mention is made of them. Werner, *Barnum*, 348; Barnum, *The Life of P. T. Barnum*, 347.

3. In another version of the story, Gaylord colludes with the prime minister of Siam.
4. "Mr. Barnum's White Elephant," *New York Times,* December 7, 1883.
5. Barnum, *The Life of P. T. Barnum*, 346.
6. "Barnum's White Elephant," *New York Times*, June 9, 1883.
7. "Mr. Barnum's Sacred Elephant," *New York Times*, January 6, 1884. 3. See also Barnum, *The Life of P. T. Barnum*, 347.
8. "The Sacred Elephant in London," *New York Times,* January 20, 1884, 5.
9. "A Car for the White Elephant," *New York Times,* January 24, 1885, 3.
10. "Barnum's White Elephant," *Janesville (Wis.) Daily Gazette,* January 30, 1884, 2, and "The White Elephant," *London Guardian*, January 30, 1884, 161.
11. "Old Tongue," *Lloyd's Weekly Newspaper*, London, February 3, 1884, 7.
12. "Dramatic Causerie," *Fort Wayne (Ind.) Gazette*, March 9, 1884, 6.
13. "An Interesting Experiment," *New York Times*, April 21, 1884.
14. Kunhardt, 295.
15. Based upon the calculation that a man was paid $31.52 per month and a woman was paid $25.99. http://www.ausbcomp.com/~bbott/cowley/Oldnews/Papers/TEACHER1.HTM, accessed March 2013.
16. "A Great Chance for Poetry," *New York Times*, April 4, 1884.
17. "Odes to the White Elephant," *New Zealand Bay of Plenty Times*, Rōrahi XIII, Putanga 1745, 30 Mahuru 1884, 4; http://paperspast.natlib.govt.nz/cgi-bin/paperspast?a=d&d=NZT18841031.2.14&e=-------10--1----0--, accessed May 2013.
18. Helen Conway, "The White Elephant," in Werner, *Barnum*, 351.
19. Saxon, 306.

20. Neil Harris, *Humbug: The Art of P. T. Barnum* (Boston: Little, Brown, 1973), 268.

21. Joaquin Miller, "The Sacred White Elephant—Toung Taloung," in Werner, *Barnum*, 350.

22. Ibid., 353. Also see "Waiting for the White Elephant," *New York Times*, March 26, 1884, 8.

23. Barnum actually paid about six thousand dollars for Toung Taloung.

24. Barnum, *The Life of P. T. Barnum,* 360.

25. His eyes were actually brown. "A Very Sea-Sick Elephant," *New York Times*, March 21, 1884.

26. Saxon, 309.

27. Werner, *Barnum*, 354.

28. Kunhardt, 295.

29. "The Death of 'Life of Asia,' " *New York Times*, November 16, 1884.

30. Barnum, *The Life of P. T. Barnum*, 360.

31. "Town Heaps Honors on Old Bet's Grave," *New York Times*, April 14, 1922.

12: Elephant Bizarre

1. Advertisement, *Philadelphia Inquirer*, September 28, 1882, 8.

2. http://www.lucytheelephant.org/index.php?option=com_content&view=article&id=43&Itemid=18, accessed March 2013.

3. According to contemporary sources, 263 men spent 129 days building the Elephantine Colossus. A day consisted of ten hours.

4. "The Elephant Burned," *Minneapolis Journal*, October 1, 1896, 7.

5. "Coney Island's Big Elephant," *New York Times*, May 30, 1885. These figures are exaggerated by 17 percent.

6. "Elephant Goes up in Smoke," *New Haven Register*, September 28, 1896, 9.

7. "Coney Island's Big Elephant," *New York Times*, May 30, 1885. He also claimed you could see church steeples in London and Paris.

8. "From the Howdah," *New Haven Register,* June 14, 1885, 1.

9. "Lost in the Elephant's Trunk," *New York Times*, July 27, 1885, 8.

10. "The Colossal Elephant of Coney Island," *Scientific American*, July 11, 1885, 15, 21.

11. Quoted in Michael Immerso, *Coney Island: The People's Playground* (New Brunswick, NJ: Rutgers University Press, 2002), 48.

12. "Loss of an Old Friend," *Brooklyn Eagle*, September 28, 1896.

13. "A World's Fair Elephant," *Illinois Morning Star*, September 2, 1892, 6.

14. Lucy's final cost was closer to thirty-eight thousand dollars.

15. "A Chicago Elephant," *New York Herald*, January 14, 1893, 6.

16. W. O. Atwater, "Primary Report on Investigation of Foods Exhibited at the World's Fair," *Report of the Committee on Awards of the World's Columbian Commission: Special Reports Upon Special Subjects or Groups* (Chicago: World's Columbian Exposition, 1893), 499.

17. The entire Stollwerk Brothers Pavilion, which was in the shape of Renaissance temple, was itself built out of fifteen tons of chocolate and cocoa butter. Louis Grivetti and Howard-Yana Shapiro, *Chocolate: History, Culture, and Heritage* (Hoboken, NJ: Wiley, 2009), 202.

18. Both the hamburger and Coca-Cola existed prior to the World's Fair but were not widely consumed. Coca-Cola was incorporated January 29, 1892.

19. Stroh's Bohemian Beer also won a blue ribbon. Later Pabst bought Stroh's.

20. Keith Newlin, *Hamlin Garland: A Life* (Lincoln: University of Nebraska Press, 2008), 175.

21. "All Midway Mourns," *Chicago Daily Inter Ocean*, August 15, 1893, 7.

22. The wheel actually made two revolutions for a rider. The first took twenty minutes as each of the cars loaded; and second rotation took nine minutes nonstop.

23. Uncle Ed's has a second elephant named Commander Robert Eli, who stands over the fish pond.

13: Born in the USA

1. *Daily Nebraska Press*, April 6, 1875, 4.
2. "Naming the Baby Elephant," *New York Herald*, March 12, 1880, 3.
3. Advertisement, *Bruce (N.Z.) Herald*, March 15, 1878, http://paperspast.natlib.govt.nz/cgi-bin/paperspast?a=d&d=BH 18780315.2.8.1&cl=CL2.1878.03&e=-------10--1----0--, accessed March 2013.
4. Based upon the assumption that men controlled their families' purse and activities, the circus catered to the family at large but to the male specifically.
5. "A Baby Elephant," *Harper's Weekly*, April 3, 1880, 219.
6. "An American Elephant," *New York Herald*, March 11, 1880, 7.
7. "The Latest Arrival," *New Haven Register*, March 22, 1880, 1.
8. "Barnum and the Baby Elephant," July 31, 1880, 4, and "Convincing Evidence," *Cleveland Plain Dealer*, August 2, 1880, 2.
9. Werner, *Barnum*, 324–25.
10. Barnum, *The Life of P. T. Barnum*, 324.
11. Stewart Craven had originally advanced these views. See William Slout, *A Royal Coupling: The Historic Marriage of Barnum and Bailey* (San Bernardino, CA. Emeritus Enterprise Book, 2000), 199.
12. "The Baby Elephant," *Indianapolis Sentinel*, March 31, 1880, 2, and "The Baby Elephant," *New York Herald,* March 12, 1880, 5.
13. The name might not have been the longest for a circus in America, but it came close. The longest—and strangest—name of any circus was no doubt L. B. Lent's Universal Living Ex-

position, Metropolitan Museum, Mastadon [*sic*] Menagerie, Hemispheric Hippozoonomadon, Cosmographic Caravan, Equescurriculum, Great New York Circus and Monster Musical Brigade of 1872.

14. *St. Louis Globe Democrat,* April 14, 1907, quoted in Slout, *A Royal Coupling,* 211.

15. Cooper had sold his share to James Hutchinson in 1880 and retired. The relationship between Barnum and Bailey remained contentious, and it would take eleven years for Barnum & Bailey to join together for good, and then only because Barnum had died and his widow sold the circus to Bailey.

16. The owners claimed the tent, which was made out of 336,000 yards of canvas, was "the Largest Tent Ever Made."

17. "The Great Show," *Patriot (Penn.),* April 18, 1881, 1.

18. According to Barnum, Charles Dickens asked Barnum, "What is it?" when he first saw Johnson. Thereafter Barnum called Johnson the *What is it?*

19. *Otago (N.Z.) Daily Times,* Putanga 5003, 1 Poututerangi 1878, 1, http://paperspast.natlib.govt.nz/cgi-bin/paperspast?a=d&d= ODT18780301.2.2.8&l=mi&e=-------10--1----0--, accessed August 2011. There were several leapers who were Batchellers during the late 1800s, including William, Frank, George, and John.

20. "The Circus Season," *New Haven Register,* May 3, 1880, 4.

21. "Barnum's Baby Elephant," *New York Times,* February 4, 1882, 8.

22. "Another Baby Elephant," *New York Herald,* February 3, 1882, 7.

23. "Baby Elephant No. Two," *New Haven Register,* February 3, 1882, 1.

24. Advertisement, *Philadelphia Inquirer,* April 26, 1882, 5.

25. A big cat trainer Toney Lowando was auditioning an act to Thompson and Dundy, the owners of Luna Park. On Lowando's command, each of three lions was supposed to jump onto

the back of an elephant and then ride her around the ring. Two big toms named Wallace and Brutus were supposedly man-killers.

Why Thompson and Dundy chose Columbia as one of the three elephants to ride around with a fully grown lion on her back remains a bit of mystery. She'd just killed a man, so if stability and security were of concern, then Columbia was obviously a bad choice. On the other hand, Columbia was a good choice when it came to box-office appeal. *A Mankiller Riding the Back of Another Mankiller* was a great stunt if Lowando could pull it off. Perhaps Skip Dundy deliberately chose Columbia because he wanted to see how well she'd tolerate having a lion on her back.

As a safety precaution they staged the audition on the little island in the middle of Luna Park's lagoon, the same island where they'd built the electrocution platform for Topsy that January. Thousands of people lined up four and five deep at the lagoon to watch Wallace ride the back of Columbia.

Dundy wasn't worried about Columbia—he thought she could take care of herself—but who knew what chaos could follow. If something did go wrong, at least the moat between the island and the promenade would protect the crowd.

Everything went according to plan. Brutus and the other lion jumped onto the backs of two elephants and continued their way around the ring. Then it was Wallace's turn to jump onto Columbia's back.

Wallace misgauged the jump and landed on Columbia's head. She tried to shake him off, which only made Wallace dig in deeper. Columbia reached up with her trunk, ripped Wallace off her head, and hurled him against the ground so hard his bones cracked. Undeterred, Wallace went for Columbia's throat. At the same time, Brutus and the other lion attacked.

"The battle royal which followed thrilled and fascinated the crowd of spectators," reported the *Dallas Morning News*. "They stood breathless and motionless, little realizing their own danger." Suddenly Brutus bolted across the lagoon into the crowd of three thousand spectators, which scattered in a panic "in which men, women and children were knocked down and trampled upon."

Brutus ran into an Irish saloon where Joseph Guinness was tending bar. "Seeing the lion coming toward him he was paralyzed with fear," a witness recalled. Brutus jumped from the door, *over* Guinness, and onto a shelf behind him, scattering glassware everywhere. Guinness tried to climb over the bar when the cat jumped on his back.

Guinness turned hysterical. But Brutus was more interested in the people staring at him through the window, and he jumped off the Irishman and ran out the door onto Surf Avenue.

Meanwhile, Columbia had fought off Wallace and the other lion. They too ran into the crowd, and for several hours three lions ran at large on Coney Island until the police finally cornered and captured them. Miraculously, no one was hurt. "Lion Thrown into Crowd," *Dallas Morning News,* September 28, 1903, 6.

26. "Greatest Show in the World," *New Haven Register*, May 30, 1882, 4.

27. Sickle's attorney, Edwin Stanton, made legal history after he argued successfully that his client was innocent by reason of temporary insanity. Sickles went on to win the Congressional Medal of Honor at Gettysburg and rose to the rank of major general. As the U.S. minister to Spain between 1869 and 1874, he was said to have had an affair with Queen Isabella II. Stanton went on to become U.S. attorney general and later, Lincoln's secretary of war.

28. "Birthday Parties," *New Haven Register*, October 17, 1883, 2.

29. "Death of a Baby Elephant," *New York Herald-Tribune*, April 15, 1886, 8.

30. Barnum actually gave Bridgeport to the Fairfield County Historical Society in Bridgeport, Connecticut, but sent her to Tufts for "safe keeping" until the historical society could find space to exhibit her. " 'Bridgeport' in the Barnum Museum," *Boston Journal*, September 4, 1886, 1. Also "A Baby Elephant's Death," *Columbus Daily Enquirer*, April 20, 1886, 6.

31. Advertisement, *Springfield (Mass.) Republican*, June 7, 1908, 19.

32. A newspaper insert to the *Bridgeton (N.J.) Herald*, May 12 1908.

33. "Circus in Hospitals, Elephant and All," *New York Times*, April 5, 1908.

34. "New Circus Rival for Baby Elephant," *New York Times,* April 12, 1908.

35. "Sagas of Pregnant Elephants Sure-Fire Attention-Getters," *Portland Oregonian,* January 14, 1961, 29.

36. Prince Utah likely lived longer as the resu lt of superior care at the Hogle Zoo.

37. "Animal-Trailing Seattleites En Route to Elephant Auction," *Seattle Daily Times*, November 6, 1958, 2.

38. "Ponderosity Prevails at Zoo Pachydormitory," *Portland Oregonian,* October 15, 1960, 1. See also "Park Board: 'Talking Books' to Be Installed at Woodland Park Zoo," December 3, 1959, 19.

39. "Zoo Draws Huge Crowd," *Portland Oregonian*, October 19, 1960, 11.

40. "Elephant Frightened by Monkey," *Seattle Daily Times,* May 21, 1959, 43.

41. "New Transportation," *Seattle Daily Times*, May 24, 1959.

42. "Stork May Need Helper," *Portland Oregonian,* October 27, 1961, 24.

43. "Impending Zoo 'Blessed Events' Stir Citizens' Interest," *Portland Oregonian,* January 12, 1962, 16.

44. "How to Tell Expectant Elephant: 'It Ain't Easy,' Experts Admit," *Portland Oregonian*, January 10, 1962, 10.

45. "Visiting Siamese Mother-to-Be Having Those Well-Known Pains," *Portland Oregonian*, January 19, 1962, 1.

46. "Weary Zoo 'Elephantricians' Wait, Keep Alert for Overburdened Stork," *Portland Oregonian*, January 20, 1962, 1.

47. *Portland Oregonian*, April 30, 1963.

48. The likely reason Belle was a good mother was that Berry used her frequently as a dry nurse for some of the ten baby elephants he'd imported to the United States. "Elephant Birth Zero-Hour Near," *Portland Oregonian*, January 15, 1962, 11. See also "Belle's 150-Pound Baby is 1st for U.S. in 44 Years," *Cleveland Plain Dealer*, April 15, 1962, 11.

49. Shana Alexander, "Belle's Baby—225 Pounds and All Elephant," *Life*, May 11, 1962, 103–20.

50. Ibid., 112.

51. Thonglaw and Belle vindicated Professor Lockhart's theory that American elephants would mate successfully under ideal conditions. The conditions in Portland were apparently ideal because not only had Thonglaw impregnated Belle, but he also got Rosy and Tuy Hua pregnant, although no one knew at the time.

52. The poem was written by Rotarian Larry Pendergrass. "Drive to Buy Elelphants Gaining City Momentum," *Portland Oregonian*, April 26, 1962, 30.

53. "Zoo's Playful Pachyderm Proves He's a Well-Behaved Critter," *Portland Oregonian*, September 21, 1963, 9.

54. "Zoo Winds 'Title' with Elephant Family," *Portland Oregonian*, October 4, 1962, 36.

55. *Circus Report* 3, No. 9 (December 9, 1974), 9.

56. The elephant was misidentified as Tonga.

57. "Did Elephant Kill Its Closest Friend?," *Seattle Daily Times*, June 28, 1979, 3.

58. "Body of Trainer Recovered from Guard of Bull Elephant," *Eugene (Ore.) Register-Guard*, June 28, 1979, 15D.

59. "Tonga Joins Elephant Herd at Washington Zoo," *Portland Oregonian*, November 20, 1979, 54.

60.   "Dream for Sale . . . if You Want Elephants," *Portland Oregonian*, February 6, 1980, 28.

14: Matriarch

1.   "Has An Elephant on His Hands," *Kansas City Star*, July 8, 1897, 8; "Have an Elephant on Their Hands," *St. Louis Republic*, February 2, 1899, 9.

2.   "The Barnum & Bailey show has something more than a quarter of a century of age [to] its credit," wrote the *Sunday Oregonian* in 1905, "and pretty nearly every year there has been a different Babe." "Intelligent Animals of the Zoo," *Portland Sunday Oregonian,* August 20, 1905, 48.

3.   "Babe Does Bit Helping Unemployed," *Dallas Morning News*, March 7, 1933, sec. II, 7; "This Elephant Picks Pockets," *Morning Star*, July 20, 1904; "Hippo Proves to Be Strongest," *Bellingham (Wash.) Herald*, April 19, 1904, 3.

4.   Barnum's Babe is also a composite of several Barnum Babes.

5.   "Ruth Offered Circus Job," *Seattle Daily Times*, January 18, 1935, 27.

6.   " 'Babe' Talks a Bit," *New Orleans Times-Picayune*, August 18, 1935, 46.

7.   The Babe that killed his keeper in Toledo was actually male.

8.   "Intelligent Animals of the Circus Zoo Prince," *Portland Oregonian*, August 20, 1905, 48.

9.   "About Elephants," *Bay City (Mich.) Times*, June 2, 1904, 6.

10.   "Certain Tendencies of Circus Elephants," *New York Times*, March 24, 1913.

11.   *Rockford (Ill.) Morning Star,* August 24, 1920, 6.

12.   "Circus Brings Joy to Old and Young," *Philadelphia Inquirer*, May 3, 1916, 4.

13.   "Big 'Babe' Will Eat Peanuts at Rockford Fair," *Rockford (Ill.) Morning Star*, August 21, 1919, 8.

14.   "Babe of the Zoo," *Rockford (Ill.) Morning Star*, September 17, 1919, 3.

15. "Oats for Dessert! It's Life! Says Babe," *Daily Register Gazette (Illinois)*, August 23, 1919, 5.

16. http://www.rockfordparkdistrict.org/home/parks/general parkinformation/, accessed August 2011.

17. "Big Babe Leaves for Old Mexico," *Rockford (Ill.) Morning Star*, April 12, 1921, 6.

15: AC/DC

1. Jill Jonnes, *Empires of Light* (New York: Random House, 2003), 171–72.

2. "Mr. Brown's Rejoinder," *Electrical Engineer*, August 1888, 369.

3. Brown and Edison maintained they had no business relationship even though Edison lent him considerable financial and technical assistance.

4. Jim Rasenberger, "Urban Tactics," *New York Times,* January 2, 2005, sec. 14, 3.

5. Francis Ellingon Leupp, *George Westinghouse: His Life and Achievements* (Boston: Little, Brown, 1918), 144.

6. The *Electrical Engineer* noted, however, that though the dog's "character had been vilified, his mild appearance suggested that there might be another side to this story."

7. Brown had considered using cats instead of dogs but disliked that they "wriggle around when you attempt to apply the electrode, and they also have claws." Tom McNichol, *AC/DC: The Strange Tale of the First Standards War* (New York: John Wiley Sons, 2011), 92.

8. "Mr. Brown's Rejoinder, Electrical Dog Killing," *Electrical Engineer* 7 (August 1888), 369.

9. Quoted in Mark Essig, *Edison and the Electric Chair: A Story of Light and Death* (New York: Walker, 2003), 143.

10. "Died for Science's Sake," *New York Times,* July 31, 1888.

11. The next issue of *Electrical Engineer* printed a ballad called "Mr. Brown and the Dog," written on the occasion of the dog's death, one stanza of which read:

> *At last there came a deadly bolt;*
> *The dog, O where was he?*
> *Three hundred alternating volts*
> *Had burst his visceræ.*

12. Leupp, *George Westinghouse*, 146.

13. State of New York, *Report of the Commission to Investigate and Report the Most Humane and Practical Method of Carrying into Effect the Sentence of Death in Capital Cases . . . Transmitted to the Legislature of the State of New York, January 17, 1888* (Albany, N.Y., 1888), 82.

14. Randall E. Stross, *The Wizard of Menlo Park: How Thomas Alva Edison Invented the Modern World* (New York: Random House, 2007), 174.

15. Ironically, one of the three members of the commission claimed to have seen animals electrocuted at the Westinghouse Electric Company in Buffalo, which means, if correct, that it too was experimenting with animals.

16. Like Edison, Dr. Guillotin was against capital punishment and felt that if the state was determined to execute its citizens, then it ought to do so expeditiously, privately, and painlessly. His comment to the French Assembly, "Now, with my machine, I cut off your head in the twinkling of an eye, and you never feel it!" forever associated his name with the guillotine. The device was actually created by Antoine Louis.

17. Besides Edison's three suggestions, the *Scientific American* proposed fifteen others, among them *electricide, thanaelectrisis, electroctasy, electrolehe,* and *electrocution.* Craig Brandon, *The Electric Chair: An Unnatural American History* (Jefferson, NC: McFarland, 1999), 66; Stross, *The Wizard of Menlo Park,* 174.

18. Essig, *Edison and the Electric Chair,* 162.

19. "Experiments with Electric Currents on Dogs," *Electrician* 12 (August 11, 1888), 72–73, and *Electrician* 22 (August 17, 1888), 478.

20. Advertisement, *Rockford (Ill.) Weekly Register Gazette,* May 25, 1876.

21. There have been claims that Topsy was eight years old when she arrived in America; however, her height and weight more closely match the physical attributes of an elephant under one year old.

22. P. T. Barnum had a *Moving Temple of Juno* that also was thirty feet tall.

23. "Hurt by an Elephant," *Philadelphia Inquirer,* May 29, 1897, 1. It is not clear whether Howard survived his injuries.

24. Although secondary sources claim Topsy killed the man in Paris (and another in Waco, Texas), there's no evidence to show this happened. She did seriously wound—if not killed— her keeper in Paris, Texas, although the *Dallas Morning News* identifies him as "Mortiman Loudett," likely a misspelled or false name since there appear to be no death records for anyone by that name. "Attacked by an Elephant," *Dallas Morning News,* October 2, 1902, 2.

25. "Flashed Light at Elephant," *Newark Advocate,* May 28, 1902, 1.

26. "Topsy the Murderer Not Vicious," *Wilkes-Barre (Pa.) Times,* May 31, 1902, 1.

27. "We Shan't See Tops," *Portsmouth (N.H.) Herald,* June 12, 1902.

28. Thompson bragged, "I think I am one of the very few who have ventured to make architecture shout my wares." Michelle Bogart, "Barking Architecture," *Smithsonian Studies in American Art* 2, No. 1 (1988), 8.

29. Reprinted from the *New York Journal* as "Cured by Hard Work," *Charlotte Observer,* December 15, 1902, 5.

30. "Defied Arrest," *Boston Globe,* January 6, 1902, 1.

31. "Elephant Alone Responsible," *Daily Inter Ocean (Chicago),* 25, No. 3, March 27, 1896.

32. "Elephant for Cuba," *Daily Illinois State Register (Springfield),* January 3, 1897.

33. Homer C. Walton, "The M. L. Clark Wagon Show," *Bandwagon* 9, no. 2 (March–April 1965), 4–11, accessed March 2013.

34. "Unexpected Performance on the Buffalo Midway," *Wilkes-Barre (Pa.) Times,* October 31, 1901, 1.

35. The three-minute film can be viewed online in the Library of Congress motion picture collection. Edison frequently produced docudramas. starting with recreations of the Spanish-American War (1898), and especially of Theodore Roosevelt and the Rough Riders.

36. In the first minute Czolgosz received seven seconds of 1,800 volts, reduced to 300 volts for twenty-three seconds, increased to 1,800 volts for four seconds, and finally reduced to 300 volts for twenty-six seconds. He was given a second jolt after a prison official said, "Give him another poke." "The Trial, Execution, Autopsy, and Mental Status of Leon F. Czolgosz, alias Fred Nieman, the Assassin of President McKinley," *Journal of American Insanity* 58, no. 3 (1902).

37. The film is available online at http://memory.loc.gov/cgi-bin/query/D?papr:6:./temp/~ammem_GTYA::.

38. "Did Not Kill Him," *Fort Worth Morning Register*, November 10, 1901, 7; "Jumbo II Still Lives," *Kalamazoo Gazette*, November 12, 1910, 2.

39. "Couldn't Kill the Elephant," *Kansas City Star,* November 10, 1901, 1.

40. "Did Not Kill Him," *Fort Worth Morning Register*, November 10, 1901, 7; "Jumbo II Still Lives," *Kalamazoo Gazette*, November 12, 1910, 2.

41. "Topsy Is Doomed," *Boston Globe*, January 4, 1902, 10.

42. Porter had filmed Topsy's approach but had stopped while Sharkey fitted her sandals.

43. "Coney Elephant Killed," *New York Times*, January 5, 1903, 1.

44. Vogelsang donated Topsy's internal organs to Princeton University for study. "Coney Elephant Killed," *New York Times*, January 5, 1903, 1.

45. "Ghost of Elephant Haunts Coney Island," *Jackson (Mich.) Citizen Patriot*, February 25, 1904, 7.

46. This discovery contradicts the claim that Herbert Vogelsang took Topsy's body, including her skull. Either Vogelsang buried Topsy's skull before leaving the site or the story is made up, which would be consistent with the showman's characteristic tactic of stirring the pot for its publicity value.

47. "What Ailed the Elephants," *New York Times,* August 7, 1905, 7.

16: Circus Day, Butte, Montana, August 23, 1900

1. Coroner's Register for January 1900 to November 1901, August 4, 1900, Inquest #80 for Patrick Murphy. Butte–Silver Bow Public Archives.

2. http://www.census.gov/population/www/documentation/twps0027/tab13.txt, accessed March 2013.

3. In August 1900, Butte registered sixty-seven people with smallpox. Ordinarily the city sent them to the county pest house at the edge of town, but someone stole the wagon they used to transfer the infected, so by August people with small-pox were still living at home while their disease matured. The county got a new pest wagon in late August.

4. Coroner's Register for January 1900 to November 1901, August 21, 1900, Inquest #83 for Lizzie Lowe. Butte–Silver Bow Public Archives. Lizzie Lowe drank enough carbolic acid to kill herself, although the coroner's inquiry did not adduce whether it was by suicide or misfortune.

5. The *Serpents* were nicknamed the *Calciners,* a reference to the smelters in Anaconda.

6. Butte also had a large Chinese population, although none played baseball.

7. Schmeer and Dunleavy recovered, quit their jobs, and went to California to play for Oakland after a single season with Butte.

8. Barnum, 337.

9. "An Ideal Circus Day," *Anaconda (Mont.) Standard,* June 29, 1899, 8.

10. "The White Man's Burden," *McClure's*, February 1899.

11. Theodore Roosevelt, *The Winning of the West*, vol. 3 (New York: Putnam, 1894), 175.

12. *The Circus Annual: Route Book of Ringling Brothers World's Greatest Shows, Season of 1897* (Buffalo, NY: Courier, 1894).

13. The crowd has been estimated at between fifteen and twenty thousand people.

14. "An Ideal Circus Day," *Anaconda (Mont.) Standard*, June 29, 1899, 8.

15. "Ringling Animals Talk," *Rockford (Ill.) Republic*, May 2, 1899, 3.

16. "The Greatest Show Ever Presented in Butte," *Anaconda (Mont.) Standard*, June 29, 1899, 8.

17. "Day With the Police," *Anaconda (Mont.) Standard*, August 26, 1900, 4.

18. Advertisement, *Idaho Falls (Idaho) Times*, August 16, 1900, 2.

19. Ibid.

20. "Trouble in Barnum's Show," *New York Times*, June 8, 1863, 1. To read about another near panic in Madison Square Garden, see "Almost a Panic," *New York Times*, April 25, 1886, 1.

21. The Lockharts were also known for a trio of elephants known as "The Three Graces." Ruth Manning-Sanders, *The English Circus* (London: Laurie, 1952), 201.

22. Frederick Dolman, "Four-Footed Actors," *English Illustrated Magazine* 21 (September 1899), 526.

23. George Speaight, *A History of the Circus* (London: Tantivy Press, 1980), 86.

24. August Heinrich Kober, *Circus Nights and Circus Days: Extracts from the Diary of a Circus Man*, trans. Claud W. Sykes (New York: William Morrow, 1931), 47.

25. The Route Book for the Ringling Brothers, Barnum, and Bailey Circus for 1941 logged 20,030 miles over 211 days. The circus used 42 railroads and gave 414 performances.

26. Larger calliopes had forty-four pipes. At least one had as many as sixty-seven.

17: Elephant Baseball

1. A *quaich* is a Scottish drinking cup.
2. Said team captain Bill Keith, "We have a deep appreciation of the absurd."
3. "Local Intelligence," *Springfield (Mass.) Republican,* June 24, 1912, 7.
4. "Ringlings' Circus Will Bring 130 Tons of Elephants Here Thursday," *Duluth News-Tribune,* July 20, 1914.
5. "Elephants That Toss Baseballs," *Tulsa World,* September 9, 1913, 2.
6. "Robinson's Circus Entertains People with Free Shows," *Montgomery Advertiser,* March 22, 1916, 9.
7. "Great Development Shown in Training of Elephants," *Springfield (Mass.) Union,* June 6, 1914, 10.
8. http://sportsillustrated.cnn.com/2010/more/07/23/honorable.hated/index.html, accessed August 2011.
9. On May 20, 1912, M. Stanley Robison died and left the St. Louis Cardinals to his niece, Helene Robison Britton. The first woman to own a professional ball club, she remarked in a newspaper interview, "If ever a woman was left with a white elephant on her hands, that woman was I when I fell heir to the St. Louis Cardinals." "Mrs. Britton Sick of Team; Calls It a White Elephant," *Salt Lake Telegram,* December 23, 1912, 15.
10. "Mack Gets an Elephant," *Chicago Daily Herald,* November 1, 1910, 6.
11. The poem/song "Elephant on His Hands" has been attributed to a variety of sources, including De Wolf Hopper, a popular entertainer who was famous for his recital of "Casey at the Bat."

18: A Lynching in Tennessee

1. Ellen Tayor Schlink, *This Is The Place: A History of Lebanon, Tennessee,* vol. 1 (Nashville, TN: Blue & Gray Press, 1975–76),

22–23. See also http://www.odmp.org/officer/18113-chief-of-police-robert-e-nolen#ixzz1kQhphh7N, accessed August 2012.

2. http://www.southernhistory.net/index.php?name=News& file=article&sid=7376, accessed August 2012.

3. "Horses Nearly Stampeded by Big, Hungry Elephant," *Augusta (Ga.) Chronicle,* March 19, 1908, 7.

4. "Elephant Ball Game," *Pawtucket (R.I.) Times,* June 3, 1916, 3.

5. C. E. Duble, "Brief History of the Sparks' World Famous Shows—Season 1916," *Bandwagon* 1, No. 8 (June 1942), 1.

6. J. O. Lewis, "The Costliest Railroad in America: A New Railroad That Cost More than Thirty Million Dollars," *Scientific American,* Supplement No. 1752, July 31, 1900.

7. http://www.executedtoday.com/2011/09/13/1916-mary-the-elephant/, accessed March 2013.

8. Charles Edwin Price, *The Day They Hung the Elephant* (Johnson City, TN: Overmountain Press, 1992), 14.

9. www.circushistory.org/Pdf/Sparks1919.pdf, accessed August 2012.

10. "Elephant Which Killed Eight People Hanged: Murderous Mary Executed by Employees of Circus," *Ann Arbor News,* November 9, 1916, 3.

11. Ibid.; "Elephant Murders, Is Legally Hanged," *Montgomery Advertiser,* November 27, 1916, 2.

12. "Sparks Circus Keeper of Elephants Killed," *Charlotte Observer,* September 14, 1916, 10.

13. Quoted in Price, *The Day They Hung the Elephant,* 37.

14. "Larger Than 'Big Mary,'" *Winston-Salem Journal,* August 5, 1920, 11.

19: How Jumbo Got His Shnozz

1. Kevin Brownlow, *The Parade's Gone By* (Berkeley: University of California Press, 1976), 31.

2. The race, which was sponsored by the tabloid *New York Sun*, also included a camel just as inexplicably as it included an elephant. The film does not survive and therefore the results of the race remain unknown.

3. Griffith's assistant director was Erich von Stroheim (who later made his living playing the role of a Prussian film director), and his scriptwriter was Tod Browning, who later wrote and directed his landmark work, *Freaks* (1932).

4. The clumsiness of the film's title is likely the result of a double translation from English to German and back to English. The only surviving copy of this film is a version in which all the title cards are in German. A retranslation from German to English produced *Lights and Shades*. A more plausible translation might be *Lights and Shadows*, clearer references to life and death.

5. The word *whipsnap* combined the swish of the leather snake followed by the snap of the tip at the moment it breaks the sound barrier. Later came *whippersnapper*, both terms of which are sexually suggestive.

6. "'Jumbo' Has Circus Touch," *Omaha World Herald*, November 24, 1935, 28.

7. Untitled review, Lawrence van Gelder, *New York Times*, October 13, 2000.

8. At an estimated cost of $4 million, the domestic box office of *Whispers* barely registered a half million. http://www.imdb.com/title/tt0185007/business, accessed August 2012.

9. The Internet Movie Data Base lists 89 feature-length Tarzan films since the first one in 1918. In addition, there are another 227 episodes made for television, making Tarzan one of the most successful and prolific franchises in film history.

10. http://www.youtube.com/watch?v=jcZUPDMXzJ8&feature=related, accessed August 2012. The elephants later reappear in sober fashion in *The Lion King* in "Elephants on Parade."

11. *The Many Adventures of Winnie the Pooh* (1977) repackaged three Disney Pooh films, including *Winnie the Pooh and the Blustery Day* (1968), which included the song "Heffalumps and Woozles," a childish corruption of "Elephants and Weasels," both of whom compete with Pooh for honey.

20: Secret Agents

1. The classic early research study of LSD can be found in Louis Cholden, ed., *Lysergic Acid Diethylamide and Mescaline in Experimental Psychiatry* (New York: Grune & Stratton, 1956).

2. Louis Jolyon West, Chester M. Pierce, Warren D. Thomas, *Science*, New Series, Vol. 138, No. 3545 (Dec. 7, 1962), 1101.

3. West and Pierce administered a doze of 300,000 micrograms intramuscularly.

4. In their final paragraph, West and Pierce assess potential social applications of LSD.

5. http://www.erowid.org/chemicals/lsd/lsd.shtml, accessed March 2013.

6. "Declaration of Ronald K. Siegel, Ph.D.," http://www.maps.org/dea-mdma/pdf/0025.PDF, accessed March 2013.

7. Unlike West and Pierce, who administered the LSD through a syringe fired into Tusko's flank, Siegel introduced the drug orally.

8. Alex Boese, *Elephants on Acid: And Other Bizarre Experiments* (Orlando, FL: Harcourt, 2007), 116.

9. *Bulletin of the Psychonomic Society* 22, no. 1 (January 1984), 53–56.

10. In 1975, the Freedom of Information Act revealed the existence of the financial history for MKULTRA, which made it possible to reconstruct its operations.

21: Seeing the Digital Elephant

1. The name Anna May refers to Anna May Wong, the first Asian-American movie star.

2. "Elephant Puts on 'Show' for Startled Oldsters," *Dallas Morning News*, August 29, 1977, sec. D, 26.

3. "Elephant's Job Is a Real Circus," *Milwaukee Journal*, August 29, 1977, 1, http://news.google.com/newspapers?nid=1499& dat=19770829&id=TGIaAAAAIBAJ&sjid=eykEAAAAIBAJ &pg=3364,5742850, accessed March 2013.

4. Jeannette Bruce, "The Great American Elephant Hunt," *Sports Illustrated*, August 4, 1975, 16–18.

5. "Search Still On for Elephants as Okies Blush," *Cleveland Plain Dealer*, July 21, 1975, 4.

6. The Hawthorn Corporation stayed in business and has been continually cited by the USDA. In June 2011 Hawthorn was cited for failing to have a written program of veterinary care and "for failing to provide a wholesome diet of sufficient nutritional value approved by an attending veterinarian." http://www.mediapeta.com/peta/pdf/Hawthorn-Corporation-pdf. pdf, accessed March 2013.

7. "Actors Speak Against Circus," *Augusta (Ga.) Chronicle*, September 13, 1997, Editions Section, 1.

8. The elephant that trampled Shirley was desperate to get at her companion, who was being removed from the tent. "This story provides another example," writes Gay Bradshaw in *Elephants on the Edge*, "of how the terms *elephant rage* or *violence* fail to capture what underlies and motivates elephant behavior: in this case, the desperate response of someone in fear of losing a loved one" (153).

9. Ibid., 153.

10. http://www.hohenwaldlewischamber.com/images/stories/ pdf/Hohenwald-TIPS2011.pdf, and http://www.city-data. com/city/Hohenwald-Tennessee.html, accessed March 2013.

11. The Memphis Branch Office of the FBI issued airtels dated December 8, 1975, and January 19, 1976, that state: "Previous investigation has determined it is a religious-type organization and is involved in no extremist or subversive activities.

[Leader] Gaskin advocated the use of marijuana but otherwise is law abiding and cooperative with law enforcement officials. They do not tolerate lawbreakers." Quoted by Albert Bates, "J. Edgar and The Farm," International Communal Studies Conference on Culture, Thought and Living in Community, 1993, http://www.thefarm.org/lifestyle/albertbates/akbp3.html, accessed March 2013.

12. http://www.youtube.com/watch?v=ZzEUayHqrRc, and http://www.youtube.com/watch?v=ZXKxgLvIS6Y, accessed March 2013.

13. "Tarra: The Sanctuary Story," http://www.carolbuckley.com/tarra.php, accessed March 2013.

14. Bradshaw, *Elephants on the Edge*, 155.

15. "Shirley Is Safely—and Wonderfully—at the Sanctuary," http://www.elephants.com/shirley/shirleyArrival.php, and "Elephants Reunited After Twenty Years," http://www.wimp.com/elephantsreunited/, accessed March 2013.

16. "Shirley's Independence Day," Elephant Sanctuary website, http://www.elephants.com/shirley/shirleyarrives.htm, accessed July 2012.

17. Personal communication with Christina Cooper, May 29, 2012.

18. The interpretation of these results has sparked vigorous debate between circus organizations such as the AZA, the Ringling Center for Elephant Conservation, and Elephant Care International. Veterinarians and policy makers disagree markedly on what constitutes a valid test for tuberculosis and how to treat and control the disease. http://www.elephantcare.org/position_files/Elephant%20Care%20International%20Open%20Letter%20on%20TB%20Issues.pdf, accessed March 2013.

19. There have been at least eight cases of the transmission of the disease from elephants to humans at the Elephant Sanctuary. Tim Ghianni, "Elephant Behind TB Outbreak at Tennessee

Sanctuary," Reuters, February 17, 2011. Of the fifty elephants that tested positive for tuberculosis between 2006 and 2010, forty-nine carried *M. tuberculosis*, the human form. One elephant was infected with *M. bovis*, a bovine form. http://www.reuters.com/article/2011/02/18/us-elephant-tuberculosis-idUSTRE71H01J20110218, accessed March 2013.

The danger of transmitting tuberculosis from humans to elephants is far more acute in places like Myanmar (Burma), which has between four thousand and six thousand *trained* elephants, each with its own mahout. Every day tens of thousands of people intersect the elephants, increasing the likelihood of transmission. Chris Furley, "Tuberculosis in Elephants," *Lancet* 350, No. 9072 (July 19, 1997), 224.

20. http://news.nationalgeographic.com/news/2006/10/061003-mastodons.html, accessed March 2013.

21. *M. tuberculosis* is a challenging pathogen. While treatment in humans is well researched and considered reliable, TB in elephants still holds many unknowns. Since the Hawthorn elephants arrived in 2006 only Misty completed a full, successful round of treatment and has been cleared to return to the general population of elephants in the Elephant Sanctuary. Misty is still tested annually and to date she remains clear of the disease.

22. Atkinson calculates that "a Free Contact elephant keeper has a chance of death or serious injury of 8.6% in a 45 year career." Personal communication with the author. Also, Stephen Roberts, "Hazardous Occupations in Great Britain," *Lancet* 360, No. 9332 (August 17, 2002), 543–44. Rob Atkinson, "Zoos Forum Review of Zoo Elephant Welfare."

23. Gail Laule and Margaret Whittaker, "Protected Contact—Beyond the Barrier," paper presented at American Zoo and Aquarium Association Annual Conference, Orlando, Florida, 2000, http://www.activeenvironments.org/pdf/PC_Beyond_Barrier.pdf, accessed March 2013.

24. In May 4, 2002, the USDA's consulting veterinarian diagnosed

Delhi with multiple lesions, a swollen tail, swollen front feet with skin damage and abscess blowouts, abscess defects on the footpads, and a split nail.

25. Bradshaw, *Elephants on the Edge*, 173.

26. McClean was the second elephant to die after falling into the moat at the Los Angeles Zoo. In 1975, a seven-month-old calf died after a fall.

27. http://www.pawsweb.org/save_the_bulls.html, accessed March 2013.

28. "A Fact Sheet About Elephants and Why the Los Angeles Zoo's Pachyderm Forest Is a Crucial Element in the World Wide Effort to Conserve This Magnificent Species."

29. "Stereotypic Behaviors in Captive Elephants," presentation given by Associate Professor Doctor Sumolya Kanchanapangka, D.V.M., Ph.D., Department of Veterinary Anatomy, Faculty of Veterinary Science, Chulalongkorn University, Bangkok, Thailand, May 8, 2012, at Hohenwald, Tennessee.

30. Carla Hall, "2 Council Panels Back Plans for New L.A. Zoo Elephant Exhibit," *Los Angeles Times,* April 11, 2006, http://articles.latimes.com/2006/apr/11/local/me-elephants11, accessed March 2013.

31. Robert Wiese, Paul Boyle, and Jennie McNary, *Facts about Elephants and why the Los Angeles Zoo's Pachyderm Forest is a Crucial Element in the Worldwide Effort to Conserve this Magnificent Species.* http://www.docstoc.com/docs/53923465/FACTS-ABOUT -ELEPHANTS-AND-WHY-THE-LOS-ANGELES-ZOOS, November 4, 2008, 4.

32. Steve Oney, "Mr. L. A.," *Los Angeles Magazine,* April 1, 2009, http://www.lamag.com/features/Story.aspx?ID=1562855, accessed March 2013.

33. "New Information on Elephant Deaths Prompts Councilman to Concur with the Decision of 12 Other Cities," press release, Councilman Tony Cardenas, 6th Council District,

October 21, 2008; http://www.lamag.com/features/Story .aspx?ID=1562855, accessed March 2013.

34. To which zookeeper Joshua Sisk replied, "No disrespect to Bob Barker, Halle Berry, Cher or any of these people, but if you want to know about acting or game shows, talk to the celebs. If you want to talk about animal care, talk to the professionals." http://www.accesshollywood.com/celebs-lose-fight-to-move-billy -the-elephant_article_13303, accessed March 2013; http://www.worldzootoday.com/2009/01/30/city-council-votes-to -keep-billy-the-elephant-at-the-la-zoo, accessed March 2013.

35. Daphne Sheldrick, "L. A. Zoo Should Free Billy the Elephant," *Los Angeles Times*, January 5, 2009, http://www .latimes.com/news/opinion/commentary/la-oe-sheldrick5 -2009jan05,0,938410.story, accessed March 2013.

36. Jack Hannah, "Let Billy the Elephant into His New Home," op-ed, *Los Angeles Times*, January 9, 2009, http://www.latimes .com/news/opinion/la-oew-hanna9-2009jan09,0,5089976 .story, accessed March 2013.

37. Hector Tobar, "Zoo Without Elephants Would Be a Loss for the Children of L.A.," *Los Angeles Times,* December 9, 2008, http://www.latimes.com/news/local/la-me-tobarnew9 -2008dec09,0,3750500.column?page=1, accessed March 2013.

38. "Rocker Slash and Golden Girl Betty White Jam for Billy the Elephant and the Los Angeles Zoo," http://www.youtube .com/watch?v=LQCnH1fURWM, accessed March 2013.

39. http://www.worldzootoday.com/2009/01/30/city-council -votes-to-keep-billy-the-elephant-at-the-la-zoo/, accessed March 2013.

40. http://clkrep.lacity.org/onlinedocs/2008/08-2850_mot_10 -21-08.pdf, accessed March 2013.

41. http://www.lazoo.org/animals/elephantsofasia/, accessed March 2013.

42. The city appealed to the California Supreme Court, but it declined to hear the case.

43. http://www.lazoo.org/animals/elephantsofasia/ conservation/, accessed March 2013.

44. "Over the past decade [Flora and Fauna International has been] researching elephant distribution and population status, and have successfully mitigated human–wildlife conflict so that elephant killings in retribution for crop damage are now a thing of the past." http://www.fauna-flora.org/species/asian -elephant/, accessed March 2013.

45. R. Sukumar, "A Brief Review of the Status, Distribution and Biology of Wild Asian Elephants," *International Zoo Yearbook* 40, No. 1 (July 2006), 1–8. Flora and Fauna International estimates a total population between 400 and 600. http://www.eleaid.com/index .php?page=elephantsincambodia, accessed March 2013.

46. http://www.aza.org/, accessed March 2013.

47. http://www.harrisinteractive.com/NewsRoom/HarrisPolls /AboutTheHarrisPoll.aspx, accessed March 2013.

48. http://www.aza.org/PressRoom/detail.aspx?id=2139, accessed March 2013.

49. John H. Falk, "Why Zoos & Aquariums Matter; Assessing the Impact of a Visit to a Zoo or Aquarium," 2007, 10. The study included 5,500 visitors to twelve zoos over three years. http:// www.aza.org/uploadedFiles/Education/why_zoos_matter .pdf, accessed March 2013.

In 2010, a study titled "Do Zoos and Aquariums Promote Attitude Change in Visitors? A Critical Examination of the American Zoo and Aquarium Study" found "six major threats to methodological validity that undermine [Falk's] conclusions." The study concludes "there remains no compelling evidence for the claim that zoos and aquariums promote attitude change, education, or interest in conservation in visitors. . . ." Lori Marino, Scott O. Lilienfeld, Randy Malamud, Nathan Nobis, and Ron Broglio, "Do Zoos and Aquariums Promote Attitude Change in Visitors? A Critical Examination of the American Zoo and Aquarium Study," *Society and Animals* 18

(2010), 126–38, http://nbb.emory.edu/faculty/personal/doc uments/MarinoetalAZAStudy.pdf, accessed March 2013.

50. "Kenya's Elephant Census Shows Slow Growth," February 14, 2011, http://s.tt/176IR, accessed March 2013.

51. http://www.nczoo.org/conservation/International/Elephant Conserv.html, accessed March 2013.

52. http://www.youtube.com/watch?v=Vd8dwtWVCXo, accessed March 2013.

53. Estimates of the total number of elephants in Cameroon range between 1,000 and 5,000. "Poachers Slaughter Half the Elephant Population in Cameroon Park," NBCNews .com, March 15, 2012, http://worldnews.nbcnews.com/_ news/2012/03/15/10707625-report-poachers-slaughter -half-the-elephant-population-in-cameroon-park?lite, accessed March 2013. Also see "Cameroon Elephant Massacre Shows Poaching, Ivory Trade Require an International Response," *Scientific American,* March 20, 2012, http://blogs.scientificamer ican.com/extinction-countdown/2012/03/20/cameroon -elephant-massacre-poaching-ivory-trade/, accessed March 2013.

54. R. E. Hoare, "Determinants of Human-Elephant Conflict in a Land-Use Mosaic," *Journal of Applied Ecology* 36 (1999): 689–700, 689. This figure varies between the 80 percent of un-protected habitat estimated by Hoare to 69 percent estimated by the African Elephant Status Report of 2007. http://www .african-elephant.org/aed/pdfs/aesr2007a.pdf, accessed March 2013.

55. The thirteen range states in West Africa are Benin, Burkina Faso, Cote d'Ivoire, Ghana, Guinea, Guinea-Bissau, Liberia, Mali, Niger, Nigeria, Senegal, Sierra Leone, and Togo.

56. P. Bouché et al., "Will Elephants Soon Disappear from West Afri-can Savannahs?," PLoS ONE 6, No. 6 (2011), available at http:// www.plosone.org/article/info%3Adoi%2F10.1371%2Fjournal .pone.0020619, accessed March 2013.

57. http://www.african-elephant.org/aed/pdfs/aesr2007w.pdf,

accessed March 2013. Accounts are not always reliable, however, since counting requires considerable investments in manpower and technology (helicopters, mainly), which some countries cannot afford.

58. Hoare, "Determinants of Human-Elephant Conflict in a Land-Use Mosaic," 690.

59. "Human-Elephant Conflict Mitigation: A Training Course for Community-Based Approaches in Africa," IUCN/SSC African Elephant Specialist Group (G. E. Parker, F. V. Osborn, R. E. Hoare, and L. S. Niskanen), March 2007, http://www .peopleandwildlife.org.uk/crmanuals/HECparticipant%20 manual.pdf, accessed March 2013.. R. E. Hoare also contended in 1999 that "the judgement that conflict is actually becoming more intense remains unsubstantiated." Hoare, "Determinants of Human-Elephant Conflict in a Land-Use Mosaic," 690.

60. "Activists Close Watching Suit over L.A. Zoo's Elephant Exhibit," *Los Angeles Times*, June 19, 2012, http:// articles.latimes.com/print/2012/jun/19/local/la-me-zoo -elephants-20120619, accessed March 2013.

61. Michael Hutchins and William Conway, "Zoo vs. Sanctuary," AZA's Communique, August 2004, 54–56, http://www. rdsinc.com/pdf/samples/sp738186.pdf, accessed March 2013.

62. This figure is based upon an estimated population of 12,000 elephants on 18,000 square miles in Tsavo and then compared to the half acre available to elephants in the United States.

63. "Asian Elephant Conservation Fund," U.S. Fish & Wildlife Service, Division of International Conservation, January 2006, http://library.fws.gov/IA_Pubs/asian_elephant_conserv06 .pdf, accessed March 2013.

64. http://www.carsonbarnescircus.com/saving-elephants/.

65. The Center for Elephant Conservation recorded twenty-five live births between December 1992 and December 2012, sired by five stud bulls (including Charlie thirteen times) and ten

cows (including Alana five times). During that period the calves suffered a mortality rate of 16 percent.

66. "Statement and Resolutions on the Role of Captive Facilities in *In Situ* African Elephant Conservation," IUCN African Elephant Specialist Group, http://www.african-elephant .org/tools/pdfs/pos_captiv_en.pdf, and http://www.african -elephant.org/tools/pdfs/pos_capvuse_en.pdf, accessed March 2013.

For some unknown factor—stress has been suggested— artificially inseminated cows give birth to 83 percent males, a figure opposite the desired outcome for the elephant industry. As a result, the AI program is producing a generation of male undesirables.

67. http://www.latimes.com/news/local/la-me-elephant -zoo-20120725,0,5329085.story?track=rss, accessed March 2013.

68. Superior Court of California, County of Los Angeles, Ruling on Submitted Court Trial BC375234, *Aaron Leider, et al. v. John Lewis, et al.*, July 23, 2012.

69. http://www.losfelizledger.com/2012/07/judge-finds-la-zoo -has-abused-elephants-but-exhibit-to-remain-open/, accessed July 2012.

70. "Bob Barker Elephants: Celebrity Picks up Tab to Move Toronto Zoo Animals," *Huffington Post*, June 21, 2012, http://www.huffingtonpost.ca/2011/12/19/bob-barker -elephants_n_1157187.html, accessed March 2013.

71. "The Toronto Zoo's Departing Elephants Have Squashed Its Accreditation. Thanks, Bob Barker," *Toronto Star*, April 20, 2012, http://www.thestar.com/opinion/editorials/article/1165620 --the-toronto-zoo-s-departing-elephants-have-squashed-its -accreditation-thanks-bob-barker.

72. "Toronto Elephants Should Head South Despite TB Test, Councilors Say," *Toronto Star*, June 14, 2012. http://www.thestar .com/news/article/1211721--toronto-elephants-should-head -south-despite-tb-test-councillors-say, accessed March 2013.

73. http://rumblingsfrompaws.wordpress.com/2012/04/27 /letter-to-the-editor-toronto-star-2/, accessed March 2013.

74. "Iringa's Custom-Made Transport Crate," *Seattle Post*, July 26, 2012; http://article.wn.com/view/2012/07/26/Elephants _move_has_to_wait_for_cooler_weather_2/, accessed March 2013.

75. The historical average is 26 degrees Celsius (78.8 Fahrenheit). "Elephants' Move Has to Wait for Cooler Weather," *Seattle Post-Intelligencer,* July 26, 2012, http://seattletimes.com/html/ nationworld/2018777974_apuspetsflyingelephants.html, accessed March 2013.

76. "Toronto Council Votes to Send Zoo's Elephants to California—Again," *Toronto Star*, November 27, 2012, http:// www.thestar.com/news/city_hall/2012/11/27/toronto_ council_votes_to_send_zoos_elephants_to_california_again. html, accessed March 2013.

77. "Toronto Zoo Elephants Transfer Held Up Again," *Toronto Star*, April 22, 2013, http://www.torontosun.com/2013/04/22 /toronto-zoo-elephants-transfer-held-up--again, accessed May 2013.

78. http://www.mediapeta.com/peta/pdf/Lydia-Elephant -Rides-pdf.pdf, accessed March 2013.

79. To see an elephant draw a picture of another elephant: http:// www.youtube.com/watch?v=He7Ge7Sogrk, accessed March 2013.

80. She actually ties for third oldest with three other elephants.

81. Ros Clubb et al., "Compromised Survivorship in Zoo Elephants," *Science* 322 (December 12, 2008), 1649.

82. http://www.elephant.se/elephant_database.php?open=- Elephant%20database, accessed March 2013.

83. Mike Keele, *Asian Elephant North American Regional Studbook*, American Zoo Association, 2010, 139; http://www .elephanttag.org/professional/2010AsianElephantStudbook .pdf, accessed March 2013.

84. Association of Zoos & Aquariums, *Standards for Elephant Management and Care*, approved March 2011, 26, http://www.aza.org/uploadedFiles/Conservation/Commitments_and_Impacts/Elephant_Conservation/ElephantStandards.pdf, accessed March 2013.

85. Iain and Oria Douglas-Hamilton (*Among the Elephants*, 1975), Cynthia Moss (*Elephant Memories: Thirteen Years in the Life of an Elephant Family*, 2000), Gay Bradshaw (*Elephants on the Edge*, 2009) and Caitlin O'Connell (*An Elephant's Life: An Intimate Portrait from Africa*, 2011).

86. "Shirley and Tarra Greet at the Lake," http://www.youtube.com/watch?v=KmxVIEoX6o8, accessed March 2013.

87. http://www.elephants.com/jenny/jennyTributes.php, accessed March 2013.

88. Personal communication, Rob Atkinson, May 8, 2012.

89. "Girl Talk," http://www.youtube.com/watch?v=tbuB7nw5a3A, accessed March 2013.

90. "Elephant Goes Out of Control Escapes but Gets Killed," http://www.youtube.com/watch?v=ym7MS4I7znQ, accessed March 2013.

91. "Asian Elephant Conservation Fund," U.S. Fish & Wildlife Service, Division of International Conservation, January 2006, http://library.fws.gov/IA_Pubs/asian_elephant_conserv06.pdf, accessed March 2013.